INTERRELIGIOUS/INTERFAITH STUDIES

INTERRELIGIOUS/
INTERFAITH STUDIES

DEFINING A
NEW FIELD

Edited by

EBOO PATEL
JENNIFER HOWE PEACE
NOAH J. SILVERMAN

BEACON PRESS, BOSTON

BEACON PRESS
Boston, Massachusetts
www.beacon.org

Beacon Press books
are published under the auspices of
the Unitarian Universalist Association of Congregations.

21 20 19 18   8 7 6 5 4 3 2 1

This book is printed on acid-free paper that meets the uncoated paper
ANSI/NISO specifications for permanence as revised in 1992.

Text design and composition by Kim Arney

Library of Congress Cataloging-in-Publication Data

Names: Patel, Eboo, editor.
Title: Interfaith-interreligious studies : defining a new field / edited by
    Eboo Patel, Jennifer Howe Peace, Noah J. Silverman.
Description: Boston : Beacon Press, 2018. | Includes bibliographical
    references and index.
Identifiers: LCCN 2018018035 (print) | LCCN 2018026483 (ebook) |
    ISBN 9780807020098 (ebook) | ISBN 9780807019979 (pbk. : alk. paper)
Subjects: LCSH: Religion—Study and teaching. | Religions—Relations.
Classification: LCC BL41 (ebook) | LCC BL41 .I47 2018 (print) |
    DDC 201/.507—dc23
LC record available at https://lccn.loc.gov/2018018035

To the memory of Brendan W. Randall
(May 8, 1966–July 9, 2017),
friend, colleague, and scholar and practitioner
of interfaith studies par excellence

CONTENTS

INTRODUCTION

Eboo Patel, Jennifer Howe Peace,
and Noah J. Silverman

You might say that this volume had its origins in a generic hotel conference room in San Diego in 2014 during the annual gathering of the American Academy of Religion (AAR). Diana Eck, senior scholar at Harvard, had wondered out loud if interreligious studies had something to offer not only in terms of content (examining what people are doing *interreligiously*) but also in terms of methodology, favoring an active learning approach over the default academic lectures. Murmurs of assent broke out among the eighty or so people gathered for the session titled "Toward a Field of Interfaith Studies: Emerging Questions and Considerations" and hosted under the auspices of the AAR's Interreligious and Interfaith Studies Unit. The panel, which included coeditors Eboo Patel and Jennifer Howe Peace, was organized around three questions: What personal history brings you to your place in interfaith studies? What are the challenges or tensions in this emerging field? (Or, as Patel put it, "What keeps you up at night?") And, from your perspective, what are some of the defining moments in the current evolution of this (sub)field?

Eck, who twenty-five years ago founded the Pluralism Project, an initiative that foreshadowed much of what has come to be called interreligious or interfaith studies, noted that she saw endless opportunities for real research in this new field. "There is a lot going on in the world that has to be brought into focus," she pointed out. Throughout the session, people were feeling their way toward what this field was, could be, or should be. "There is no frame for what we are doing," said one participant. He elicited nervous laughter when he jokingly commented, "I'm pretty sure I'm going to be fired for what I did here today."

Patel observed that a distinctive contribution of the AAR was to offer "direction, depth, and definition," along with rigor as this field emerged. He quoted from his recent article "Toward a Field of Interfaith Studies":

> Scholars from a range of fields have long taken an interest in how people who orient around religion differently interact with one another. . . . As the activity in this area increases, one crucial role for the academy is to give some definition to what is clearly an emerging field of research, study, and practice. Another role is to recognize the importance of training people who have the knowledge base and skill set needed to engage religious diversity in a way that promotes peace, stability and cooperation—and to begin offering academic programs that certify such leaders.[1]

Further elaborating his hopes for the field, Patel named five civic goods associated with interfaith work: reducing prejudice, strengthening social cohesion, building social capital, strengthening the continuity of identity communities, and, finally, creating binding narratives for diverse societies.[2]

Peace argued that interfaith studies is more than an academic exercise, given the reality of religiously motivated violence, bigotry, and a lack of mutual understanding across religious traditions. In her definition, interfaith studies is a field that values scholarship accountable to community, the dynamic link between theory and practice, and the centrality of relationships at every level (from subject matter to methodology and motivations).

Other scholars weighed in. "Interreligious studies is a subfield of religious studies," said panelist Jeanine Diller. This was clear in her context at a large secular university and mirrors Kate McCarthy's argument in her chapter for this book. Barbara McGraw (also a contributor to this volume) noted that in her setting at Saint Mary's College of

California she defines this as an interdisciplinary field under the rubric of leadership. Her model includes a focus on (1) leadership in an organization; (2) communication and dialogue; (3) identity and bias; and (4) religious literacy.

John Thatamanil, associate professor of theology and world religions, mentioned that his institution, Union Theological Seminary, had added "interreligious engagement" as their newest field within theological education. He outlined Union's approach, which includes theory from comparative religious studies, in-depth knowledge of a particular tradition other than one's own, and appreciation for cultivating dispositions that promote interreligious understanding (based in part on Catherine Cornille's work).

Oddbjørn Leirvik, who wrote *Interreligious Studies: A Relational Approach to Religious Activism and the Study of Religion*, suggested three categories for the range of concerns we were discussing: (1) *interreligious work*—a broad term referring to practical efforts; (2) *interreligious education or formation work*, which Leirvik noted is less common in Europe than in the US; and (3) *interreligious studies*, which he described as being focused on studying interreligious dialogue as well as broader efforts related to building interreligious relations. He also noted that an important critical contribution of this area involves attending to the power relations and gender dynamics that are part of interreligious engagement. (This last point is taken up by several contributors to this volume, including Elizabeth Kubek and Jeannine Hill Fletcher.)

The session's conversation continued with animated dialogue about goals and definitions, both compatible and competing. All of it underscored a key concern articulated at the outset of the panel—that we lack a current consensus about the nature of this emerging field. What does it mean to do this work well?

Sixteen months later, in March 2016, over one hundred faculty members from across the United States came together for a conference at California Lutheran University to discuss curricular programs in the emerging field of interfaith and interreligious studies. Robert Jones, a sociologist and the CEO of the Public Religion Research Institute, was one of the keynote speakers. He caught up with the three coeditors of this volume after one of the conference sessions and commented, "Well, interfaith studies is certainly a thing."

As recently as even five years ago, that statement would have been unlikely. Indeed, when Patel published his article calling for the creation of an academic field of interfaith studies in 2013, the argument was almost entirely speculative.[3] Five years later there are enough "facts on the ground" within the academy that are referred to as "interfaith and/or interreligious studies" to constitute a discernible "thing." An incomplete list includes

- The AAR approved a new unit in 2013, cofounded and co-chaired by Jennifer Howe Peace, one of the coeditors of this volume, focused on "Interreligious and Interfaith Studies." The group receives between sixty and eighty proposals per year and regularly draws seventy-five to ninety participants to each of its sessions.
- Building on the momentum of the AAR group, in 2017 an affiliated Association of Interreligious/Interfaith Studies was launched by Peace in conjunction with the annual AAR gathering held that year in Boston.
- There are now more than one hundred undergraduate courses on college and university campuses that focus on interfaith topics.[4]
- Tenure-track faculty positions in "interfaith studies" (or labeled similarly) now exist at Andover Newton Seminary, Candler School of Theology, Claremont School of Theology, Regis University, and Villanova University, with similar positions at other undergraduate and graduate institutions currently under development.
- Academic programs—such as majors, minors, and certificates—in interfaith and interreligious studies have been approved at more than twenty undergraduate institutions in the US, alongside more than a dozen graduate-level degree programs in the US and abroad.[5]

- Academic journals and publications such as the *Journal of Interreligious Studies* and *Interreligious Studies and Intercultural Theology* regularly publish new scholarship in the field.
- Academic centers focusing fully or partly on interfaith education, engagement, and leadership proliferate at undergraduate and graduate institutions. These include the Center for Jewish, Christian, and Islamic Studies (Chicago Theological Seminary), Forum on Faith and Life (Concordia College, Minnesota), Center on Religion, Culture, and Conflict (Drew University, New Jersey), Center for Interfaith Engagement (Eastern Mennonite University, Virginia), Center for the Study of Religion, Culture, and Society (Elon University, North Carolina), Berkley Center for Religion, Peace, and World Affairs (Georgetown University, Washington, DC), Kaufman Interfaith Institute (Grand Valley State University, Michigan), Pluralism Project (Harvard University, Massachusetts), Center for the Study of World Religions and the Religious Literacy Project (Harvard Divinity School, Massachusetts), Miller Center for Interreligious Learning and Leadership (Hebrew College, Massachusetts), Leadership and Multifaith Program (LAMP) Initiative (Ivan Allen College of Liberal Arts at Georgia Institute of Technology and Candler School of Theology at Emory University), Center for the Study of Jewish-Christian-Muslim Relations (Merrimack College, Massachusetts), Hickey Center for Interfaith Studies (Nazareth College, New York), Of Many Institute for Interfaith Leadership (New York University), Boniuk Institute for Religious Tolerance (Rice University, Texas), Center for Engaged Religious Pluralism (Saint Mary's College of California), Dialogue Institute (Temple University, Pennsylvania), Jay Phillips Center for Interfaith Learning (University of St. Thomas, Minnesota), Center for Religious Understanding (University of Toledo, Ohio), Lumbar Institute for the Study of Abrahamic Religions (University of Wisconsin–Madison), and Center for Interfaith Community Engagement (Xavier University, Ohio).

- The increasing number of grants from the Teagle Foundation, Henry Luce Foundation, Arthur Vining Davis Foundations, and Andrew W. Mellon Foundation—all major funders of higher education—seek to advance research, theorizing, and teaching in interreligious leadership, religious literacy, and other areas under the rubric of interfaith or interreligious studies.
- Major higher education associations such as the Council of Independent Colleges and the Association of American Colleges and Universities have formed collaborative partnerships for interfaith conferences, faculty development seminars, and institutes.

A central goal of this book is to draw a circle around these various "facts on the ground"—the courses, journal articles, degree programs, faculty positions, and common questions—and see what pictures emerge. How does this "thing" called interfaith (or interreligious) studies relate to similar things, such as religious or theological studies? What are the key questions, motivations, and outcomes that animate this emerging field? What are its signature pedagogies? In other words, what is the shape of interfaith/interreligious studies, and what is its distinct contribution?

The coeditors of this volume have had a long commitment to these questions and have played a significant role in putting some of the aforementioned facts on the ground. Jennifer Howe Peace held the first tenured faculty position in interfaith studies at Andover Newton Theological Seminary (what is now Andover Newton at Yale Divinity School). As mentioned above, she also cofounded and cochaired the AAR's Interreligious and Interfaith Studies unit and founded the AAR-affiliated Association for Interreligious/Interfaith Studies in 2017. Eboo Patel and Noah Silverman, as staff members at Interfaith Youth Core (IFYC), received grants from each of the foundations mentioned above for partnerships with major higher education associations, which helped (and continue to support) many of the undergraduate courses and degree programs in interfaith and interreligious studies mentioned above. Each of us has published in this new field and taught courses, designed curriculum, and led faculty seminars in interfaith and interreligious studies. In the process, we have encountered hundreds of college and university faculty and administrators who have come to identify themselves with this emerging field.

While the existence of interfaith or interreligious studies is increasingly hard to ignore, its meaning and import is still being debated. Bill Drayton, who coined the term "social entrepreneur," once responded when asked how he felt about that term's rapid proliferation, "I only wish people knew what it meant." Similarly, Eboo Patel notes that when IFYC gets résumés listing "interfaith experience," there is little to no agreement on what this means. This points to a practical question at the heart of this volume: what can one expect as a potential employer if someone has an academic pedigree in interfaith studies? As interfaith or interreligious studies has taken shape over the past five years, it has been defined in multiple ways, with disputes and disagreements among scholars with conflicting visions of the field's scope and purview. This book thus builds on the panel discussions, conferences, and debates over definitions to explore the state of the emerging field. The contributions in this volume attest to the range of research and work taking shape under the rubric of interreligious or interfaith studies.

OVERVIEW OF THE VOLUME

When the coeditors issued a call for chapters for this volume, more than fifty scholars responded. From those, we chose the eighteen essays that appear in this collection. To develop an edited volume that was more than the sum of its parts, we gathered all the contributors for a conversation in August 2016 in Chicago. At that meeting, Mary Elizabeth Moore, dean of the Boston University School of Theology, shared opening remarks about the challenges and possibilities inherent in defining a field.[6] A field, by definition, is an area of open land often designated for a particular purpose and bound by signs of its outer limits—a fence, a stone wall, a creek. By analogy, an academic field frames a particular area of study both in terms of what it includes and excludes. The project and purpose of this volume is to offer multiple views on a field in formation.

Contributors to this volume do not necessarily agree on how to define, name, and bind the outer limits of this field (or subfield) or on what belongs in it (and what does not). This is by design. We hope the book will inspire conversations and lively debates among scholars, teachers, and religious practitioners about the kinds of questions and concerns interreligious/interfaith studies is uniquely positioned to explore.

The first section of the book, "Constructions: Mapping the Field," includes five chapters from authors with a range of disciplinary backgrounds and in diverse institutional settings—factors that shape and influence their approach to, and understanding of, interreligious/interfaith studies. Kate McCarthy writes from her position at a large public secular university and advocates for interreligious studies to be embraced as a subfield of religious studies, while suggesting that both the field and the subfield have something important to learn from each other. Deanna Womack, a pastor and seminary professor, describes interfaith studies as a "third way" that takes the best from the twin disciplines of her own intellectual formation: history of religions and theology. Taking a different tack, Elizabeth Kubek, shaped by women's studies and gender studies, argues for interfaith studies as a new inclusive and interdisciplinary field akin to other area studies. Coauthors Amy L. Allocco, Geoffrey D. Claussen, and Brian K. Pennington take readers through the concerns and questions they confronted while designing a minor in interreligious studies at Elon University and differentiating their curricular project from the civic project of interfaith engagement. Finally, Kristi Del Vecchio and Noah Silverman, program staff at Interfaith Youth Core, identify six key themes that have emerged from existing interfaith and interreligious studies curricular growth over the past five years. Each of these essays offers constructive proposals and lingering questions—valuable signposts as we continue the work of collectively mapping the boundaries of this emerging field.

Having traced the outlines of how this field might be constructed, we turn to the second part of the book: "Pedagogy and Classroom Practices." There are a set of teaching strategies that are becoming increas-

ingly common or even "signature" ways of doing interreligious and
interfaith studies that are simultaneously impacted by and impacting
our understanding of the field. In Kevin Minister's chapter, we see the
transformation of one professor and his classroom as he moves from a
more traditional "world religions" approach of teaching religions to an
"interfaith studies" approach. Minister's piece is a helpful bridge from
the previous section of the book as he considers the wider implications
of this move for departments of religious studies in general. In the second chapter of this section, Ellie Pierce, research director at the Pluralism Project at Harvard and pioneer in producing a set of case studies
on religious pluralism, offers a detailed look into the benefits and limits
of using the decision-based case method in the interfaith studies classroom. Beyond formal case studies, Matthew Maruggi and Martha E.
Stortz look more broadly at the power and importance of narrative
storytelling as part of the tool kit for teaching interreligious studies.
Postulating another key aspect of teaching in this field, Michael Birkel
in "A Pedagogy of Listening: Teaching the Qur'an to Non-Muslims"
homes in on the importance of listening as a pedagogical commitment
in his experiences as a Quaker and professor of religion at Earlham
College. The final contribution to this section is a chapter by Wakoh
Shannon Hickey and Margarita M. W. Suárez focused on articulating
key affective goals for their students and describing exercises designed
to take students beyond acquiring data to cultivating qualities such as
reflexivity, empathy, inquiry, and a commitment to pluralism—core dimensions of the coauthors' definition of what constitutes an interfaith
studies approach in the classroom.

Part 3 of the book, "Challenges and Choices," includes four chapters that explore tensions, complications, and wider considerations
that, these authors argue, should inform how interfaith studies is defined and constructed. Rachel S. Mikva begins this section by outlining
six issues that complicate interreligious engagement, as seen from her
experiences in the field. Jeannine Hill Fletcher focuses on one of the
issues named by Mikva—the history of white Christian privilege in the
United States—and argues that acknowledging this history and commit-
ting to structural transformation are needed if interfaith studies fulfills

hopes of contributing to a "religio-racial" project that can be inclusive of all persons. Thinking about what—or who—is included (or left out) of interreligious/interfaith studies as it is currently being conceived, the two final chapters in this section focus on this issue from very different angles. Marion H. Larson and Sara L. H. Shady look specifically at evangelical Christians in the interfaith movement in ways that pose larger questions about the ideological commitments and inclusivity of this field. Finally, Lisa E. Dahill widens the perspective appreciably by arguing that any approach to interreligious engagement that is relevant and responsive to our times needs to consider not only an interreligious model of understanding and solidarity but also an interspecies and holistic ecological model, one embodied, located in specific places, and with an express commitment to being in relationship not just with each other but also with the "more-than-human-world."

The fourth and final section of the book, "Applications Beyond the Classroom," explores a range of contexts and settings in which interfaith leadership, interreligious education, and interfaith studies approaches are having an impact on everything from religious leadership formation to advocacy work for adherents of minority religions in prisons and to training for diplomatic work. In the section's first chapter, Or N. Rose and Jennifer Howe Peace argue for a model of interreligious education that can broaden the way future religious leaders understand their role and their calling. The next chapter reveals how encountering religious prejudice in prisons and teaching religious literacy to prison officials led Barbara A. McGraw to develop an "interfaith leadership for institutional change model," which she now applies to other institutions and professions. Turning to the applicability of interfaith studies for professions beyond the academy, Mark E. Hanshaw and Usra Ghazi in the next chapter offer views from their respective locations about the important role interfaith studies can play in preparing people for the religiously diverse workplaces they will encounter once they graduate. In the final chapter, coauthors Heather Miller Rubens, Homayra Ziad, and Benjamin E. Sax turn their attention to the possibility of fostering an "interreligious city," using their home city of Baltimore as a case study. Writing from their positions as scholars at the Institute for Islamic, Christian, and Jewish Studies, their chapter considers the potential role of educational nonprofits as resources for education, training, and activism as they imagine the potential for greater interreligious solidarity.

The coeditors hope that this book's essays, on their own and taken together, provide timely and relevant insights for the emerging field of interfaith/interreligious studies—and beyond—as the engagement of religious diversity continues to shape and influence the affairs of our world.

I

CONSTRUCTIONS: MAPPING THE FIELD

(INTER)RELIGIOUS STUDIES

Making a Home in the Secular Academy

Kate McCarthy

As interfaith and interreligious studies programs—majors, minors, certificates, and concentrations—emerge in American colleges and universities, it is worth noting that the larger field of secular religious studies is not necessarily throwing a welcome party. While many of these new programs are housed or affiliated with religious studies departments, the relationship between the fields has not yet been clearly established, and tensions between them are deep and complicated. The case for establishing such programs as part of, or even allies to, religious studies requires careful mapping of purposes, methods, and values.

I come at this issue with double vision. I earned my PhD in systematic theology with a focus on Christian theologies of religious pluralism, and I am committed to a particular understanding of religious diversity as a public good. But I have spent my academic career in the religious studies department of a public university, where the word "theology" is sometimes suspect, and I am equally committed to the project of secular critical inquiry that is religious studies. Interreligious or interfaith studies as it is beginning to be defined is not a theological endeavor, yet its normative agenda and deep ties to the US interfaith movement whose roots and frameworks are Christian, as well as its friendly disposition toward religion itself, raise difficult challenges for an academic partnership. What's more, the creation of interfaith and interreligious studies programs is often closely linked to extracurricular programs aimed at promoting intergroup understanding and inclusive campus climates, often under the auspices of larger diversity initiatives. Scholars of religion, then, may have trouble seeing this work as an area of academic research, relegating it instead to the world of student affairs.

But it is clear that serious secular academic work is being done in the area of interreligious relations, in a wide range of disciplines. Beyond the fields of philosophy of religion and philosophical theology, American religious studies scholars working out of varied disciplinary frameworks have brought increasing attention to religious diversity, as evidenced by the success of Diana Eck's *A New Religious America* (2001), Robert Wuthnow's *America and the Challenges of Religious Diversity* (2005), and Robert Putnam and David Campbell's *American Grace: How Religion Unites and Divides Us* (2010). The American Academy of Religion's establishment of the Interfaith and Interreligious Studies Group in 2013 is an institutional marker of the growing size and legitimacy of this area of religion research.

Beyond religious studies, peace and conflict programs like those of the Kroc Institute for International Peace Studies at the University of Notre Dame and the Berkley Center for Religion, Peace and World Affairs at Georgetown University rely on the work of political scientists, anthropologists, sociologists, and psychologists to understand the complicated role of religion in both fomenting and helping to resolve international and intercultural violence. Cognitive and moral psychologists like Joshua Greene and Jonathan Haidt have brought attention to the deep dynamics of social polarization and its interreligious implications. And of course historians and area studies scholars have always had to reckon with interreligious conflict and cooperation as important dimensions of their research. To conceptualize this diverse work as a coherent field of study—interreligious relations—is to make an important move toward cross-disciplinary engagement and the kind of critical mass that can give academic work significance beyond the academy. To locate it in the already multidisciplinary field of religious studies is both apt and problematic.

In 2013, Eboo Patel offered an outline of what "interfaith studies" might look like: "As an academic field, interfaith studies would examine the multiple dimensions of how individuals and groups who orient around religion differently interact with one another, along with the implications of these interactions for communities, civil society, and global politics."[1] In what follows I examine the current contours and possible future of such a field in the secular discipline of religious studies.

CONTEXTS: ACADEMIC, CIVIC, RELIGIOUS

Three overlapping contexts frame the relationship between interreligious studies and what would seem to be its logical disciplinary home: religious studies. The first of these is the *institutional context* in which religious studies, and the humanities more broadly, face decreasing enrollments and increased pressure to justify themselves on market grounds. Media analyses over the past several years, triggered in part by Harvard's Mapping the Future report, have raised alarms about the "decline," "crisis," or "threat" facing traditional humanities disciplines.[2] In this regard, anxiety is clearly felt in the halls of university religious studies departments.

Our students, influenced by the triple threat of educational debt, stagnant job markets, and a wider culture that increasingly defines the value of education in terms of its immediate economic payoff, are likely to leave their religious studies education at a single general education course—or nothing at all. And because a low number of majors is often given as justification for reducing or eliminating academic programs, many religious studies departments are indeed in crisis mode. While it is the stuff of eloquent essays in the *Chronicle of Higher Education*, the case for the long-term and intrinsic value of humanities degrees has not yet been made effectively to the relevant populations. An infusion of new disciplinary energy from interfaith and interreligious studies programs, with their promise of practical, employment-relevant outcomes, would be a welcome development but only if the purpose, values, and methods of the emerging field can be aligned with those of the existing discipline, which is rightly wary of selling out to market-based measures of educational significance.

The second important setting in which this new field is emerging is the *civic context* of increased public concern to reduce interreligious intolerance and promote intergroup understanding. Increasing public anxiety about interreligious conflict and extensive media coverage of the changing US religious landscape have fueled countless initiatives to improve religious literacy and reduce prejudice and bigotry. These efforts are seen at the local level in the proliferation of community-based interfaith organizations, at the national policy level in the State Department's establishment in 2013 of the Office of Religion and Global Affairs, and in the educational arena in such programs as the Religious Literacy Project at Harvard Divinity School, which launched in 2015 and whose massive open online course (MOOC) in religious literacy enrolled over thirty-two thousand students in the spring of 2016.[3]

The project of strengthening the social fabric by reducing ignorance and promoting engagement across lines of difference is vital given nativist responses to shifting demographics and fears of violent extremism, both of which played a role in the US presidential election of Donald Trump in 2016. Once accustomed to life in a somewhat obscure and widely misunderstood academic discipline, then, religious studies scholars now find ourselves in the less familiar terrain of public interest and relevance. These developments invite the discipline to turn a fresh eye outward.

Finally, the American *religious context* of decreasing religious affiliation and increasingly dynamic, plural, and hybrid religious identities complicates established models of both interreligious relations and the academic study of religion. In many American cities it has become common to see church buildings that now house antique stores or yoga studios rather than religious congregations. A Pew Research Center report in 2012 provides some numbers behind this repurposing: The "nones," those who report no religious affiliation in particular, now account for nearly one-fifth of the US population and an even greater percentage among those eighteen to twenty-five years old.[4] What are the academic study of religion and the study of interreligious relations to do with this development? Programs for the study of nonreligion and secularity are quickly emerging, but they have yet to be woven into the fabric of the discipline, especially at the level of undergraduate education.[5]

Scholarly work on the nones has explored causes for the decline of religious affiliation.[6] It has also analyzed the identity subcategories of the unaffiliated, including atheists, agnostics, seekers, and the "spiritual but not religious."[7] But in this research, religious identities are usually understood as relatively stable things. One is a Christian, a Jew, a Muslim, a Buddhist, a Hindu, or a "none," and movement among categories is referred to as "switching," suggesting an either/or binary that may not accurately reflect Americans' increasingly eclectic religious lives. Interreligious studies and the established discipline of religious studies (whose departments and introductory courses are still largely built on "Big Five" world religion models) will both have to confront not only the new prominence of nonreligious identities but also the degree to which all religious identities are plural, partial, and hybrid, the ways many religiously affiliated people might *not* belong to their religions, and the ways many nones may in fact not be *not* religious.

CURRENT CONFIGURATIONS

One way to explore the relationship between religious studies and the emerging interreligious field is to compare descriptions and mission or goal statements. I was able to identify seventeen interfaith or interreligious studies programs currently offered by US colleges and universities and compared them to those of thirty-two religious studies programs.[8] The former are diverse in their curricula—some emphasize interfaith leadership, while others are more traditionally academic—but all but two of the seventeen surveyed are located in private colleges and universities, twelve of which are religiously affiliated. This in itself contributes to the suspicion with which secular religious studies might initially view such programs.

In reviewing their published self-descriptions, I identified thirteen salient traits across the two sets of programs:

1. Scholarly method
2. Multidisciplinary method
3. Comparative method
4. Explicitly neutral, objective, or critical method
5. International or global scope
6. Religious literacy as purpose
7. Promoting dialogue as purpose
8. Understanding diversity as purpose
9. Contributing to citizenship or the public good
10. Fostering empathy, sympathy, or appreciation of other religions
11. Personal development or critical self-awareness
12. Professional preparation
13. Attention to nonreligious perspectives

The graph "Percentages of Interfaith/Interreligious and Religious Studies Program Descriptions Featuring 13 Traits" shows the percentage of the two program types that featured each trait. While it is certainly likely that the programs surveyed do more (or perhaps less) than their public statements indicate, these characterizations give a broad sense of self-understanding in the field(s).

For both religious studies and interfaith/interreligious studies programs, a multidisciplinary method and a global perspective are high priorities. Many programs also are understood to be serving practical goals by improving skills for citizenship and equipping students with professional competencies. What is striking, though, are the traits that are common in one set of programs and rare in the other. Among the traits that showed up least frequently in religious studies program descriptions, for instance, are the development of empathy or sympathy for other religions, promoting dialogue, and personal development and critical self-awareness. Each of these is relatively prominent in interfaith/interreligious studies program descriptions, with dialogue being the second most common trait for those programs overall. On the other hand, while 35 percent of interfaith/interreligious studies programs cite the development of empathetic, sympathetic, or appreciative views of religious

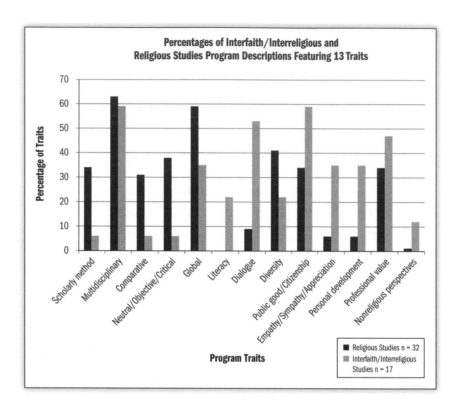

others as a goal, only 6 percent of religious studies programs include any such language (none of which were affiliated with public institutions). Similarly, religious studies programs tend to draw explicit attention to their scholarly, comparative, and critical methods, while this language is nearly absent from the interfaith/interreligious studies program descriptions, each trait appearing only once each. An obvious conclusion to draw from this comparison is that religious studies' emphasis on critical scholarship is, at least on the surface, at odds with the more affective and religion-friendly goals of interfaith and interreligious studies.

Some of the tension evidenced in this analysis can be explained by the history of religious studies as an academic discipline. The post–World War II establishment of departments of religion in American universities was largely the work of Protestant scholars who argued for the study of religion not only as preparation for ministry but also as a vital element of the science-driven modern university. But academic interest in religion remained largely limited to those religion departments themselves.[9] Especially as higher education shifted from mostly private to mostly public institutions and from a liberal arts to a professional focus, the study of religion was increasingly marginalized.[10]

When the US Supreme Court ruled in 1963's *Abington School District v. Schempp* that school-sponsored Bible-reading was unconstitutional, it also legitimized the nonconfessional academic study of religion in public education systems, declaring in fact that "it might well be said that one's education is not complete without a study of comparative religion or the history of religion and its relationship to the advancement of civilization. . . . Nothing we have said here indicates that such study of the Bible or of religion, when presented objectively as part of a secular program of education, may not be effected consistently with the First Amendment."[11] But that ruling also intensified concern among academics to keep hard and fast the boundary between the study and endorsement or practice of religion. Thus in the many now well-established religious studies departments in public universities across the country, there is wariness about practicing meditation in the Buddhism class, and even more wariness about hiring a Protestant pastor to teach the introductory Christianity course.

This concern for legitimacy and boundary maintenance extends beyond public universities to the wider self-understanding of the field, as seen in the last of historian of religion Bruce Lincoln's famous "Theses on Method," in which the religious insider is barred entry to the discipline.[12] Especially as the public *practice* of religion becomes increasingly associated, rightly or wrongly, with intolerance and violence, religious *studies* practitioners will rightly highlight these distinctions. If religious studies is to make room for interreligious studies, with its orientation to empathy and engagement, this boundary will have to be carefully renegotiated.

NAMING THE FIELD

Perhaps the most important step in defining the relationship between these two areas of study is terminological. One need not aim for orthodoxy here. The larger field of religious studies is also variously called religion, comparative religion, and history of religions, each with a different inflection but all mutually intelligible. The most widely used terms for the newer field, though, are more freighted. "Interfaith" appears to be the most widely used in the academic programs launched to date. But I believe "interreligious" is the better term, for two reasons.

First, "interreligious" more accurately denotes the inclusive scope of the field. "Faith" is a heavily freighted term, one that emerged from Western religious systems and is prominent especially in Protestant Christianity. Leonard Swidler has noted that "interfaith" came to be used more than "interreligious" as more Protestants got involved in interfaith dialogue programs in the mid-twentieth century.[13] "Faith" connotes personal disposition ("being faithful") and propositional assent ("having faith in this or that"), religious features that may not be central to non-Christian traditions in which ritual or ethical practice may be more prominent, or in which communal identity rather than individual piety is paramount. To ask the word "interfaith" to do the work of including Theravada Buddhists and Reform Jews—let alone secular humanists—is akin to asking "mankind" to stand for all humans. We can make the mental translation, but why not define the field more openly at its inception? If we begin from Patel's wonderfully inclusive naming of the object of study as "individuals and groups who orient around religion differently," "interreligious" would seem the better choice, especially as it pertains to those whose different orientation does not include religious affiliation of any kind. Any academic program in interreligious relations must ask whether students and scholars of all religious affiliations (including none) would find themselves at home in the discipline; "interreligious" is the more capacious term.

A second reason to opt for "interreligious" over "interfaith" is methodological. If this is to be an academic discipline suitable to secular higher education, it must not be construed as an auxiliary of the interfaith movement. Countless national and international initiatives, from community interfaith councils to high-level institutional consultations, use the word "interfaith" to refer to their work of mutual understanding, bridge-building, and peace-making. These are vital projects, now more than ever. But, as Lincoln would insist, they cannot be confused with scholarship. The interfaith movement, to which the word "interfaith" is I believe ineluctably tied, is decidedly an insider affair, the work of practitioners with normative visions emerging from both their own faith commitments and the dialogue project itself. Religious studies scholars resolve the insider/outsider problem in a range of ways, from Wilfred Cantwell Smith's insistence that any scholarly statement about a religion should be recognized as true by the practitioner of that religion to Russell McCutcheon's insistence that the religious insider's viewpoints, behaviors, and institutions are only data for the scholar to theorize.[14] Precisely because its subject matter includes the interfaith movement, though, the academic field of interreligious studies will need to work through the insider/outsider problem in a way that emphasizes critical distance, and "interfaith" will not help in that effort.

The prefix "inter-" is less contested in naming the field, but Anne Hege Grung has made an interesting case for "trans-religious" over "interreligious" because the former "requires the acknowledgement of *intra-religious* differences and a larger fluidity in the encounter between people of different religious affiliation."[15] This is an important move that emerges from feminist and postcolonial analysis of the complex nature of religious identity, especially for those—women, racial and sexual minorities, etc.—who are simultaneously insiders and outsiders in their social worlds. These theorists call attention to the power relations inherent in interreligious encounters, which remain dominated by white Christians and in which doctrinal and institutional conceptions of religion edge out those of practice, culture, and internal flexibility.[16] While "trans," with its suggestions of crossing over, through, and beyond, may speak well to plural, hybrid, and power-imbalanced religious realities, I believe "inter," with its own evocation of betweenness, can do the same job. The spaces that the "inter" in "interreligious studies" bridge must include those between different religious institutions, texts, belief systems, and practices; between practitioners of those diverse traditions; between those affiliated with the same tradition who differ in culture, race, gender, sexuality, literacy, and so forth; between religious and other social systems; and, finally, between religion and secularity.

TOWARD A FIELD OF INTERRELIGIOUS STUDIES

Interreligious studies belongs within the secular study of religion because (1) there is a great deal of research on the subject already being done in that setting that justifies a unified (though multidisciplinary) field, (2) religious studies scholars are equipped to address the subject with unique depth and focus, and (3) perhaps most importantly, the secular academy affords the critical intellectual space where the very terms and frameworks of interreligious interaction—such as religion, faith, pluralism, dialogue—can be interrogated and theorized. The practical aspect of interreligious studies that is captured in program traits like promoting dialogue and contributing to the public good, as well as affective traits such as fostering empathy, would be recast in a secular religious studies context as civic and professional outcomes.

We might then define the field this way: Interreligious studies is a subdiscipline of religious studies that engages in the scholarly and religiously neutral description, multidisciplinary analysis, and theoretical framing of the interactions of religiously different people and groups, including the intersections of religion and secularity. It examines these interactions in historical and contemporary contexts, and in relation to other social systems and forces. Like other disciplines with applied dimensions, it serves the public good by bringing its analysis to bear on practical approaches to issues in religiously diverse societies.

The *scholarly and religiously neutral* quality of interreligious studies is what establishes its place in the academy. Interreligious studies therefore must underline its commitment to critical inquiry by including, among other things, systematic analysis of conflict, domination, and contestation in historical and current interreligious encounters. That is, medieval Cordoba must be set against ISIS and the antigay Westboro Baptist Church. In this sense, McCutcheon is right that it should not be the task of interreligious relations scholars to be caretakers of the traditions. Such programs must also attend to the full range of dispositions toward religion itself, including those of the evangelical atheist. It is problematic, especially given the data on American nones, that so few of the surveyed religious studies programs (one of thirty-two) and interfaith/interreligious programs (two of seventeen) listed explicit attention to nonreligious worldviews.

The idea of pluralism that underlies much of the discussion of interfaith and interreligious work in the United States is due for particular scholarly scrutiny, and *theoretical framing* is a critical part of the endeavor. Critics of initiatives like the Harvard Pluralism Project and Interfaith Youth Core have argued that in these settings pluralism can function in the service of American exceptionalism, in the universalizing of elite cultures, and even in "the expansionist logic of empire" by incorporating more and more identities—such as religious conservatives, atheists, and racial minorities—into configurations of difference that make real difference invisible.[17] These are important and sophisticated critiques. If interreligious studies is to achieve the status of an academic discipline, central theoretical constructs such as this must be subject to critique and reformulation.

To say that it is religiously neutral, though, is not to burden interreligious studies with the standard of objectivity. Ironically, while religious studies has continued to pursue strict detachment in the quest for academic legitimacy, most other academic disciplines have long acknowledged that there is no view from nowhere and that scholars inevitably bring predispositions to their research questions. But religious studies scholars are up against a unique problem when this is acknowledged. As Bruce Grelle argues, "The language of neutrality is one of the main things that helps us distinguish between an academic and a devotional approach to the study of religion, a distinction that has never occurred to a surprising number of people."[18] Ongoing critical reflection on the scholar's role and self-understanding in relation to the subject matter must accompany the growth of interreligious studies.

The establishment of interreligious studies as a subdiscipline of religious studies creates a space in the field for clear articulation of the *intellectual* and *civic* values that drive it. These can align with those of the diverse secular institutions in which the programs will be housed. Grelle includes among these values "free and open inquiry, respect for multiple perspectives, and evidence-based argumentation," as well as freedom of religion and the promotion of tolerance, which, he acknowledges,

"undoubtedly aligns [the field] with liberal pluralist democratic poli-
ties."[19] Ongoing conversations with critiques of these alignments will
be an important aspect of interreligious studies as a secular discipline.
But it will be vitally important to ally the field with values that are
constitutionally sound, civically relevant, and clearly distinct from con-
fessional approaches.

The last feature of this conception of interreligious studies that
needs further explication is its *applied* element. Given the civic context of increased attention to the problems of religious intolerance and
the real-world consequences of religious illiteracy, religious studies can,
through the interreligious subfield, develop programs that substantively
engage students in real-world concerns. While other academic disciplines
have been building relations with community institutions for decades,
secular religious studies programs have generally resisted such partnerships, both because of concerns for maintaining critical distance from
the practice of religion and because there is not yet a robust infrastruc-
ture for getting students to do practical work around religious diversity
in the community. Those of us invested in the long-term flourishing of
religious studies would do well do to embrace an applied dimension
to our mission, framed in terms of civic and professional (rather than
religious) values and skills. Many religious studies programs, as noted
above, already include civic and professional outcomes in their program
statements. Interreligious studies programs can provide opportunities
to achieve those outcomes by involving students in the theory and practice of effective interaction in professional and civic contexts with those
who are religiously different. The challenge for such programs will be
to find sites for community engagement that are themselves religiously
neutral. It would be appropriate, for instance, for a student pursuing a
degree in education with an interreligious studies minor to work with
a public elementary school teacher on developing religiously inclusive
and constitutionally sound curriculum, while it would not be appropriate for that student to intern with her church's youth group. Carefully
identifying and developing suitable community partnerships is one of
the first tasks that secular interreligious studies programs must take on.

Religious studies scholars, especially those of us who work in American public university settings, know that our students come to our classes with misconceptions about the study of religion and about religion itself, often including essentialist views that religions are stable things and that all religions are basically the same (good or bad), or the hope that our courses might help them answer life's hard questions. Most of us aim to disabuse them of these assumptions and expectations with opening lectures on the academic study of religion and lists of learning objectives that assiduously avoid promises of personal meaning-making. But most of us also, I believe, hope that our courses *are* transformative, that our students become less dogmatic, more open-minded, curious, and tolerant. Incorporating the study of interreligious relations into our field offers us a legitimate site for the development of these dispositions by locating them in the civic sphere, where questions of religious identity and difference shape policy and inform the daily practices of life and work in democratic societies. Our public universities' mission statements typically include reference to preparing students for responsible participation in these communities, and interreligious studies programs could make a substantive contribution to that effort. This expanded model of the discipline can offer a substantive— but civic rather than capitalist—rationale for the vitality of academic religious studies, while responding to a real and urgent social challenge. By bringing a focus to the instability and betweenness of religious categories, interreligious studies also provides a space to explore some of the most interesting recent developments in both the lived practice and the theoretical interpretation of religion.

FROM THE HISTORY OF RELIGIONS TO INTERFAITH STUDIES

A Theological Educator's Exercise in Adaptation

Deanna Ferree Womack

The construction of a field of interfaith studies is both a pressing need and an exciting opportunity to build upon and move beyond the achievements of academic programs in theology and religion. Despite tensions between the central goals of Christian theology (the articulation of knowledge about God) and religious studies (the value-neutral investigation of religion), both fields have had an immense impact upon my understanding of how and why one ought to study religion. Yet, like other scholars, I was drawn to interfaith studies as I considered questions that traditionally neither comparative religion nor systematic theology has sought to answer. Although it is a multidisciplinary field with implications that reach far beyond the humanities and social sciences, interfaith studies can become an established area of research and teaching only in conversation with these two existing fields. As a theological educator trained in the history of religions, I look to interfaith studies as a third way of approaching questions of human religiosity and spirituality in the classroom and on the increasingly diverse campuses of American institutions of higher education.

Indeed, as I aim to demonstrate in this chapter, this emerging field might become a point of connection and reconciliation between religious studies and theology as it equips students with "the knowledge base and skill set needed to engage religious diversity in a way that promotes peace, stability, and cooperation."[1] What sets interfaith studies apart is the explicit aim to make such competencies available to students who "orient around religion differently."[2] This goal has been hampered by the ongoing divisions between theology and religious studies. Although university programs in religion attract students with diverse religious and spiritual orientations, the field has mandated objectivity as a guard against religiously motivated impositions. As a consequence, the sort of knowledge privileged in religious studies courses is often cognitive rather than affective, limiting the practical implications of students' studies for interreligious engagement inside and outside of the classroom.

Christian seminaries and schools of theology face the opposite problem. As the purpose of theological education is to train Christian leaders for service in the world, many seminaries now include the study of world religions or interfaith dialogue in their curricula. Yet such courses often take place in religious enclaves of students and faculty with similar Christian commitments or denominational affiliations. Even in schools with significant religious diversity or in seminaries that partner with Jewish, Muslim, or Buddhist institutions, the conversation remains limited by its theological nature.[3] In contrast, interfaith studies offers possibilities for a learning environment of disciplinary diversity and religious plurality. This is apparent from several recent college and seminary programs that take an innovative approach to interfaith studies, some of which are featured in this volume.[4]

In order to highlight the potential contributions of interfaith studies, this chapter places the academic study of religion in historical perspective. Focusing primarily on the North American context, it considers how the pioneers of interfaith studies might learn from and move beyond the methods, motivations, and accomplishments of previous generations of scholars. I begin with an overview of the shifting patterns in approaches to religion in the modern West. The second section explores how this trajectory evolved into the present-day movement of certain theological schools toward programs of interfaith engagement.

The final section considers what the history of religions and models of interreligious theological education together might contribute to interfaith studies as a distinct academic field.

SHIFTING PATTERNS IN THE STUDY OF RELIGION

The genealogy of Western Christian thought about "non-Christian" religions is important because of the dominant and enduring influence of European and American Christian scholars upon the study of world religions. Even today, Protestant assumptions about religion still color much of the academic and activist work on interfaith relations in the US. I begin this historical survey with the emergence of the modern study of religion in the nineteenth century. It was then that scholars and missionaries took up the Enlightenment concept of world religions and contributed to a global process of "religionization" and new ways of teaching about global faith traditions.[5] I am not concerned here with the various prevailing theories of religion.[6] Nor am I concerned with the pioneering scholars of the history of religions (*Religionswissenshaft*, also known as comparative religion) such as Mircea Eliade, Wilfred Cantwell Smith, Ninian Smart, and Joseph Kitagawa.[7] Rather, I am interested in historical shifts in the study of religion and the implications of such trends for relations between individuals of different faiths.

One key moment in American Christian engagement with "other" religions was the 1893 World's Parliament of Religions at the Chicago World's Fair (Columbian Exposition).[8] This significant gathering revealed a growing receptivity on the part of American Protestants (who dominated the leadership and constituted the majority of the attendees) to "foreign religious ideas or persons in the last decade of the nineteenth century."[9] This open disposition nevertheless operated under the same imperialistic approach of the larger Columbian Exposition, which put the achievements of the United States and Europe on display along with the cultures of the world that Western travelers had "discovered."[10] At the parliament, representatives of non-Christian traditions delivered 41 of the 192 papers, and the Christian speakers included scholars in the emergent field of comparative religion (for example,

Max Müller, the German-born Orientalist) and foreign missionaries (for example, Henry Harris Jessup of the American Syria Mission).[11] Both groups—scholars of religion and missionaries—had contributed substantially to knowledge production about religion in the decades leading up to the World's Fair. In the 1870s, when comparative religion gained much public attention, the movement of American missions also rose to new heights, with a post–Civil War increase in personnel and publications on "other" religions.[12] As a result of such traveling scholars and missionaries who encountered the religions of the world in Africa and Asia, the typical Western categorization of humans into Christians, Jews, Muslims, and "heathens" shifted, in what Tomoko Masuzawa has termed the "invention of world religions."[13]

The way Western Christians conceived of other religions and their adherents was changing, yet as new discourses on religious plurality replaced claims of Christianity's universality in the first half of the twentieth century, the logic of European supremacy remained.[14]

Although the agendas of scholars and missionaries were not always aligned, the study of religion in American institutions was still tinged with an air of Christian superiority, parallel to the ethos of the World's Parliament of Religions, which sought unity among the religions while also lifting up the ideal of America as the "redeemer nation" and of Western Christianity as a force for uniting all religions under one truth.[15] It would be decades after the parliament before those scholars who advocated an objective approach to studying world religions could carve out a place to do so in an environment not wholly dominated by denominational ideologies or Christian theological presuppositions. In an effort to avoid ecclesiastical control, university reformers first contributed to the growth of the "science of religion," which flourished in American institutions between 1890 and 1930. Such efforts to apply scientific methods to the study of religion did not aim to exclude religion from American higher education, however. Thus, this period saw "not the secularization of education but rather a 'desectarianizing' of it."[16]

Interest in the study of religion surged again following World War II. It was only in the 1960s, however, that scholars succeeded in establishing the first departments of religion in public universities and colleges in the US, despite concerns that such programs might violate the separation of religion and state.[17] With emphasis upon the "pursuit of objectivity" and a rejection of apologetics, religious studies advocated a sensitivity to "non-Christian" religious experiences that was not often demonstrated in Christian theological seminaries or in missionary training courses in comparative religion.[18] Although tied, at least initially, to the sort of Euro-American hegemony that Masuzawa identified in her study, over time the field of religious studies opened doors for scholars and students of all religious backgrounds or none. In this sense, as a field that (in theory) does not require or privilege any theological affiliation, it offers an important model for interfaith studies to build upon, in a way that approaches to world religions and interfaith engagement within most theological seminaries cannot. Because classical approaches to religious studies privilege cognitive abilities over practical application, however, I find it helpful to examine how Christian discourses on the religions and concrete practices of interfaith engagement in theological institutions have shifted since the late nineteenth century.

FROM THEOLOGIES OF EXCLUSION TO INTERFAITH ENGAGEMENT

While the Western Christian missionary enterprise of the nineteenth and early twentieth centuries is one source for contemporary American Christian feelings of rivalry with "other" religious traditions, the missionary encounter also contributed much to the present-day movement for interreligious dialogue. Besides prompting an increase in scholarship and teaching on non-Christian religions in theological schools by the early twentieth century, the publications of missionaries and mission supporters also provided a range of views on the subject of world religions. Many missionaries were profoundly changed by experiences of living among Muslims, Hindus, and Buddhists, and by their Asian and African Christian colleagues' more appreciative characterizations of non-Western traditions. This prompted a shift in some Christian theologies of religion from theological exclusivism (a belief in the absolute impossibility of salvation outside of Christianity) to more inclusive orientations in the early twentieth century.

Take, for example, the work of William Temple Gairdner, an internationally renowned scholar and missionary leader in Egypt, who came to believe that the Christian gospel was meant to fulfill rather than to destroy the religious values of Islam.[19] By the time the International Missionary Council convened its famous conference in Jerusalem in 1928, such fulfillment theologies had cultivated greater openness within the ecumenical-missionary movement toward the spiritual value of world religions.[20] Here we find echoes of the call of the World Parliament of Religions to "unite all religions against irreligion."[21] Gairdner's colleague Constance Padwick took this emphasis further as her encounter with popular Muslim piety and her study of Sufi prayer booklets with Egyptian friends led her to seek "a basis for Christian-Muslim encounter through the experience of the life of worship rather than through questions of doctrine or apologetics." Padwick suggested that Christians might incorporate into their own practices some liturgical expressions of Islam like the *basmala*, the invocation central to the Islamic prayer-rite ("In the name of God, the Merciful, the Compassionate").[22] By recognizing their theological affinities and common devotional experiences with members of other faiths, such missionaries (along with local Christians around the world) laid the groundwork for the more formal commitments to interfaith dialogue that emerged after the mid-twentieth century. These included the Second Vatican Council's affirmation of non-Christian religions and the World Council of Churches' first multifaith dialogue session in 1970 between Hindu, Buddhist, Muslim, and Christian participants in Ajaltoun, Lebanon.

With the influence of such early endeavors toward formal dialogue and the growing religious plurality of American society spurred by the Immigration and Nationalization Act of 1965, theological schools began turning their attention beyond the study of world religions to the establishment of curricular programs in interfaith dialogue. This shift is relevant for interfaith studies because the goals of such dialogue initiatives are different than the traditional goals of the history of religions or of systematic theology, reaching beyond academic inquiry to life practices, as interreligious awareness becomes essential to the formation of Christian leadership in the twenty-first century.[23]

In a 2009 study of 150 Christian, Jewish, and Muslim theological institutions in the United States, the Center for Multifaith Education at Auburn Theological Seminary found "a surprising and impressive range of academic course offerings about other faith traditions." Nearly half of the schools surveyed offered five or more courses in this area, indicating a commitment to promoting students' deep understanding of religious traditions different from their own.[24] Some scholars in these institutions—like Paul Knitter at Union Theological Seminary, Richard Fox Young at Princeton Theological Seminary, and Diana Eck and Francis Clooney at Harvard Divinity School—are building upon long legacies of the Christian study of religions within their institutions.[25] Other schools have developed new degree programs or centers for interfaith engagement since the year 2000, like the multifaith doctor of ministry degree offered by New York Theological Seminary in conjunction with Auburn Theological Seminary, the Master of Theological Studies program in global religions at Emory University's Candler School of Theology, Catholic Theological Union's Catholic-Muslim Studies Program, and the MA degrees offered through Graduate Theological Union's Institute of Buddhist Studies, Center for Islamic Studies, and Center for Jewish Studies.[26] Still other theological schools, including Hartford Seminary, Claremont School of Theology, and Andover Newton Theological School, have transformed traditional Christian theological education into interreligious theological programs. Hartford offers an Islamic Chaplaincy Program and master's degrees with a focus in Islamic studies and Christian-Muslim Relations, and Claremont has trained pastors, imams, and rabbis in collaboration with the Islamic Center of Southern California and the Academy for Jewish Religion, California. Andover Newton's long-term partnership with Hebrew College led to its Center for Inter-Religious and Communal Leadership, and more recently the school launched a Master of Arts program in global interreligious leadership.[27] In each of these cases, theological educators have given significant attention to the way that interfaith sensitivity and leadership should be conceived of and taught in seminaries to Christian students and—in select interreligious programs—to future Jewish, Muslim, or Buddhist leaders. Although such initiatives carry great potential for promoting peace, stability, and interfaith cooperation, their target audience remains limited to the clergy and to specialists in theology. In the final section below, I consider how interfaith studies might achieve a broader impact by building upon and integrating the work of theology and religious studies.

ADAPTING HISTORICAL AND CONTEMPORARY MODELS FOR THE STUDY OF RELIGION

Pioneers of interfaith studies today have the opportunity to pick and choose from earlier approaches to the study of religion and to adapt them to the needs of undergraduate and graduate students who will not major in religion or theology. Adaptation means that we need not start from scratch and also that we have the freedom to avoid becoming entrenched in old ways of doing things. We can be open to contemporary needs and experiences rather than limited by the contours of established academic fields and by methodological rivalries. While we face the daunting challenge of integrating interfaith studies into the academy, I also believe that we can make use of a space on the margins to accomplish what our predecessors have failed to do in the area of multifaith relations.[28] I will conclude with four points of guidance toward using insight from theology and religious studies to nurture effective interfaith leaders.

First, as an adaptive discipline, *interfaith studies has the potential to transcend the tension between religious studies and theology with regard to religious confessionalism.* In interfaith studies, a student is not required to leave her faith at the door, but she is expected to learn how to listen to the perspectives of her classmates and of the religious communities that the class engages together. The Enlightenment dichotomy between public facts and private belief could be challenged in such courses, while each student also learns to be one participant at the table of many religious and spiritual traditions rather than presuming to speak for everyone's theological truth. In cases where the scholars, instructors, or students of interfaith studies represent the dominant Protestant majority in the US, special care will have to be taken not to project a Christian or

Eurocentric viewpoint. This is just as important for Christian-affiliated institutions as for state-funded secular universities.

Second, *interfaith studies can place front and center the pressing issues of diversity and participation* that many scholars are still working to integrate into long-established fields. For example, feminist/womanist/*mujerista* theologies remain subcategories of systematic theology and are not fully incorporated into the traditional curriculum in many seminaries. We have the opportunity to create a field where "women's issues" are not merely the concern of some, but where women's voices are a natural and expected part of the pluralism that interfaith studies seeks to cultivate. The same would be true also of many other perspectives that have been marginalized (including LGBTQ, non-Western, and liberation theologies) and of newer subjects of exploration like interreligious theology that remain outside traditional areas of study.[29]

Third, *interfaith studies can become a bridge linking the question of religion to STEM fields and pre-professional degree programs* that no longer require students to show any knowledge of religious and theological studies. It may even be that the addition of interfaith studies into religious studies programs could add to the attractiveness of such departments that have sought in recent years to justify the need for religious study as a supplement to other majors. Rather than making the argument that a religious studies course might be helpful for a career outside of the humanities, interfaith studies courses would train pre-med students in an interreligious competency that is directly relevant to their field and equip business majors with a skill set for communicating with diverse clientele, for example.

Finally, while breaking from patterns that are detrimental to dialogue and collaboration, *we do not have to give up valuable principles that have already been established in the study of religions and interreligious engagement.* In my own teaching on the history of religions and interfaith relations, these principles include the following:

- The history of religions principle of seeking to understand a religious community on its own terms. (Interfaith studies might challenge students and scholars to become empathetic listeners seeking to understand each community studied or each individual in the classroom.)

- The history of religions distinction between emic (the perspective of participants or insiders) and etic (outside theories) approaches to a religious tradition.[30] (Scholars of interfaith studies should not make an independent judgment on the reality of a religious tradition but should reflect upon and recognize their own values and biases while also learning from others. Moving beyond the insider-outsider dichotomy, this means working together to build a common life.)
- The theological language of formation (faith formation or ministerial formation). (Interfaith studies courses should provide leadership formation for professionals in a multifaith world.)
- New theological initiatives in interreligious learning. (Interfaith studies can cultivate an interreligious or interfaith learning environment that goes beyond comparative theological reflection.)

Thus, whereas Christian studies of world religions developed in service of world missions, and religious studies emerged due to the need for non-apologetic study of religious traditions, interfaith studies is a response to the growing plurality of American society. Young people—whether they are religious studies majors and theologians or not—will need to demonstrate interreligious awareness in their private and professional relationships. Rather than reinventing old academic and cultural patterns, the success of interfaith studies will be tied to the next generation's ability to live out the values of pluralism in a multifaith world.

COMMON GROUND

Imagining Interfaith Studies as an Inclusive, Interdisciplinary Field*

Elizabeth Kubek

*And feminist methodologies can assist us all
in major ways as researchers, academics,
and as activists and organizers.*

—ANGELA DAVIS,
Freedom Is a Constant Struggle

As a scholar and teacher, I come to the conversation represented by this volume along a different path than that of my fellow contributors. A graduate student in literature during the 1980s, I benefited from the groundbreaking work of earlier feminist scholars, who had fought to create a new academic field that embraced the lives and creativity of women. For my generation of students, the shared rediscovery of women as artists and activists, whose concerns seemed to reflect our own, was exciting and transformative. Previous to this discovery, we had learned to practice a form of what Kenji Yoshino, following Erving Goffman, terms "covering": treating our embarrassing gender as a disability, at best irrelevant to scholarly practice.[1] Sometimes it was worse

* Thanks to Jennifer Peace for the subtitle and to both Jenny and Noah Silverman for patient and collegial editing, done in the collaborative spirit this essay attempts to describe.

than embarrassing; we were told explicitly that as women we were in-capable of mastering the "purer" fields of philosophy, science, or math-ematics. The boundaries of the disciplines were laid out and patrolled by men, and we had turned to the humanities as our natural refuge. But women's studies offered us a space of our own, one from which we could boldly raid the territory of others, claiming and transforming their scholarly tools and practices.

As women's studies became an established field, it also offered us a new vision of the American academy. The "theoretical turn" of 1980s feminist scholarship, while potentially divisive, marked the moment when a critical interdisciplinarity emerged within the field. Feminist the-ory not only drew upon the traditional disciplines but also transformed them, challenging their blind spots and patriarchal complicities. The interdisciplinary nature of women's and gender studies also allowed us to form collegial relationships in which narrow expertise was less im-portant than shared dedication to positive change. At its finest this field was (and remains) collaborative and creative, open to examining the relevance of personal experience, and prepared to empower unheard voices, enrich pedagogies, and transform teaching and learning.

Across the United States, while many institutions now have formal programs in women's studies, feminism and questions of sexual identity remain controversial, and I have come to accept that the work of gen-der studies may always be in progress. In the current decade, however, questions of religious identity and faith have come to carry a similar burden of social and ethical urgency. Like women's and gender studies, an interdisciplinary field of interfaith studies has the potential to meet this challenge and in the process change the academy (and the world, one hopes) for the better. My contribution to this conversation, then, is to reflect on my own experience as a student, a teacher, and a scholar of the transformative potential of inclusive, interdisciplinary teaching and learning. In the process, I hope briefly to sketch answers to three questions: how the model of women's and gender studies might help us imagine an interdisciplinary field of interfaith studies as a site of dis-covery; how women's studies classroom practices can create collective awareness, collaboration, and "common ground"; and, finally, which interdisciplinary or transdisciplinary practices might nurture the activist potential of interfaith studies.

UNCOVERING: INTERDISCIPLINARY RESEARCH AS (SELF) DISCOVERY

In graduate school, I experienced women's studies classes as discovery zones: reading the works of early modern women writers (many of them back in print after long neglect), I saw not only literature but history emerge as new fields, enriched by women's varied experience and inspiring struggles. My definition of art underwent a similar transformation, as feminist scholars brought to light previously undervalued forms: genre novels, textiles such as quilts and embroideries, diaries, private "closet" plays. At the same time, my own experience as a woman was given value by classroom practices that reassessed the relationship between personal experience and systems of power and knowledge.

Along the way, I came to reassess writers I had previously dismissed as trite and fussy. Frances Burney's eighteenth-century heroine Evelina, a naïve young woman overwhelmed by her first visit to London, initially struck me as absurdly anxious about her reputation. Feminist history helped me see that Evelina's fears reflected limits still affecting my own freedom: in a patriarchal society, women are judged in terms of their surroundings. Energized by this connection between scholarship and life, I wrote my doctoral dissertation on eighteenth-century women's writing about the city of London and the ways their authors exploited urban space to carve out new identities. The research for this project required me to step outside disciplinary boundaries, to draw upon the insights and methods of history, urban studies, and psychology, and to connect my own struggle for independence with the complex social structures of capitalist modernity.

The discovery of one's own place within a living narrative of resistance and risk is an origin story shared by many feminist and area studies scholars. These fields also share interdisciplinary traits: focus on a "problem or issue or intellectual question" rather than on a single body of knowledge; "broad dissatisfaction with traditional knowledge structures"; and a conviction "that the kinds of complex problems facing humanity demand . . . new ways . . . to order knowledge."[2] For interfaith studies, an interdisciplinary approach would allow scholars to reassess the ways we define "faith" in terms of its intersectional relationships with multiple areas of human behavior and culture. Rather than following the "traditional knowledge structures" of the academy, we can imagine how an integrative research approach might (for example) help a scholar contextualize her own faith experience and her encounters with faith "others" as part of an ongoing cultural narrative manifest in art, urban space, and mass media communication. The history of women's studies provides models and resources for interfaith studies as an interdisciplinary field—one that might free a new generation of students to contextualize their own stories and empathize with the stories of others.

TEACHING IN THE (MINE)FIELD

In the opening essay to *The Evolution of American Women's Studies*, Alice E. Ginsberg succinctly tracks four decades of the development of women's studies as an academic field. One of the great strengths of feminist teaching and scholarship, she points out, is that these practices empower students to challenge privileged aspects of teaching, learning, and research that conceal patriarchal hierarchies. Women's studies thus requires of faculty, staff, and students a shift in practice, toward a more experiential and learner-centered system. According to Ginsberg, this system can allow subjects to "creat[e] and own . . . knowledge based on their own personal and political experiences"; stimulate creation of flexible programs and courses where "process and purpose" may be privileged over the acquisition of a fixed body of knowledge; challenge the idea of expertise as the main source of authority; and nurture multiple, sometimes dissenting voices within the discipline (entailing race or ethnicity, class, and other "identity" questions, for example).[3] The validation of lived experience as a source of insight can transform the classroom into a shared space where the attitudes of participants can (and should) be addressed directly, rather than simply buried in the syllabus under rules of participation and conduct.

At this point a truth must be acknowledged: actively engaging the discursive behaviors of students, and encouraging them to speak in a classroom "based on their own personal and political experiences," is terrifying. Many students are convinced that they will be graded on their beliefs; many instructors dread student complaints and negative evaluations. Both parties fear embarrassment, loss of "professionalism," and the group disapproval of the class. But women's studies and other interdisciplinary approaches assume a decentered authority and provide "common ground"–based strategies for identifying and resolving areas of tension and disagreement.[4]

Finding common ground can be as simple as allowing students to create connections and build shared strategies for confronting new ideas. Early in my teaching career, having emerged into a dwindling job market, I was hired to teach a class in women's literature for Empire State College at the State University of New York. At the first class meeting, in a run-down former office building, I found that my students were all working women, most of them older than I was. Initially, I felt deeply uncomfortable. What did I have to offer that these women would find worthwhile? And how had I ended up in what I had been taught to regard as the backwater of adult education? But the students were motivated, excited (if a bit apprehensive) to be back in a classroom, and giddy with a sense of possibility: they expected education to change their lives. Most importantly, they were willing to open up to each other and to me. At our last meeting, one student lingered behind to tell me that, because of what we had read and her conversations with her classmates, she had just left an abusive relationship. That moment changed everything for me. I knew I could not take credit for her act of courage, but my ideas of professional prestige seemed shallow compared with the working community that had emerged in that shabby classroom. As different as we were, we had found our "common ground" in our intentional, shared reading of women's narratives as models for positive change.

Finding common ground doesn't have to be this personal; it can begin with a simple acknowledgment of the cultural systems in which our students already live and work. These systems cut across disciplinary boundaries, representing a deep unconscious knowledge base that includes both variations and normative features. For my Gender and Literature class, which fulfills a general education requirement, I don't assume any feminist motivation or theoretical background in my students. Instead, we start the semester with an exercise I call "The Gender Game," in which small groups collaborate to create lists of objects they associate with masculinity and femininity, starting with food. The low stakes and apparently humorous nature of this exercise let students relax and get to know each other. When the groups report out, they agree more than they disagree: sweets are feminine, meat is masculine; women bake, men grill. At the same time, not everyone fits the categories: some women like steaks, some men confess to craving chocolate. Yet, as students who have worked in restaurants confirm, the server, when in doubt, presents the steak to a male diner; standard food service training holds that a woman might be offended by the assumption that she ordered meat. This seemingly innocuous exercise reveals both the extent to which we unconsciously gender behavior and the ways we practice what I think of as "I don't think this, but *they say*." In other words, we attribute to others the stereotypes that quietly govern our own lives. When we make this visible in the classroom, we are like the proverbial fish that become aware of the water in which they swim. For students, this process bypasses a lot of potential shaming and blaming behavior: they see themselves as part of a common system, one of which they can be critical. We can then move on as a community to discuss more serious examples of gender bias than those posed by what is on our plates.

Across the board, the ability of interdisciplinary fields to reimagine knowledge encourages this sort of "aha moment," in ways that traditional scholarship may not permit. In 2009–10, journalist Tracie Mc-Millan went undercover in the US food industry, as a picker, stocker, and restaurant worker. In the process, she became aware of the gap between academic knowledge and how we actually lead our lives: "There's a world of scholarship on these topics, and I've read some of it, so in strictly intellectual terms I should not have been surprised. But the narrative trailing along in my subconscious was different."[5]

Students may know that their perceptions of others' identities and beliefs are affected by cultural stereotypes but not know where the boundaries lie between myth and person. By distancing themselves from "the narrative trailing along in [their] subconscious," students can get past the fear of insulting those unlike themselves. This fear of misrecognition may be even more intense where faith forms the ground of difference: students may be uncomfortably conscious that a certain idea may not be what a particular person or group believes but rather what others think they believe. Yet they also know that a religion ideally constitutes a privileged object of "right" information. Addressing the faith of another person thus carries with it the threatening prospect of being doubly wrong: faith is both an attribute of selfhood that may be attributed (correctly or falsely) to another and an identity derived from a (potentially unknown) system. But in order to change our false attributions and misconceptions, we need to express them in a broad, interpersonal context, one where questioning and being present are emphasized over being correct. Starting with "nonscholarly" and interdisciplinary aspects of cultural systems, such as food practices, can create a safe common ground from which to acknowledge both positive differences and dangerous stereotypes.

FIELDWORK: TRANSDISCIPLINARY KNOWLEDGE AND STUDENT ENGAGEMENT

In interdisciplinary theory, a fieldwork approach is sometimes referred to as "transdisciplinary" because it allows "integration . . . of insights generated outside the academy," often leading to a localist focus.[6] In an age when academic privilege is being questioned on multiple fronts, the stakes here are not simply theoretical. A contemporary trope of community engagement that activist movements should "do nothing about me without me," reminds us that taking others as passive objects of knowledge creates resentment, widening an already dangerous gap between academia and the larger world.[7]

Recognition of the learner's experience as relevant fits well with both contemporary "high impact practices" and the current demographics of the American academy. Increasingly, students are "nontraditional," with multiple identities as parents, employees, veterans, and immigrants. Contemporary "andragogical" teaching methods for adult learners are designed to take advantage of this resource by engaging students in personal reflection and other integrative exercises. Paulo Freire, whose work with adults is foundational for theorists of andragogy, asserts that it is neither possible nor morally right to divorce practitioners from practice: "To deny the importance of subjectivity in the process of transforming the world and history is naive and simplistic. It is to admit the impossible: a world without people. This objectivistic position is as ingenuous as that of subjectivism, which postulates people without a world. World and human beings do not exist apart from each other, they exist in constant interaction."[8] Born of the same liberating impulses that actuated the contemporary feminist movement, Freire's praxis grounds insight in dialogue, rejects the power relations inherent in disciplinary knowledge, and privileges the experience, voices, and aspirations of those present. Embedded in his activist vision is a theory of knowledge as inherently interdisciplinary: living and collaborative, goal-driven, and valuing multiple strategies.

In the last fifty years, experiential learning and other "high-impact practices" (HIPs) were pioneered by scholars in women's studies and area studies fields, especially those with agendas focused on social justice and cultural change. Current trends in the academy offer at least a core of support for integration of HIPs into curricula, yet this trend runs counter to a century of scholarly tradition that derives prestige from abstract thought, objective methods, and "correct," reproducible results. Even in the humanities, the theoretical turn has meant an emphasis on specialized approaches, a trend that (ironically, for feminists) in effect "genders" scholarship as masculine—opposed to the personal, the broadly defined, and the immediate. This focus, valuable though it may be, ignores the contextual and contingent nature of active human learning in educated adults as well as in young children. It also tends to marginalize the activist origins and social engagement strategies of fields like women's studies, a trend of concern to some feminist scholars. The 2011 National Women's Studies Association report *Women's Studies as Civic Engagement: Research and Recommendations* examines the degree to which the field "has key lessons to offer about fostering civic engagement at the course level that will deepen student learning in the college setting, contribute respectfully to communities in which they become involved, and produce lifelong civic learners."[9] This report notes that service learning and community building are always at risk of being seen as "student life" functions and thus denied the prestige granted more traditional practices.

Yet when we examine the needs and interests of our current students and the world that we hope they will shape, the image of the scholar as an isolated, specialized researcher begins to seem like a remnant of nineteenth-century industrialism. Instead, interdisciplinary fields and collaborative practices are shaping research-and-development processes and redefining crisis management. Contemporary professions are increasingly intercultural, interpersonal, and contingent, with project teams and even "flash organizations" dominating headlines.[10] More seriously for a discipline with activist leanings, global environmental and humanitarian crises are rendering disciplinary boundaries obsolete while heightening the risk and the costs of miscommunication. Interdisciplinary fields harness integrative and collaborative approaches to approach a wide range of problems, but collaboration may be impossible without strategies for productive dialogue on divisive issues. In this context, a field of interfaith studies that provides students with skills for collaboration and global activism seems not only ethically imperative but also vital as a tool set for the continued relevance of American education.

It may be objected that the prospect of an independent identity for interfaith studies runs counter to the social-change agenda of activist teaching and learning. For some institutions, a preferred approach may be broad-based, an "across the curriculum" strategy that ultimately aspires to make the need for a specialized field obsolete. Certainly, feminism and women's studies have always hoped to make inclusion normative, but I would argue that one virtue of area studies fields is their ability to remain responsive to new voices and forms of oppression. For American women's studies, as the field broadened to include women of color, LGBTQ groups, and gender studies and men's studies, finding common ground grew more challenging. Arguably, the specialist logic of the academy made it easier to turn a movement into a profession. Yet the ideal of commonality endures, derived from a shared dedication to theorizing and challenging structures of power. To find its place on this shared ground, interfaith studies must be critical of authoritarian, objectifying discourse and open to acknowledging everyday experiences of faith (including "none"). Because it would actively seek out the participation of nonspecialists, an interdisciplinary field of interfaith studies would be more prepared to develop effective approaches to misunderstanding and prejudice. Feminism has been able to oppose patriarchy on so many disciplinary fronts (including the "objective" physical sciences) precisely because it has extended its theoretical framework (gender and liberation) to individuals within multiple contexts. This brings out another key commonality between interfaith studies and women's and gender studies: faith, like gender, is a quality of individuals and thus unknowable except as it is manifested in human lives and actions.

Seen in this light, interdisciplinary fields emerge as better equipped to create new knowledge and engage new demographic groups without objectifying those outside the academy. The "unknowability" of relatedness for an activist interdisciplinary field represents not the surrender of ethical responsibility but rather its acceptance. By refusing to "talk about them without them," we truly become agents of potential change. Women's studies, with its decades of struggle and vast body of theoretical and practical models, thus represents only one of many possible models for imagining a similar scope for interfaith studies, but it provides an excellent place to start.

CONSTRUCTING INTERRELIGIOUS STUDIES

Thinking Critically About Interfaith Studies and the Interfaith Movement

*Amy L. Allocco, Geoffrey D. Claussen,
and Brian K. Pennington*

Driven by a vision of cooperation between individuals of diverse religious identities, the civically oriented American interfaith movement has successfully established cocurricular interfaith engagement programs on many college campuses. We value these programs and the vision of "making interfaith cooperation a social norm," as the leading interfaith organization, Interfaith Youth Core (IFYC), articulates it. But as scholars who teach about interreligious encounter, we are also concerned that efforts valorizing cooperation may provide fertile ground for essentialism and generalization, fail to fully engage with histories of interreligious conflict, and unwittingly provide cover for the secular nation-state, hegemonic forms of Christianity, the globalizing capitalist order, and other systems and approaches that are in fact responsible for many of the tensions that the interfaith movement aims to address. In this chapter we extrapolate from our experience of developing the curriculum for an "interreligious studies" minor at Elon University to argue that the academic field of interreligious studies must maintain independence from the interfaith movement in order to critically assess discourses and practices that promote tolerance, pluralism, and respect for diversity.

OUR CONTEXT

A commitment to promoting interfaith dialogue and interreligious education was written into Elon University's 2010 strategic plan. Along with other faculty who aspire to teach about religion in ways that advance understanding and reduce conflict, we responded enthusiastically to this signal that the university supported our interests and was willing to invest resources in pursuing them. Three years later, when we joined IFYC's national effort to develop academic programs in interfaith studies, we found ourselves asking a series of questions prompted by this endeavor as well as by our experience as architects of, participants in, and observers of a campus initiative to foreground interfaith projects.

At Elon, we faced challenges posed by our relatively homogenous student body, which is dominated by Anglo-American, Protestant Christians and has significant Roman Catholic and Jewish populations but only the tiniest minorities of other "faith" traditions. The university's strategic plan had nevertheless begun to successfully build vibrant and well-staffed chaplaincy and cocurricular interfaith programs via its Truitt Center for Religious and Spiritual Life. These programs included multifaith internships and engagement programs for a small but dedicated cohort of students. The initiative energized our classrooms and helped our campus to begin to seriously engage with questions of religious diversity. Although popular and transformative, some of these programs—for example, a springtime Holi celebration consisting almost entirely of raucous, powder-throwing, non-Hindu students—are appropriately critiqued by students of diverse backgrounds as superficial and homogenizing.

As participant-observers in national conversations about an emerging field of interfaith studies, we find ourselves unexpectedly at the leading edge of related disciplinary and curricular innovations. In what follows, we describe and assess Elon's efforts to build a program of multireligious education as one site of the production of interfaith (or, to use the language we prefer for reasons similar to Kate McCarthy's in this volume, interreligious) studies. We are scholars trained in religious studies disciplines, intellectually habituated to historical and critical theorizing. When we and our colleagues began, with encouragement from Elon's leadership and an IFYC grant for this purpose, to design an "interreligious studies" minor, we reflected not only on the specific conditions of a campus early in its experimentation with interfaith programming but also on the terms in which the national conversation was taking shape. As we studied the handful of similar programs at other institutions, which may include coursework in leadership or conflict management, for example, we recognized that by contrast our commitments lay squarely in the realm of the humanities disciplines. When we listened to IFYC founder and coeditor of this volume Eboo Patel describe the interfaith movement he was helping to lead as a "civic project," we asked ourselves how interreligious studies, as a *curricular* project and a mode of intellectual inquiry might make a distinct contribution. And as we observed our students spray powder on each other at Holi and saw Elon's campus embrace programs like Christian yoga and mindfulness meditation, we deliberated about how to promote alternative modes of encounter and critical reflection on encounter.

OBJECTIVES FOR INTERRELIGIOUS STUDIES

With this context in mind, we embarked on a yearlong investigation into curricular programs that would reflect our institutional and intellectual circumstances. We hoped thereby to complicate the questions that the emerging field of interfaith studies might ask and to spearhead innovation and new models for structuring and assessing interreligious encounter. The distinction between the interfaith movement as an action- and engagement-oriented *civic project* and interreligious studies as a *curricular project and academic field* assumed a certain prominence in our thinking, and we posited the analogue of the relationship between social programs of poverty alleviation and the discipline of sociology.

At an important and fundamental level, those pursuits are often allies in their commitments to social justice and equality, but the first is a project of direct action, intervention, and policy development, while the second is an effort to understand social forces through research and assessment and to teach students to critically evaluate, improve, and enhance direct action programs. Thinking along these lines, we determined that fidelity to the principles and methods of the humanities would demand that we think and teach historically and theoretically. It would require firsthand engagement with communities and their interactions with one another as well as critical reflection upon those experiences, and it would ask us and our students to seriously consider critiques of the methods and emphases of the American interfaith movement.

In the end, we determined that a guiding principle for our curriculum development should be something like this: securing the *relevance* of interreligious studies to the wider academy and contributing to the *advancement* of the field requires ongoing critical engagement with models of interfaith cooperation and a rigorous interrogation of their ramifications.[1] With these ideas in mind, we concluded that as a counterpoint, complement, and correction to the interfaith movement and cocurricular models of interfaith engagement, interreligious curricular development should equip students to accomplish three overarching objectives: (1) to analyze the character of interreligious encounter; (2) to think critically about interfaith dialogue; and (3) to historicize diversity, pluralism, and tolerance. In contrast to modes of encounter predominant in the interfaith movement, which privilege direct encounter and individual experience, and in cocurricular campus programming by students and student life professionals, which promotes appreciation and celebration but may drift toward appropriation and caricature, we concluded that three other paradigms were necessary for us to consider: historical contextualization of encounter, ethnographic engagement through the carefully framed site visit, and critical reflection on discourses of pluralism and projects of the neoliberal nation-state.

In consultation with our own department, the Truitt Center, and colleagues in other disciplines, we sought and received approval for an interdisciplinary minor in interreligious studies that requires students to meet six learning outcomes:

1. Students will produce nuanced reflections on ways that religious traditions and religious communities have interacted with other religious traditions and communities throughout history.
2. Students will recognize and explain the ways in which religious traditions and interreligious encounters are embedded within cultural, political, and economic systems.
3. Students will recognize and appreciate the contours of religious difference both within and between particular traditions.
4. Students will interact with communities and hear from practitioners, gaining firsthand experience of worship, ritual practice, gender dynamics, the use of sacred texts, political dynamics, and/or interreligious encounters.
5. Students will analyze the category of religion and the field of interreligious studies, including the histories and theoretical models that inform them.
6. Students will critique existing models for understanding and facilitating interreligious encounter and offer constructive suggestions for improving these models.

While the required courses for the minor are all located within the Religious Studies Department, elective courses may come from a variety of departments. Minors must complete:

1. The Religious Studies Department course Religion in a Global Context that introduces students to the field of religious studies and gives particular attention to learning outcome 2 (and, in some sections, outcome 4).
2. Two courses that provide breadth and historical perspective with regard to particular traditions (e.g., Buddhist Traditions, Hindu Traditions, Islamic Traditions, Christian Traditions, and Jewish Traditions) and give particular attention to learning outcomes 2 and 3 (and, in some sections, outcome 4).

3. Two elective courses that focus on encounters between different religious communities or traditions, giving particular attention to learning outcome 1 (and, in some sections, outcome 4).
4. A capstone course titled Interreligious Encounters, in which students will meet all six learning outcomes.

The following sections of this chapter offer examples of how some of our elective courses and our capstone course help students to meet learning outcomes 1, 4, 5, and 6.

THINKING CRITICALLY ABOUT HISTORIES OF INTERRELIGIOUS HATRED

In choosing elective courses that meet learning outcome 1, students may elect to explore encounters between a variety of religious traditions and communities across time periods and locations. Offerings include, for example, an art history course on visual cultures of Judaism, Christianity, and Islam, looking at points of contact, continuity, and conflict among those traditions; a German course that devotes substantial attention to relations between Christians and Muslims in contemporary Germany; a religious studies course focusing on conflicts and confluences along the Silk Road in late antiquity and the early Middle Ages; a Spanish course that examines the history of Spanish Christian imperialism and the conquest of indigenous peoples; or an Elon study abroad course located in Ethiopia and Tanzania, taught by a historian and an anthropologist, that scrutinizes encounters between and among multiple religious communities.

All of these courses are historically oriented in one way or another and thus require students to study histories of interreligious conflict and hatred. Co-curricular interfaith programs readily acknowledge these histories, but in their effort to cast approved religious traditions in a positive light they are more likely to conclude that, nevertheless, none of our faiths *in their essence* truly promotes hatred and conflict. By contrast, our interreligious studies faculty are more likely to point out that what Americans like to call "faiths" have historically been political traditions as much as anything, and that members of so-called "faith communities" have often been interested in asserting political power over others and fostering hatred of those who challenge what they see as their rightful power.

One example of an elective course that explores these historical dynamics is a course taught by Geoffrey D. Claussen and Jeffrey Pugh, Jewish-Christian Dialogue (Real and Imagined). This course examines the ways that Jews and Christians have constructed Jewish and Christian identities in relation to the other in diverse historical, geographic, cultural, and political contexts. We underscore that the history of Jewish-Christian dialogue has often been less about actual conversations between human beings and more about imaginary dialogues in the minds of Jews and Christians, reflecting the way that both Jews and Christians have imagined the other as idolatrous, impure, demonic, or the source of any number of evils that must be eliminated from an ideal world.

The work of history that stands at the center of this course is David Nirenberg's *Anti-Judaism: The Western Tradition*, which gives particular attention to how diverse Christians have thought about Jews as the other in opposition to whom they have constructed their identities. As Nirenberg demonstrates, many of the Christians who engaged in influential patterns of thinking about Jews had no contact with actual Jews themselves but often used rhetoric about Jews in their fights with other Christians. Their concepts of Judaism, however, frequently had dire political consequences for actual Jews, given the historical realities of Christian political power (and Jewish political powerlessness) throughout most of the past seventeen hundred years. Even as they see the striking parallels between how Jews have demonized Christians and Christians have demonized Jews, students come to appreciate the ways in which these hatreds have had very different levels of influence on the course of history, and also the ways in which Jewish-Christian relations have dramatically shifted with the tides of political power in the twentieth century. Students are able to recognize how studying the dynamics of political power is essential for understanding the encounters between different communities.

Significantly, Nirenberg also argues that the history of Christian thinking about Jews has had serious consequences for all of us who are heir to Western intellectual traditions. Nirenberg argues that "anti-Judaism" has not been marginal to the development of dominant patterns of thinking in the West but rather "one of the basic tools with which that edifice [of Western thought] was constructed."[2] With regard to this history, Nirenberg writes, "The peril of fantasizing our freedom from the past is great."[3] Quite the contrary, even the very language that we use to speak about "interfaith" or "interreligious" encounters—including words like "faith," "religion," or "politics" (not to mention words like "spirit," "freedom," "reason," "law," "love," and "justice")—is burdened by the way it has functioned in the past as part of an arsenal of Christian ammunition used against Judaism (though, to be sure, such language is also burdened by its roles in other forms of intergroup conflict). And students discover that even many of the critics who may provide them with resources for "critical thinking" about religion (such as, for example, Marx or Kant) developed their critical tools for thinking about religion precisely through their anti-Judaism (though, again, other antipathies have played a similar role for other critics). Studying such histories helps students to realize how their contemporary ideas are affected by this history of ideas, how even their visions for interreligious harmony may be fashioned by histories of interreligious hatred, and how, even as they seek to be critical thinkers, they may be insufficiently critical of their own habits of thought.

CRITICAL THINKING THROUGH EXPERIENTIAL LEARNING: THE SITE VISIT

Elon has earned a national reputation for its emphasis on experiential and engaged learning in its core curriculum and across university departments and programs, and we have capitalized on these strengths in our interdisciplinary minor. Its fourth learning outcome—that students will interact with communities and hear from practitioners, gaining first-hand experience of worship, ritual practice, gender dynamics, the use of sacred texts, political dynamics, and/or interreligious encounters—is accomplished through ethnographic site visit assignments that bring students into different religious communities and spaces. These site visits, which owe a great deal to Amy Allocco's design, feature in the capstone

Interreligious Encounters course and are threaded through several other courses in the minor. While we acknowledge that there are a number of limitations and pitfalls involved in including ethnographic site visits in university courses focused on religion and religious traditions, particularly when a single encounter with a community is all that is feasible in a given semester, we persist in using such experiential assignments in our courses because we recognize the potential that even one such fieldwork encounter holds for moving students toward a more informed appreciation of others' religious beliefs, practices, and commitments.

Although including site visits in our interreligious studies curriculum may appear to blur the lines of distinction we drew earlier between cocurricular models and our own vision, we would point to some key differences in the framing and execution of these experiences. In contrast to these cocurricular paradigms, where encounter is sometimes uncritically offered as an end unto itself, we privilege a trajectory that includes careful academic preparation followed by independent ethnographic participant-observation, classroom reflection and discussion, and written analysis to catalyze an informed and nuanced awareness of religious diversity in our students that we believe classroom learning alone cannot.

Students require adequate preparation in advance of the site visit, both personally in terms of the rigors of the ethnographic process, as well as academically, so that they are familiar with relevant histories and basic content and are therefore minimally prepared to navigate and interpret what they observe. While preparation levels will vary in relation to the course topics and foci, we know that spending significant time—ideally beginning on the very first day of class—discussing the logistics, goals, and expectations for this assignment is crucial. Still, even the best-prepared students sometimes find the site visit daunting or uncomfortable.

Substantive handouts prime students for the site visit by outlining the participant-observer methodologies they will employ as well as guidelines related to dress, etiquette, and bodily comportment. Other documents list key terms and sample questions students might ask of those with whom they interact during the visit and offer models for how to bring this experiential learning into explicit and sustained conversation with course categories and readings. We generally favor a model whereby students undertake site visits solo or in small clusters rather than arranging for the class to visit together (the approach most cocurricular interfaith engagement programs take). Two reasons underlie this preference. First, sending students out to navigate new religious spaces and communities independently offers them the opportunity to test drive course material in real-world settings and conversations, thus revealing the applicability and limits of the knowledge they have gleaned in the course thus far. This process shifts the locus of authority temporarily away from the course instructor to those they encounter on their visit and forces students to assume the responsibility for interpreting what they see and hear there (and for framing questions about what they do not feel competent or comfortable analyzing without assistance). Second, when students recount their experiences to their colleagues in subsequent classes, we all benefit by learning about an array of places, practices, and exchanges. Their rich narrations sometimes confirm or corroborate others' experiences but also frequently act as foils or highlight significant differences. In these sessions students extemporaneously and critically engage course categories and readings as they collaboratively hypothesize about what may account for such divergences. Identifying these variances and analyzing them in conversation with material presented in the course is a key aim of the culminating site visit report.

David Pinault observes that it is the physicality of site visits involving ritual that his students sometimes find "challenging or even threatening."[4] Pinault's students report being discomfited by the necessity of removing their shoes and getting their fingers sticky from contact with food offerings, bodily inconveniences that signal that getting out of the relative safety of the classroom to learn about living religions entails putting their bodies on the line in ways no amount of groundwork can fully prepare them for. Elon students' concerns about somatic involvement most often coalesce around gender dynamics, particularly among those who experience gender-segregated prayer on their site visits or encounter menstrual taboos in the communities they visit.

Because the site visit offers students the chance to temporarily embody gender-specific religious and ritual practices, it frequently prompts these participant-observers to raise more nuanced questions about gender roles and expectations in various religious communities than more detached classroom knowledge typically elicits.

These moments of literal cold feet are as crucial to the process of our interreligious studies model for interreligious encounter as the flashes of mutual recognition and appreciation are, and we render our fullest service to our students if we can help them to grapple with both. Successful site visits will make students palpably aware of difference as well as similarity, as attuned to incommensurable categories as they are able to recognize shared vocabularies and devotional idioms. These direct, real-time exchanges will alert students to the many ways that histories of conflict, exclusion, and distrust may still be present in contemporary communities and to think critically about the received categories of diversity, pluralism, and tolerance. And they will push us as pedagogues to embrace the role of colearner with our students as we hear and read about what they saw and did and heard, to be nimble in assisting them in contextualizing and deciphering without giving in to the temptation to overdetermine their interpretations and evaluations, or to make messy pasts and relationships overly tidy even as we push toward a more civil and respectful future.

THE IMPORTANCE OF DISCIPLINARY THEORY

Our capstone course for the minor, Interreligious Encounters, developed by Brian Pennington, helps students to meet all six of our learning outcomes, but it has two goals particular to this course: that students can analyze the category of religion and the field of interreligious studies, including the histories and theoretical models that inform them (learning outcome 5), and that students can critique existing models for understanding and facilitating interreligious encounter and offer constructive suggestions for improving these models (learning outcome 6). Capstone courses in major and minor programs very often familiarize students with the history of a disciplinary discourse and help them develop some self-awareness about that discipline's commitments and limitations, especially as it relates to other disciplinary approaches. This one devotes particular attention to the ways in which theoretical models used in the field of religious studies can help students to critically analyze the Christian pedigrees of categories such as "religion," "faith," and "interfaith" and appreciate their potentially hegemonic, normativizing tendencies. Alongside pluralism's scholarly advocates such as Diana L. Eck, for example, they read Talal Asad to grapple with the Protestant suppositions inherent in some versions of pluralism and Russell T. McCutcheon to consider the potentially ideological character of pluralism projects such as the interfaith movement.[5]

Students taking this course also study the particular historical contexts that gave rise to the goals of such movements. They are led to consider the roles of Western colonialism and Christian missions in establishing the very racial, ethnic, national, and religious identities that structure the contemporary social order and the interfaith movement itself. The course encourages students to ask: Who benefits from interreligious harmony and interfaith cooperation? Which values, communities, or interests are empowered by them and which are marginalized? They analyze critiques of interfaith studies as an academic field: for example, that it suppresses and stigmatizes conflict;[6] that it naturalizes and normativizes a bland and interiorized spirituality;[7] that it provides domestic cover for racist and imperialist projects abroad;[8] that it makes the world safe for global capital; that the logic of the incorporation of difference on which it is based is part and parcel of the imperialist US project;[9] that it co-opts difference for its own purposes and manufactures hegemonic depictions of minority difference;[10] that it compels an accommodation to Protestant secularism;[11] that it foregrounds projects of identity recognition over analysis of material sources of conflict; and that it normalizes US-style pluralism and thereby advances American exceptionalism.[12] If the field of interreligious studies is to have a healthy future, we maintain that, as with all disciplines, it must work to identify and deconstruct its assumptions, even if some of those assumptions are foundational to the interfaith movement itself. Just as anthropology came to an awareness of its facilitation of the violent colonization of the non-European world, and just as religious studies has successfully (at least as of this moment) survived the disembowelment of its foundational category, "religion," interfaith studies will have to contend with concerns about the interfaith movement's relationship to neoliberal projects of the postcolonial nation-state. Engaging with and assessing critiques such as these, we think, can help students think constructively about the future of interreligious dialogue and contribute toward building the field of interreligious studies.

Our goal is not that our students emerge from our courses as cynical detractors of good-faith intentions and actors, and our hope for the future of interreligious studies, we must be clear, is not that it collapses under the weight of its own self-assessment. Our challenge to our students and to interreligious studies is the same we pose for ourselves. A long, cruel, and racist history of European Christian colonialism and its intellectual products has generated the very lexicon and conceptual apparatus by which we apprehend one another and structure our social actions, a critical underpinning of what Jeannine Hill Fletcher in this volume calls the West's religio-racial project. A world globalizing at an ever-accelerating pace in service of the concepts and values born of the Enlightenment and the West's unremitting efforts at domination have put us all in an epistemological bind that we have not yet thought our way out of. Its social and political consequences are ever more obvious. With historically unprecedented resources at its disposal, the neoliberal nation-state is relentlessly committed to the defense and preservation of the modern episteme and the global capitalism that it undergirds. Rather than building on the very values that got us here in the first place, the field of interreligious studies could set its sights on addressing the problems that give rise to the very perception that we need an interfaith movement. A more radical critique could contribute to a fundamental reimagining of our social order. In our view, that would be an approach to interreligious studies worth pursuing.[13]

LEARNING FROM THE FIELD

Six Themes from Interfaith/ Interreligious Studies Curricula

Kristi Del Vecchio and Noah J. Silverman

In 2013, coeditor Eboo Patel published an article arguing for the development of the academic field of interfaith studies and theorized how curricula in this field might take shape in undergraduate contexts.[1] At the time, Patel noted that scholars have long been interested in interactions between people who orient around religion differently—and have produced academic works accordingly—but have not seen themselves as contributors to this distinct academic field. Seeking to clarify and develop this area of research, study, and practice, Patel offered the following preliminary definition for interfaith/interreligious studies: "As an [interdisciplinary] academic field, interfaith studies would examine the multiple dimensions of how individuals and groups who orient around religion differently interact with one another, along with the implications of these interactions for communities, civil society, and global politics."[2] Throughout the remainder of the article, Patel provided a list of hypothetical courses that might contribute to an undergraduate academic program in interfaith/interreligious studies.

Five years later, these academic courses and programs—including minors, concentrations, certificates, and even majors—are no longer hypothetical. As stated in the introduction to this volume, Interfaith Youth Core (IFYC) estimates that at least one hundred interfaith-focused courses and about twenty interfaith-focused programs have taken shape at undergraduate institutions in the US, and more are in development. This vast and rapid accumulation of curricular engagement with interfaith/interreligious studies provides tremendous data from which to analyze and draw preliminary conclusions about this field in its nascent development. In this chapter, we seek to identify and analyze themes found across undergraduate interfaith curricula that have developed since the writing of Patel's article.

As an organization that collaborates with colleges and universities in the US to advance interfaith initiatives, IFYC is uniquely well situated to conduct this analysis. Although not itself an academic institution, IFYC has partnered with higher education funders for the past five years to offer grants that support the development of interfaith-focused courses and curricular programs.[3] Through these collaborative partnerships with campuses across the country, we have gathered significant data from these grant projects—primarily in the form of syllabi, program models, and grant reports from dozens of undergraduate institutions—to perform this analysis.

As such, this chapter will discuss six principal themes that we have seen emerge across interfaith curricula thus far: (1) experiential and engaged learning, (2) interdisciplinarity, (3) intersectionality, (4) professional relevance, (5) personal reflection, and (6) religious literacy. These themes speak to the content seen within interfaith courses and programs, as well as the methodologies and pedagogies employed by scholars in the field. It is important to note that these six themes are not completely distinct. For example, components of religious literacy are involved in experiential and engaged learning, and interdisciplinarity tends to intersect with professional relevance. While not mutually exclusive, each theme contains unique qualities that will be described in the following sections, using examples from courses and programs that illustrate the theme particularly well.

EXPERIENTIAL AND ENGAGED LEARNING

Interfaith educators have long prioritized direct encounter, or, as Patel would say, *interaction*, between people who orient around religion differently.[4] Simply stated, putting students in interactive situations often drives home interfaith learning outcomes more effectively than traditional texts or lectures. While professors may use academic texts to introduce and analyze interreligious encounter, learning through engagement can bring to life some of the concepts that students learn in the classroom. This recognition has driven educators to create and experiment with a wide range of experiential or engaged learning activities both within and outside of the classroom.[5]

One successful method of experiential learning in the classroom entails case studies, wherein students are asked to consider the perspectives of different religious or nonreligious actors in a given scenario or to role-play exercises that require students to fully inhabit one such actor.[6] Outside of the classroom, experiential learning often comes in the form of site visits to houses of worship and faith-based civic organizations, short- or long-term service learning, and internship programs.[7] The following examples, all from faculty with whom IFYC has worked, illustrate the range of experiential and engaged learning practices within interfaith courses or across academic programs.[8]

Role-Play Activity

Rose Aslan of California Lutheran University often includes role-playing exercises in her courses to give students a better understanding of how moments of interfaith tension or cooperation might manifest. One such example is Aslan's "Park 51 Role Playing Activity," wherein students research stakeholders involved in—or opposed to—the development of Park 51 (the "Ground Zero mosque") in New York City shortly after the terrorist attacks of September 11, 2001.[9] After conducting research on their assigned characters, students defend their respective positions in front of one of Manhattan's community boards and "Mayor Michael Bloomberg" (also assigned roles in the activity), who then decide if Park 51 can be built.

Service Learning

As part of his Interreligious Encounter course at the University of St. Thomas, Hans Gustafson asks students to complete fifteen or more hours of service with a chosen community partner.[10] Service opportunities include volunteering at a local Jewish senior and assisted living center, tutoring elementary students at a Muslim after-school program, and working with teens at a local interfaith organization. When their service requirement is complete, students write reflection papers that integrate classroom readings with their experiences in the community.

Internship Course

To complete the new Certificate in Interreligious and Intercultural Studies at California State University, Chico, students are required to complete an internship course. Developed by Sarah Gagnebin, this internship course partners students with a local interfaith organization—such as the Chico Area Interfaith Council, the Center for the Public Understanding of Religion, and the California Pluralism Project—for a full semester. Students typically spend about nine hours per week conducting fieldwork, meeting with an internship coordinator, and completing assigned readings and writing. At the end of the semester, student interns develop and execute a plan that focuses on improved interreligious competency for the organization or its constituents or both. These final projects range from training modules to workshops, web resources, and community dialogue events.

INTERDISCIPLINARITY

As other authors in this volume articulate, interdisciplinarity is inherent to the goals of interfaith/interreligious studies in ways both theoretical and practical. Theoretically, interdisciplinarity leads to a more holistic, accurate study of interfaith interaction.[11] Practically, viewing interfaith/interreligious studies through an interdisciplinary lens better trains leaders who will work within a wide range of professional sectors.[12]

With both theoretical and practical implications in mind, most interfaith/interreligious studies curricula are developed with interdisciplinary learning goals. In the context of a course, interdisciplinarity often manifests as readings and assignments that integrate research, methodologies, and theories from other academic disciplines, such as sociology or business ethics. Given the time and content restraints of a single course, however, it is more common to see interdisciplinarity in the context of interfaith/interreligious studies programs, where courses from a wide range of academic departments are integrated.

Much of IFYC's learning around interdisciplinarity manifested throughout a grant project funded by the Teagle Foundation, in which IFYC partnered with more than a dozen colleges and universities from 2014 to 2015 to support the development of interfaith-focused programs. While most of these programs now are formally housed within religion, theology, or philosophy departments, some are situated more broadly within an academic center or a college of arts and sciences. In one case, at Saint Mary's College of California, faculty and administrators building the college's Interfaith Leadership Studies minor determined that it would be best situated within the School of Economics and Business Administration.

It is worth noting that, even if the interfaith/interreligious studies programs built through this grant project were placed within a religion or theology department, students were always required to take at least one course—but usually more—outside of these disciplines. The range of courses that fulfill program requirements span the humanities, social sciences, and occasionally hard sciences, including communications, biology, business, history, journalism, literature, management, marketing, pre-health professions, psychology, and social work.

From this grant project, we learned from our campus partners that interdisciplinarity was a key trait in designing interfaith programs. Building on this first project's success, an extended partnership with the Teagle Foundation allowed IFYC to offer a second set of grants to fourteen campuses from 2016 to 2017 to support the development of interdisciplinary interfaith programs within pre-professional contexts. At the time of this writing, most of these curricular programs have yet to launch. But programs currently under development include minors, certificates, and concentrations in interfaith studies or interfaith leadership designed specifically for students entering the fields of business, health, hard sciences (such as engineering), social work, criminal justice, and education. Many of these programs also feature courses in the core curriculum, allowing a greater breadth of students to encounter interfaith themes through their required or elective general education courses.

INTERSECTIONALITY

Religious and worldview identities do not exist in a vacuum. As authors in this volume have discussed, identity is intersectional. Worldview identity is influenced, complicated, and given nuance by other human characteristics such as race, gender, sexual orientation, political ideology, and ability.[13] To capture this nuance, scholars in the field are increasingly and intentionally focusing on these intersections in their research, which is also affecting the development of interfaith/interreligious courses and programs.

In the context of a course, readings and assignments about the diversity within a particular tradition or life stance often illuminate the importance of intersectionality. For example, Reform Jews in Ethiopia are likely to practice Judaism differently than Reform Jews in the Bronx; majority-black Baptist congregations are likely to worship differently than majority-white Baptist congregations; and atheists in the US differ vastly along political lines, as some claim libertarian values while others align themselves with American liberalism.

In some cases, entire courses focus directly on intersectionality. One such example is Matthew Cressler's Interfaith Atlanta Across the Color Line course at the College of Charleston, which examines the intersections of racial justice and interfaith cooperation in a fifteen-day summer seminar. After one week of course work, students spend a week in Atlanta visiting centers and organizations that have historically approached activism across racial and religious lines (such as Habitat for Humanity, Interfaith Community Initiatives, Koinonia Farm, the Center for Civil and Human Rights, and the Martin Luther King Jr. Center for Nonviolent Social Change). The course concludes with a final essay about the possibilities and/or tensions between racial justice and interfaith cooperation, as informed by the students' visits in Atlanta.

PROFESSIONAL RELEVANCE

Amid well-circulated critiques of the liberal arts when it comes to pre-paring students for the workforce, scholars and educators are creating interfaith programs with an eye toward professional applicability.[14] In-deed, Mark Hanshaw and Usra Ghazi's chapter in this volume, "Inter-faith Studies and the Professions," focuses exclusively on the applied dimensions of interfaith education, particularly as it relates to career and vocation discernment. Within courses and academic programs in interfaith/interreligious studies, professional applicability is addressed in a few different ways. More robust opportunities include internships, capstone projects, and volunteerism in professional settings wherein stu-dents are required to analyze how religious diversity is relevant within a given workplace or professional context. Less time-intensive projects include interview assignments in which students interview professionals in their future fields to better understand how issues of religious diver-sity manifest.

The importance of professional relevance is exemplified in Miriam Rosalyn Diamond's Understanding and Valuing Spiritual and Religious Diversity at Work for Professional Success course at Simmons College. In this course, students consider how to be effective professionals—across a diverse range of fields—in cooperating and connecting with colleagues, patients, or clients whose worldviews, beliefs, and customs may differ vastly from their own. To investigate the importance of inter-faith competencies in their future fields, students interview at least two professionals to learn how an organization or company engages issues of spiritual or religious diversity. Combining these interviews with official company resources (annual reports, websites, policies and procedures manuals, etc.), students write an integrated report, including recom-mendations for how the organization can enhance its religio-spiritual inclusivity or effectiveness.

PERSONAL REFLECTION

While IFYC's work tends to focus on the civic value of interfaith coop-eration and leadership, students and faculty alike are attracted to this field because of the relationship-building and personal growth that it affords. Many interfaith/interreligious courses or programs deliberately create opportunities for students to reflect upon their own religious or spiritual journeys, as well as their own capacities for interfaith leadership. Common approaches to fostering personal reflection in courses include journaling throughout the semester, writing a spiritual autobiography, and designing classroom activities that prompt ongoing, personal conversation among students.[15]

One course that exemplifies personal reflection is Spiritual Autobiographies: Many Paths, One World, created and taught by Nancy Klancher at Bridgewater College. In this course, students read autobiographical texts written by practitioners and adherents of multiple traditions, including Native American religions, Christianity, Islam, Hinduism, Buddhism, secular humanism, and Creation Spirituality. One of the course's main learning goals is for students to develop "perspective-taking"—a practice described by Klancher as taking seriously the ideas of others, reframing them by restating what was heard, and exploring their implications from multiple, often contradictory points of view.[16] The final assignment for the course is a ten-page autobiography, wherein students reflect upon the development of their own personal, intellectual, and ethical perspectives within the context of their own spiritual journeys.

RELIGIOUS LITERACY

The question of how much students need to know about a religious tradition before engaging with its adherents is still widely discussed among scholars teaching interfaith/interreligious courses. Undoubtedly, religious literacy continues to be an important learning goal in interfaith/interreligious courses.[17] Most professors agree, however, that students do not need to be experts in Buddhism, for example, before visiting a Buddhist temple. In this way, the need for religious literacy often emerges in the context of real-world examples or assignments, such as during a site visit or when workshopping a case study. This challenge has led to innovative solutions, mostly in the form of course assignments and projects, by professors teaching interfaith/interreligious courses.

One such example is Caryn Riswold's Interfaith Studies course at Illinois College, which requires students to attend worship services at a nearby synagogue, mosque, and church. Before visiting each, students complete a "Religious Literacy Report" about Judaism, Islam, and Christianity, respectively, to ensure that they have some level of familiarity—and know how to present themselves respectfully—before entering each sacred space. Together, these site visits and Religious Literacy Reports achieve the goal of integrating classroom knowledge about interfaith cooperation with concrete experiences in the local community.

CONCLUSION

While the field of interfaith/interreligious studies is still relatively young and continues to be theorized and articulated by scholars in the field, institutions of higher education are nonetheless moving forward with the development of robust curricula for their students. In examining and analyzing syllabi, program descriptions, and grant reports from IFYC's curricular grant projects, we have observed that these courses and programs share six major themes: engaged and experiential learning, interdisciplinarity, intersectionality, professional relevance, personal reflection, and religious literacy.

We acknowledge that these themes are not exclusive to interfaith/interreligious studies. They are in fact larger trends within academia, especially as the academy increasingly values interdisciplinary approaches, lived experience, and intersectionality as legitimate "ways of knowing" or sources of information. Furthermore, we recognize that these themes are also found in spaces of social advocacy and activism. Because interfaith/interreligious studies centers fundamentally around human relationships, the field is also (appropriately) impacted by the public discourse around issues of identity.

Thus, as the contours of interfaith/interreligious studies continue to develop and evolve—amid the ever-changing landscapes of academia and social advocacy work—we expect curricula to adapt accordingly. We anticipate revisiting and refining these six themes as even more courses and programs develop in the years to come.

II

PEDAGOGY AND CLASSROOM PRACTICES

TRANSFORMING INTRODUCTORY COURSES IN RELIGION

From World Religions to Interreligious Studies

Kevin Minister

As we bumped along a rural Himalayan road in the back of a jeep a few years ago, my university president asked me, "Why do we still teach World Religions?" This casual but incisive question struck at a tension in my own feelings about one of our discipline's foundational courses, a course I taught every semester. The importance of educating undergraduates about how different religious traditions are shaping society in an interconnected world has never been clearer, but I understood my president's question to interrogate whether the model of world religions was relevant and effective in accomplishing this objective in the academy today. Indeed, when I took a world religions course as an undergraduate, it was boring, outdated, and mostly irrelevant to the students' lives. As I worked with colleagues with similar concerns about the world religions model, I found that interreligious studies offers an alternative model for introductory undergraduate education in religious studies that is more relevant and effective in preparing students to understand, work, and live in a religiously diverse world.

Interreligious studies, however, is not just a niche academic field; it transforms the very foundations of religious studies curricula. This chapter examines why and how interreligious studies is transforming the introductory world religions model that still functions as the foundation of many undergraduate religious studies curricula. By focusing on both why and how interreligious studies is transforming introductory religion courses, this chapter seeks to persuade readers of the theoretical justification for focusing on interreligious engagement in introductory courses as well as provide concrete steps and practical examples for making this transition. As I have worked to transform my own introductory approach to teaching about religion from a world religions model to an interreligious studies model, I have become convinced that focusing on interreligious engagement helps students develop the knowledge and skills for navigating religious diversity.

THE "WHY": DECOLONIZING WORLD RELIGIONS WITH MORE THEORETICALLY COHERENT ALTERNATIVES

The world religions course I inherited fits the classic model of an introductory survey course in the origins, beliefs, and practices of "major" religious traditions, serving as both the gateway to upper-level religion courses and as a general education course. In the world religions model, a series of religious traditions are taken up as singular, global phenomena to be comprehended and then compared to other religious traditions. The structure of the world religions model is undergirded by assumptions that reflect its colonial origins that have been critiqued, most notably by Tomoko Masuzawa. In this section, I argue that teaching interreligious engagement addresses Masuzawa's critiques of the world religions model, offering a more theoretically coherent model for education about religious diversity in the twenty-first century.

As Masuzawa recognizes at the outset of her book *The Invention of World Religions*, we all have a general idea of what we mean when we say "world religions"—even "college students with no previous instruction on the subject seem to understand what it is when they decide to enroll in a course by that name."[1] But this consensus understanding reflects problematic assumptions about the nature of religion that ground the course I inherited and most world religions textbooks. These assumptions include, first, the ability to identify, extract, and prioritize religious beliefs and practices from other social and cultural ways of being and, second, the ability to essentialize universal forms of religion that can be compared and contrasted. On the basis of these assumptions, Masuzawa argues that the field of world religions has been from its origins "a discourse of secularization; at the same time, it was clearly a discourse of othering."[2] Through a genealogical critique of the field, she argues that these two generative assumptions of the nature of world religions "conjointly enable this discourse to do the vital work of churning the stuff of Europe's ever-expanding epistemic domain, and of forging from that ferment an enormous apparition: the essential identity of the West."[3]

Seeing the justification of these critiques in my own attempts to teach world religions, I have spent the last few years working to transform the way I teach the class. Throughout this ongoing process, two alternative theoretical commitments have developed in the structure of my course. The first is a focus on the "glocal" interaction of religions. "Glocal" is a telescoping of the words "global" and "local" that names the complex interrelation of the ways we experience global realities locally and the ways we locally shape global realities.[4] In terms of teaching world religions, this means religions are networked, interrelated phenomena embedded in local communities and cultures. World religions are not "somewhere out there," they are right here in Winchester, Virginia, where I teach.[5] Students cannot understand religion in Winchester, though, without a global understanding of religion, because how religious traditions are lived out in Winchester is shaped by global religious realities. Likewise, how religious communities interact locally has global implications. This means that the classroom cannot be an objective space for the study of world religions. Instead, the classroom, teacher, and students are all located in communities with global implications, and our approach to studying religious traditions, even at the introductory level, should reflect this.

The second alternative commitment, which follows from the first, is a focus on religions as lived realities, inherently relevant to students' lives. This is to say that the goal of an introductory, undergraduate course in religious studies is not primarily conceptual understanding of religions, much less an opportunity for students' self-discovery through the "exploration" of others' religious ideas. Instead, my classroom has become focused on the ways religious communities interact with the lives of the students and the knowledge, skills, and ethical awareness necessary to engage in these interactions well.[6]

These two alternative commitments, a glocal approach to religious interactions and a focus on religions as lived realities, have reoriented my world religions classroom around interreligious engagement. I do not intend to suggest that this is the only way to teach an introductory, undergraduate course in religious studies today. But I contend that transforming world religions courses in the model of interreligious studies provides a more theoretically coherent approach to introductory, undergraduate education. This interreligious studies model takes responsibility for addressing the colonial legacy of religious studies still present in its curricular structures and more accurately reflects the global interactions of religious traditions today.

THE "HOW": PRACTICAL WAYS INTERRELIGIOUS STUDIES TRANSFORMS THE INTRODUCTORY CLASSROOM

Having established the theoretical coherence of the interreligious studies model for introductory, undergraduate education, I want to build on this argument with practical examples of how shifting from a world religions model to an interreligious studies model has practically transformed the way I teach. I hope that these examples will serve both to clarify the difference between the world religions and interreligious studies models and to inspire the concrete transformation of introductory, undergraduate classes in the interreligious studies model. This section identifies how teaching interreligious engagement transforms introductory religious studies courses in four practical ways, drawing on examples from my own teaching as well as from other faculty teaching interreligious engagement at an introductory, undergraduate level.

First, I replaced the previous learning outcome—that students would be able to "display familiarity with the central concepts and practices of the major religions of the world"—with the learning outcome that students will be able to "demonstrate the knowledge and skills to navigate a religiously diverse world." The new learning outcome directly reflects the shifts from the classic assumptions of the field of world religions to my alternative theoretical commitments. It organizes the course around the students' lived interactions with different religious traditions, not diminishing the importance of knowledge about religious traditions but grounding that knowledge in lived interactions and pairing knowledge with interpersonal skills and ethical awareness. Moreover, this new learning outcome gives the course an interreligious orientation throughout the semester because I introduce it on the first day as the guiding question for the class: "How do we live well in a religiously diverse world?" This question serves throughout the semester to orient students to the practical, ethical nature of our inquiry.

Second, I added a unit that invites students into the ongoing process of theorizing religious interaction during the opening week of the course. As a class we analyze and critique four existing models of religious interaction ("Different Paths up the Same Mountain," "Different Paths up Different Mountains," "Religious Houses," and "Sheilaism"), before developing our own model.[7] I am upfront with the students that, as a discipline, we don't have a model of religious interaction with which I am fully satisfied and that we need a model that better accounts for how interreligious interactions shape lived religion. With that in mind, each student is responsible for identifying and describing an interreligious interaction from one's own life as a case study to test the models in class. With each model, we ask, first, "What does this model help explain about your case?" and then "What does this model miss, hide, or get wrong about your case?" I will briefly introduce these four models for religious interaction that we analyze in the class before giving a more detailed description of a model we have developed as a class, because the development of these models is key to differentiating an interreligious model from a world religions model in the class.

The first two models that we analyze, Different Paths up the Same Mountain and Different Paths up Different Mountains, provide frameworks for conceptualizing religious difference. The Different Paths up the Same Mountain model suggests that, while the present differences of religion are undeniably clear, ultimately all religions are headed toward a single, common goal in which their differences are reconciled.[8] The Different Paths up Different Mountains model suggests that religions share a common starting point, recognizing that something is wrong in the world, but their diagnosis of the problem and corresponding identification of a solution actually leads them on divergent paths toward different goals.[9] While these two models help students reflect on their own assumptions about the nature of religious difference, both of these models remain within what I have termed the world religions model because they tend to extract religions from other cultural ways of being and universalize religious traditions into a singular phenomenon. As a result, both models oversimplify and essentialize the nature of religious interactions.

The third and fourth models that we examine as a class, Religious Houses and Sheilaism, provide frameworks that explicitly aim to explain interreligious interaction. The Religious Houses model depicts distinct religions as different buildings, not unlike a mosque, church, synagogue, and temple standing side by side on a city street. Within this model, religious interactions tend to be envisioned as voluntary encounters on clearly demarcated sacred ground belonging to a single tradition or as consensual encounters in a secular, third space (conceptualized as a community center) where religious persons can meet on neutral ground.[10] The Sheilaism model arises from an interview in which Sheila named her religion after herself because she did not participate in institutional religions but believed in a God who wanted her to love herself and take care of others.[11] Sheilaism functions as an archetype of a model for privatized religious pluralism that focuses on the acceptance and interrelation of individuals and their unique religious identities instead of models that focus on the institutional or public interrelation of religious traditions. While these models clearly fall within what I have termed an interreligious studies model, the privatized sense of the houses model and the individualized sense of Sheilaism do not account for, as one of my students recently said, the unavoidable public interactions that we have with religious persons and traditions in our everyday lives and professional activities.

The limits of these four models have given rise to a fifth model that my introductory course continues to critique and revise every semester. The model that we have worked on developing together has been alternately termed the "Gravitational Model," "Atomic Model," and "Nuclear Model" by different classes. This model expresses lives as tracing paths that are pulled by centers of religious gravity, along with other centers of social gravity.[12] Religious traditions are identified by the many paths that individuals trace around the religious centers. Religious traditions may have multiple centers that are proximate to one another, but they are not identical, and they are only identifiable as centers because of their relationship to those who trace the paths of their lives around them. But the life of every individual pulled by a distinct religious center is also pulled by other social centers of gravity, including those of work, class, gender, sexuality, family, race, ethnicity, and nationality. How individuals trace their paths around these common pulls of social gravity is deeply shaped by how they trace their path around their religious centers of gravity. As individuals trace their distinct paths around these shared centers of social gravity, they unavoidably come into interaction with persons from different religious traditions. These interactions may be constructive or conflictual, but it is these interactions to which the course intends to attend. Much to my surprise, students have gotten palpably excited during the construction of a common theoretical model for the course because they are able to shape a model for religious interaction that reflects their experience. Among the elements of this model that students find most helpful are that it accounts for the interrelation of religion and other elements of cultural identities, the diversity of paths traced by followers of the "same" tradition, the potential for religious conflict and cooperation, the existence of persons shaped by multiple religious identities, and the presence of "nones" in relation to religions. Students also express critiques of the model as we continue to develop it, including that it does not account for the journey motif in which some of them figure their interreligious experience and that the messiness of the model complicates its application. This is certainly not the only model we could develop as a class, but the process of collaboratively critiquing and designing models provides an alternative understanding of the nature of religion from what the students arrive at the class assuming and orients the course of study to how religions interact and why students are invested in navigating these interactions.

Representing a third way that teaching interreligious studies can transform introductory religious studies courses, I changed the organization of the course schedule from a series of units on individual religions to units organized around case studies of interreligious conflict. Each of the case studies engaged introduces a key question for navigating religious diversity. For example: How do we disagree well in a religiously diverse world? How do we cooperate in a religiously diverse world? The case studies create concrete avenues into exploring the glocal interactions of different religious traditions.[13] This change has shifted the meta-structure of the course to acknowledge religious interaction as the site for learning the knowledge and skills for living in a religiously diverse world, while still providing the requisite knowledge of major religious traditions required by the department. For each case study, we spend a class period practicing ethical reasoning skills for analyzing religious conflict, collaboratively developing concrete plans of action in response, and articulating ethical justification for such responses. Throughout this process, it tends to become clear to the students that they need to know more about the traditions involved to respond ethically to a conflict. So we use the questions about religious traditions raised by the interreligious conflict to orient our study of the relevant religious traditions. Subsequently, the class reads short essays from *My Neighbor's Faith*, written by scholars coming out of the traditions we have just discussed, each telling a story of an interreligious encounter that was significant personally, and we analyze in class how the ethical reasoning latent in these essays illuminates the case study.[14] This culminates in a "Case Study Analysis Paper" in which students draw on the ethical reasoning skills and knowledge of the religious traditions to develop their own response to a real-life case of interreligious conflict.

Finally, I have integrated formative and summative assessments that enable students to practice skills for living in a religiously diverse world. Students develop a résumé of religious experience through which each locates one's own religious influences and interactions. As individuals or groups, students develop, execute, and evaluate a plan to use their right to free expression well on a religiously diverse campus. I have the students practice their interpersonal communication skills about religion, including explaining their perspective on religion in a way that helps others understand why it matters to them, asking questions of someone else's perspective on religion to better understand where they are coming from, and explaining how they relate to a different religious tradition in a publicly accessible manner. Finally, students visit local religious communities in which they employ their interreligious skills to learn about a local religious community and its perspective on and experience of religious diversity. Students are then responsible for demonstrating the skills to communicate what they learned about a regional religious community in a publicly accessible manner with the rest of the class and reflect together on the interreligious context in which we live. These assessments have enabled me to intentionally develop and evaluate students' skills for living well in a religiously diverse world.

These four practical transformations of my teaching manifest my theoretical commitments to introduce undergraduates to the study of religion through glocal interactions that highlight the inherent relevance of religious traditions to students' own lives. Knowledge about religious diversity remains important to the learning objectives in the class and prepares students for upper-level work in religion. The pursuit of knowledge about religious difference, however, is grounded in the lived interactions of religious communities and tied to the students' own ethical commitments to living well in a religiously diverse world. Furthermore, in the interreligious model, learning skills for interreligious engagement is just as important as gaining knowledge about religious diversity. As these practical examples attest, embracing the interreligious studies model transforms the very structure of introductory, undergraduate education in religious studies.

THE "SO WHAT": BENEFITS AND LIMITS OF TRANSFORMING THE INTRODUCTORY RELIGION COURSE

I opened this chapter with the valuable question that my college president asked about why we still teach world religions. While this question was part of a positive interaction that encouraged the development of our religion curriculum, it still reflects a broader shift in the academy in which religious studies needs to find new ways to articulate its role in undergraduate education. Using the interreligious studies model in introductory undergraduate courses helps justify the relevance of religious studies in an increasingly career-oriented academy because it highlights the relevance of engaging well across religious difference in students' lives and communities. As a result, I have experienced increased faculty and administrative support for the value of all students taking the course because they perceive its relevance to professional fields. But focusing on interreligious engagement is not just a sales pitch; it brings real benefits to the classroom experience.

The benefits that I have observed in my students' experience since I began focusing on interreligious engagement have been significant. I have observed increased student engagement from general education students. Students seem to experience greater respect for their own perspective on religion and, as a result, demonstrate a higher level of commitment to understanding the religious perspectives of others. For example, one student who grew up with parents from two different religious traditions and identified as both an evangelical Christian and as Jewish found acknowledgment of her own complex identity and, in doing so, became more comfortable with learning about other religious traditions that she had previously found threatening. Another student, majoring in global studies, who had no personal experience with religion entered the class unsure of the relevance of the religion classroom to her, but she quickly became the most engaged student in the section because she realized the relevance of being able to interact with the religious perspectives of others to achieving her professional ambitions. Perhaps the most pertinent benefit is that students demonstrate improved skills for navigating religious diversity, including the ability to articulate their own perspectives on religion, to continue learning about the religious perspectives of others in the future, and to develop an ethical framework for negotiating interreligious conflict. Their sense that they are more fluent in navigating religious diversity at the end of the semester is what comes through most clearly in the student evaluations of the course. In what is likely to be the only course dealing with religion in students' education, they don't just gain knowledge about religious traditions; they also learn the skills that will help them to live well in a religiously diverse world.

But once you change the starting point of how we introduce undergraduate students to the field of religion, we shift the trajectory of the religious studies major and the relationship of the religious studies program to the rest of the university. The major cannot proceed as normal because the world religions model on which it is built has been dislodged from its foundational position. The interreligious studies model sets a trajectory in which the inquiry into the nature of religion begins from the real-world interactions of different religious traditions. Upper-level courses must fulfill this trajectory by taking students more deeply into the study of how different religious traditions interact to shape the society in which we live. Because Kate McCarthy's chapter in this volume coherently articulates the theoretical and methodological transformations involved in shifting a religion program from a world religions model to an interreligious studies model, I will just offer a few examples of what this has concretely looked like in my context.

In my department, this has meant a shift from upper-level courses focused primarily on the history and beliefs of a single tradition (for instance, Judaism, Islam, Christianity), toward a model in which upper-level courses focus on the interaction, conflict, and collaboration of multiple religious traditions around global issues of common social concern (for example, "environmental sustainability," "gender and sexuality," "violence and peace"). This new trajectory for the study of religion has also opened up new opportunities for religious studies to permeate the undergraduate curriculum, including developing a focus on interreligious understanding in first-year seminar courses and a new curricular program that bridges religious studies and pre-professional education to better prepare undergraduate students to navigate religious diversity in their professional lives.

This chapter has argued that an interreligious studies model offers a more theoretically defensible and pedagogically engaging framework for introductory undergraduate classes in religious studies than the world religions model. In light of the history of colonialism, the reality of globalization, and ongoing challenges of living in a religiously diverse world, the interreligious studies model presents an intellectually and civically responsible alternative to the world religions model. Because the interreligious model refuses the secularizing and othering foundations of the world religions model, it opens the bounds of the discipline to flow out across the rest of the undergraduate curriculum and to allow the rest of the curriculum to flow in to inform religious studies. As a result, the interreligious studies model creates opportunities for collaboration with new disciplines (especially pre-professional disciplines) and for educating broader populations of undergraduates, which promises to expand the impact of religious studies in a time when it is much needed.

USING THE CASE METHOD IN INTERFAITH STUDIES CLASSROOMS

Ellie Pierce

In 2005, Diana Eck and I began an experiment: Could we creatively apply the case method to the dilemmas and disputes of multireligious America? How might this change the way we teach about interfaith engagement, and how students learn?

This chapter begins with the opening of our first case study, "A Mosque in Palos Heights," to illustrate the form and function of a case study. Then I step back to explore the origins of the case initiative, the fundamentals of the case method, and Diana Eck's reflections on using this pedagogy. Finally, I examine the wider use of the case method in interfaith studies, bringing in perspectives on practice from the field.

CASE STUDY: FORM AND FUNCTION

Dean Koldenhoven has the large, weathered hands of a former bricklayer, the long, distinct name of his Dutch ancestry, and the colorful bolo ties of a man who likes to do things his own way. Koldenhoven enjoyed being mayor in a city with a small-town atmosphere, where people know each other by their first names. Many people in Palos Heights, Illinois, referred to him simply as "Mayor Dean."

After many years of working in construction, Koldenhoven was appointed to serve as the city's zoning commissioner. He knew the construction trades and had a straightforward, no-nonsense attitude. After eight years working with an increasingly divided city council, Koldenhoven ran for mayor. He was elected in a close race: the margin was just 156 votes. As Koldenhoven joked, "It only takes one vote to win."

In March 2000, Mayor Koldenhoven started hearing some talk around town, rumors mostly, that "Arabs" were going to buy the Reformed Church of Palos Heights. It wasn't clear who exactly these people were, but it was clear from the rumors that they were not welcome in Palos Heights. Koldenhoven began receiving phone calls and letters from concerned citizens. They asked: "What are you going to do about this?"[1]

Decision-based case studies ask us, like Koldenhoven was asked, "What are you going to do about this?" and challenge those engaged in the field of interfaith studies to prioritize skills and action over theories and abstraction. As the above opening suggests, a case is fundamentally a story: it has characters, setting, tension, and a narrative arc. In a case study workshop, readers and discussion participants are asked to make an imaginative leap in order to inhabit the particulars of the case in time and place. While the scope of this chapter does not permit the inclusion of the full text of "A Mosque in Palos Heights," this section will walk through some of its elements as an example case, offering a glimpse of how the text is designed to elicit discussion through the case method.

After the case introduces the characters and the conflict, it establishes the context. Palos Heights is a small bedroom community outside of Chicago and with a population of just twelve thousand. Many of its citizens are of Dutch ancestry, and all of its eleven houses of worship are Christian. In this predominantly, if not presumptively, Christian town, the Al Salam Mosque Foundation plans to purchase the Reformed Church of Palos Heights. Yet local opposition is strong, and angry. Mayor Koldenhoven grows concerned over the rumors and fear arising in his community.

Even with limited information, the character—and by extension the reader—begins to explore the issue. Key questions related to assessment, diagnosis, and action help unpack the case and facilitate class discussion: 1) Assessment: "How serious is this?"; 2) Diagnosis: "What is the most significant challenge Koldenhoven faces?"; and 3) Action: "What would you recommend to the mayor?"[2]

As the case continues, Koldenhoven recognizes that he needs to learn more about the Muslim community and reach out to religious leaders for support. Again questions arise for the character and the reader: What does Koldenhoven need to know about Islam? How might he research this? What risks might he face? Is this a question of religious literacy or of civic responsibility? Does he really need to know anything about the religion to support the Muslim community's right to purchase a building? What should he do next?

The story is told as it unfolded for him *at the time*, without the case writer's analysis but with the limited information and suboptimal conditions that often characterize real-life decision-making. Primary and secondary materials, such as quotes from newspaper articles or from transcripts of city council meetings, help establish the chronology and move the story forward. At the same time they suggest some of the complexity and competing values and help engage the reader in both the facts and emotions of the story. The controversy intensifies, and tensions build for Koldenhoven. Some residents in Palos Heights are angry and afraid that the proposed mosque will change their city; others are shocked by the vitriol of the opposition to the mosque. Both sides are distressed to read newspaper coverage of the dispute, which includes a new label for their small city: "Palos Hates."

After weeks of debate, the city council offers $200,000 to Al Salam to walk away from the real estate offer. Koldenhoven is deeply disappointed by the offer—and with the fact that Al Salam accepts it. At the same time, Koldenhoven's son passes away after a long illness. The case concludes at a low moment, which is also the point of decision: at the next regular city council meeting, Koldenhoven must decide whether or not to veto the buyout offer, and he must decide how to move forward.

"A Mosque in Palos Heights" follows the traditional decision-based case structure: the (A) case presents the problem and the (B) case details the resolution. In between, there is ample space for reflection and discussion. Again, both the protagonist and the reader are called upon to assess, diagnose, and act. Students might be asked to draft the speech for Koldenhoven to deliver at the next city council meeting, or they might imagine themselves as citizens of Palos Heights and draft a letter to the editor of the local paper expressing their own perspective.

Context-specific and rich in detail, "A Mosque in Palos Heights" is also generalizable: How might the challenges faced by Mayor Koldenhoven, or, indeed, the Al Salam Mosque Foundation that is planning a mosque, be emblematic? How might the themes of this case—fear, change, courage, and managing crisis—inform our training of interfaith and civic leaders? What do we need to know? How do we get this information? How do we find our voice and the courage to speak? What do we say? And, fundamentally, in the field of interfaith studies, how do we teach about the interfaith encounter in such a way that builds the skills and capacities to effectively assess, diagnose, and act?

ORIGINS AT HARVARD

Diana Eck first encountered the case method in the 1970s at a seminar for new teachers at Harvard University. Led by Chris Christensen and Bill Poorvu, esteemed faculty at the Harvard Business School, those cases described classroom and pedagogical dilemmas. Eck was drawn to the participant-centered methodology and wondered how it could be translated to the study of religion. As she began her teaching career, she could not find anyone in the field who was using the case method. Yet, in the discussion sections of her classes, she would experiment with the method by setting the agenda for discussion with provocative study questions.

When Eck's academic focus expanded to the multireligious America, she developed the Pluralism Project. From the very beginning, the project took what might be broadly understood as a "case study" approach. As researchers, we in the Pluralism Project documented the changing religious landscape of the United States. Each in-depth study of a mosque, temple, or gurdwara (Sikh place of worship) served as a specific, situated example of a larger phenomenon. These narrative cases were at the foundation of Eck's books *On Common Ground: World Religions in America* (1997) and *A New Religious America* (2001).

Eck and I continued to follow media coverage of the encounter across lines of difference through the Pluralism Project's Religious Diversity News, an online compendium. Eck recalls, "Over the years we had a series of what we thought of as micro-histories of the transformation of American cities and towns through the struggles and creativity of Muslim, Hindu, or Sikh communities. This was the archive that seemed worth mining for teaching material—and this field of teaching seemed just right for the case method."[3]

After some fifteen years of researching religious pluralism, we were witnessing an ever more complex and contested religious reality. With the terrorist attacks of September 11, 2001, came an emerging interfaith movement and interfaith studies field, along with the *will* to manage change, contend with conflict, and build effective forms of collaboration, but what about the *skills*? Indeed, if pluralism is understood as more than "mere diversity," perhaps we needed more than "mere stories" to teach and learn about religious diversity.[4] Together, Eck and I wanted to dive a bit deeper into the stories of encounter and explore the case method.

The case method originated at Harvard Law School in 1870. It has been the dominant pedagogy at the Harvard Business School (HBS) for more than a century. Today, more than 80 percent of HBS classes are built on the method, and some 85 percent of class time is spent on student discussion.[5] The school's first dean referred to it as "the problem method" and understood its value for training agile, adaptable leaders.[6] The case method is now regularly and successfully used at all of Harvard's professional schools—of Law, Business, Medicine, Government, and Education—but rarely at the Divinity School or in the Faculty of Arts and Sciences, where the Pluralism Project is based.

CASE AS TEXT AND METHOD

We began our exploration of the case method in 2005 by asking questions of colleagues at other schools at Harvard. We sought the expertise of HBS faculty, attended case classes, and pored over cases and teaching notes. We observed how, through case discussion, students practiced varied skills such as analysis, decision-making, applying frameworks, oral communication, time management, and interpersonal interaction.[7] We learned that the case method also fosters critical thinking; encourages student responsibility for learning; transfers information, concept, and technique; develops a command of a body of material; blends affective and cognitive learning; enlivens the classroom dynamic; develops collaborative skills; and teaches questioning and self-directed learning.[8]

The HBS case study "An Introduction to Cases" explains, "The case method is built around the concept of *metaphors* and *simulation.*"[9] Although a case describes a unique, specific situation, it serves as "a metaphor for a particular set of problems." The HBS case study continues: "The best way to learn a skill is to practice in a simulation-type process. Thus, the swimmer swims and the pianist plays the piano. The swimming novice might drown if thrown into deep water after reading a set of books. And few of us would want to hear a concert pianist who had never before touched a piano, but who had attended many lectures on piano playing."

Within the field of business, definitions of "the case method" often refer both to the form and function of a case study: "A case is a description of an actual situation, commonly involving a decision, a challenge, an opportunity, a problem or an issue faced by a person (or persons) in an organization. A case allows you to step figuratively into the position of a particular decision maker."[10] The "case method" we sought to adapt for our field included these two inextricable aspects: (1) the decision-based case-study text and (2) the participant-centered case discussion pedagogy.

As Boehrer and Linsky write in *The Changing Face of College Teaching*, "The relation between the artifact of a case and its functional purpose is a crucial aspect of the case method. To grasp this, it is useful to think of a case in several ways: as a document or text, as a story, as a vehicle for discussion, and as an event."[11] Indeed, as we witnessed in person at HBS, the case method in practice functioned like an event: although highly structured, the discussion was new each time the case was taught. And the students were engaged in ways one rarely sees in a religious studies classroom.

Taking the HBS cases as a model and using their resources as a guide, we took the stories of encounter in multireligious America and began developing decision-based cases.[12] At the same time, we started integrating the case method more intentionally into how these materials were taught, beginning with Eck's classroom at Harvard.

A CASE-STUDY COURSE

In 2007, when the Pluralism Project developed enough decision-based cases and proto-case material to create the spine of a curriculum, Diana Eck launched her first formal case-study course: Religion in Multicultural America: Case Studies in Religious Pluralism. A General Education course, open to both Harvard undergraduates and graduate students, it carried forth our ongoing experiment with the case method. It was Eck's first class that used case discussion as the primary pedagogy and decision-based cases as the primary texts. Among these texts, then and now, was "A Mosque in Palos Heights."

While Eck enjoys lecturing, she notes, "I realized over the years that as the one who gets to put my thoughts together and present them to students, I was the one who was learning the most in the class, not the students. They might be inspired by what I said or the energy and passion I bring to it, but this is not the most effective learning experience for students." She explains, "While I do lecture for five or ten minutes occasionally at the outset of a case discussion, I really have learned to step back and enable students to take an active part in the classroom experience. I ask questions. I write on the board. I referee a discussion, but I don't take the authoritative teacher role."[13]

The case-study course has evolved since its inception, integrating new cases and scholarship, including essays from Martin Marty, Robert Bellah, and Martha Nussbaum. The course has shifted from a tradition-based approach to one in which thematic "sites of encounter" structure the course. In its seminar form, the course also integrates field visits, and students develop four papers: one on an encounter with a person of another religious tradition (or, if the student does not identify as religious, an encounter with someone who does); reflections on site visits to a local gurdwara and mosque; and the analysis of a news article related to the issues of the course. For the final paper, students choose between writing a research paper or developing a case study.

Eck explains, "The primary challenge is making sure that students understand the nature of the class. They will have to come to class prepared to think on their feet and talk. For students who are used to taking notes on a lecture, this is a new format. In many cases, the background work required to enter into and 'inhabit' a case will mean learning more about Islam or the Sikh community." She continues, "In many cases, the dilemmas presented in the case are quite new, and they can't just rely on their wits or their bravado. They need to learn, to think, and to express themselves—out loud. This is an experience that can be quite unsettling, especially for reticent students. It is active learning because the students have to take a very active role in their own learning. One of the other challenges is getting students to inhabit a case, to enter into it, rather than just talk about it and discuss it."

Jennifer Howe Peace joined Eck in the teaching of her 2016 seminar, as well as a 2014 summer program for seminarians. Peace had begun integrating cases into her courses at Andover Newton Theological School years earlier after she recognized their value for helping to cultivate both the skills and the qualities needed for religious leaders engaged in interfaith work. These skills, Peace explains, include "critical thinking, flexible thinking, ability to analyze sources of authority within their own faith tradition, [and] religious literacy."[14] Beyond skills, she adds, cases also cultivate qualities such as "an increased tolerance for ambiguity, self-reflection on one's own hierarchy of values in order to weigh choices, and empathy, as students are asked to put themselves in the shoes of the protagonist."

Peace considers the case method to be a signature pedagogy for interfaith studies: "A key dimension of interfaith studies is a balanced attention to both theory and practice—it is focused on understanding across religious lines/religious literacy not for its own sake but because it is essential for the healthy functioning of a religiously diverse democracy.

Our understanding or ignorance of each other religiously has profound implications in the civic sphere—which case studies illustrate beautifully." Yet Peace cautions that cases are not simply documents to add to a syllabus: "Case studies are a tool for teaching, and, like any tool, the key to using them well is to focus on the learning goals—what skills and knowledge are you looking to cultivate? How can you organize a case discussion to serve your goals?"

Peace notes, "I also like teaching with cases because they provide rich data without being didactic or prescriptive. They leave plenty of room for creative teaching." The case classroom is a dynamic one, and both Peace and Eck explain that they learn more about the text and the method each time they teach a case.

THE CASE STUDY IN PRACTICE: NOTES FROM THE FIELD

In decision-based case studies, dilemmas and problems are generative: they structure the narrative, engage the reader in problem solving, and enliven the discussion. While this chapter has focused on the promise of the case method, it is also important to consider the problems that emerge in the practice of teaching with cases. Three perspectives from the field of interfaith studies follow.

Reverend Marcia Sietstra

When the Reverend Marcia Sietstra encountered the case method in Eck's graduate seminar, she describes having "an aha moment." "I finally found a way to work with my congregation on interfaith issues."[15] Sietstra, a minister with twenty-eight years of congregational and community experience, explains, "I wanted to find a way to teach people in rural South Dakota something about other religions so they would not be so afraid." She developed her own curriculum, brought in speakers, and used books and videos, but she found these methods lacking. Many South Dakotans couldn't visit a mosque in their hometowns, and few local speakers were available to speak in a nuanced way about their differing traditions. Cases, Sietstra feels, brought some of the richness, complexity, and empathy that she wanted to offer her congregation and community.

When Sietstra started teaching with cases, she found that her biggest challenge was "overcoming the personal need as a pastor to take an advocacy position." At times, she wanted to steer the class toward a particular theological position or civic response or was too eager to cover a particular issue. "I don't want to shut them down or disagree. I just need to wait and see what they bring up. . . . It was about letting go of advocacy and my own need to make sure the participants recognized every important aspect of the case." Instead, she found the key to case teaching was simply "good questions" to help structure the discussion and unpack the case.

In congregational settings, Sietstra found mixed success. "Few congregants were prepared to read in advance. While many were eager to discuss the case, some were uncomfortable with the large-group discussion format or expressed the need to have more time to think about their responses before being asked to participate." Sietstra observes that the case method proved most effective in courses with the Osher Lifelong Learning Institute (OLLI), where highly motivated learners over the age of fifty were eager to prepare and discuss. She adds, "I'm thrilled when people come away from case discussions feeling empowered to be engaged and to become problem solvers in their communities."

Matt Hoffman

Matt Hoffman's first exposure to cases was in an emerging leaders seminar with Shoulder-to-Shoulder, an interfaith group working to counter anti-Muslim sentiment. After discussing a Pluralism Project case with a Muslim protagonist, Hoffman was eager to use cases in his new course on interfaith dialogue at Warren Wilson College. "Our student body is mostly white: 70 percent don't identify with a religious tradition." Hoffman recalls, "I was hoping it would allow a different set of voices to be present."[16] Like Sietstra, he was motivated by his context: "There is not a lot of religious diversity on our campus, which is located near Asheville, where there is not a lot of religious diversity."

Hoffman's students were bright and engaged, but their perspective on religion was profoundly different from the interfaith leaders from Shoulder-to-Shoulder. Some students tended to take a "legalistic" approach, rather than inhabiting the perspectives of others. Another complicating factor was a lack of religious literacy. When students discussed my case study "A Sign of Division," in which a rabbi is asked to remove a sign supporting Israel from his synagogue lobby for an interfaith event, his students thought the decision was simple: take it down. "They didn't have an understanding of the central, complex relationship of the American Jewish community with Israel to be able to understand why the decision was complicated."

Although Hoffman was disappointed with his first experience with case teaching, he notes, "I will try a case again. . . . Students are hungry for practical use and ready to think about these issues in a practical sense." He found the case studies engaging and enjoyable to teach, and they were highly rated on student surveys of the class. Hoffman will continue to experiment and will choose different case topics now that he better understands his student population.

Brendan Randall

When Brendan Randall enrolled in Diana Eck's case-study course as a master's student, he sought ways to apply the case method to his high school history classroom. "It wasn't just about being a better teacher but to have students who are more capable of living in a pluralistic society."[17] He recalls that, in traditional history classes, students would often ask: "Why do I need to know this?" Cases provided an answer: "You are going to be living in this diverse community. While this scenario might not be exact, do you want the first time you encounter it to be real-life, or do you want practice?"

Randall went on to become a teaching fellow in Eck's class and led case workshops in community settings. Over time he recognized the potential risks of using cases with self-selected interfaith audiences, including "groupthink" and not representing more exclusivist positions. He explains, "People can start to reaffirm each other and form an echo chamber. You need someone who puts on another persona as a pedagogical tool . . . imaginatively and with empathy." Otherwise, he warned, those who don't share the dominant view may be uncomfortable sharing their dissent. He adds, "This doesn't occur in business school cases because they can be less politicized, with questions like: 'How do we turn around a struggling company?'"

Yet Randall also recognizes the value of the case method in teaching interfaith studies: "It touches on not just cognitive, knowledge-based skills, but [also] affective skills, dispositions, and ways of thinking." He notes that "the benefits are less qualifiable and tangible . . . and the outcomes are difficult to assess accurately, as the results occur longitudinally." Randall adds, "It may not even be that class, that semester . . . but it happens when the student finds [oneself] in one of these dilemmas."

Later, Randall used the case method on college campuses across the US in his role as director of campus engagement at the Interfaith Youth Core. "With faculty, we introduce them to research about why the case method is an effective pedagogy for developing flexible expertise, not just concrete knowledge." He concludes: "We are not giving students answers but tools."[18]

As Sietstra, Hoffman, and Randall suggest, the case method in practice brings its own challenges: How to adapt the method for the teaching context? How to engage exclusivist, nonpluralist, or humanist perspectives? How to balance the need for depth, complexity, and ambiguity with the need for short, simple, accessible cases that need not be studied in advance? And, fundamentally, how do we ensure that students still learn content and build theoretical understandings and frameworks, and that the study of cases enhances, rather than replaces, other methods of teaching?

AN ONGOING EXPERIMENT

The experiment continues at the Pluralism Project and well beyond. Our cases are now regularly—and creatively—integrated into interfaith studies courses, as Kevin Minister describes in his chapter above; in

Salma Kazmi and Yehezkel Landau's Interfaith Peacebuilding course at Boston University; in Hans Gustafson's Interreligious Dialogue course at the University of St. Thomas; and in Barbara Brown Taylor's Religions of the World course at Piedmont College, to name just a few. Some may use the case study but not the discussion method. Others may use the method but not a formal case. Broadly speaking, news articles, brief scenarios, films, and literature can be taught using the case method. Ideally, these would have some of the essential elements of a teaching case, including context, complexity, ambiguity, and relevance.[19]

The case method has proven suitable for a broad audience, which might include theologians, civic leaders, and negotiators, as well as teachers and students in a religious studies classroom who no longer see the world religions approach as sufficient or relevant. The wider adaptation and integration of the case method signals—and supports—this shift to the new field of interfaith studies, which is interdisciplinary in nature and seeks to be innovative in its approach.

Colleagues from many fields have been partners in this work, including Willis Emmons at the Harvard Business School, Rabbi Justus Baird at Auburn Seminary, and Wendy Cadge at Brandeis University, as well as those quoted in this chapter. We continue to develop new cases and refine our approach, together with students, colleagues, and the community leaders who help us to craft their stories into case studies. After ten years of experimentation, Diana Eck reflects, "For the Pluralism Project, this is certainly a signature pedagogy." More than "mere stories," she observes, "it is a dialogical method of teaching in which context matters, listening is critical, and learning to speak in one's own authentic voice is essential."

TEACHING THE "MOST BEAUTIFUL OF STORIES"

Narrative Reflection as a Signature Pedagogy for Interfaith Studies

Matthew Maruggi and Martha E. Stortz

In his book *God Is Not One*, religious historian Stephen Prothero offers a four-part analytic for comparing religious traditions. He posits that each identifies a *problem*, a *solution*, a series of *practices* that move believers from problem to solution, and an *exemplar* or figure whose life embodies the tradition. Accordingly, in Buddhism, the problem is suffering; the solution, nirvana. In Judaism, the problem is exile; the solution, return. In Christianity, the problem is sin; the solution, salvation.[1]

Yet we argue that these problems are addressed not so much with "solutions" as with stories that are subtle, expansive, and filled with mystery. Jews reenact the story of the Exodus in Passover seders. Christians offer four biographies of Jesus. Buddhists return to the story of their exemplar, Siddhartha, a rich prince whose first encounter with suffering sent him out of his palace and into pilgrimage. According to the Qur'an, Allah is a divine storyteller, revealing "the most beautiful of stories."[2] Prothero's fourfold analytic handles the content of the great traditions, but narrative captures their heart.

We teach at Augsburg University in Minneapolis, a church-related institution rooted in the Lutheran tradition and located in an urban hub that is home to the one of the largest Somali communities in the United States. The neighborhood is one of the most diverse zip codes west of Chicago and east of Seattle. The undergraduate student population includes 37 percent students of color, a large group of first-generation and immigrant-American students, as well as students in recovery from substance abuse. The undergraduate curriculum requires two courses in religion and vocation, an introductory course in the student's first year and an upper-level course. A keystone or capstone course in the student's final year returns to the question of vocation and meaning-making within the context of the student's major. Augsburg's mission commits to educating "informed citizens, thoughtful stewards, critical thinkers, and responsible leaders."

We take seriously the university's mission, particularly the challenge to educate responsible leaders for religiously plural environments. While few students will become religion majors, they will all need interreligious literacy and interfaith competence to be "responsible leaders" in whatever profession they choose. Interfaith competence entails certain knowledge of the world's religious and philosophical traditions (the "what" of interfaith studies), skills that include conflict management, appreciative inquiry, and deliberative dialogue (the "how" of interfaith studies), and distinctive sensibilities like humility, empathy, and resilience (the "why" of interfaith studies).[3]

We have found narrative to be a powerful pedagogy for training interfaith leaders in the undergraduate classroom. Yet, we have also found that stories matter differently depending on the curricular level. For example, the introductory course uses core narratives from the world's religions, as well as spiritual autobiographies of their key exemplars, inviting students to see their own journeys as narratives. The upper-division course places these core narratives in conversation with the students' own. Finally, the keystone course asks students to craft case studies from their own experience, drawing out interfaith dimensions for discussion and analysis.

In this chapter, we will look at why and how stories matter, at the narrative aspect of transformative learning, and finally at effective narrative strategies for the different curricular levels of entry-level, upper-division, and graduating students.

NARRATIVE: WHY AND HOW STORIES MATTER

Theologians and philosophers of religion note the unique role of narrative in forming and transforming religious identity. Muslim philosopher Tariq Ramadan notes the importance of historical memory, which invites one into an ongoing, collective story: "Without roots, without memory, without belonging to a group, [humankind] is left prey to economic logic."[4] He underscores the need for stories that young people can inhabit and exemplars whose lives they can emulate.[5] Similarly, Protestant theologian Stanley Hauerwas argues that "the mysterious thing we call a self is best understood exactly as a story."[6] Roman Catholic moral theologian Richard M. Gula notes that all transformation involves a repatterning of the imagination to attend to stories that make life worth living.[7]

Religious traditions offer thick, complex webs of narrative meaning, but all stories are not equal. In Plato's *Republic*, Socrates argues that caregivers should be persuaded to tell their children only "noble stories."[8] He understood that stories have the power to inform and transform, but also to malform and deform.

Stories matter—but what constitutes a good and worthy one? Theologians and philosophers of religion have long wrestled with the criteria.[9] We distill these criteria in three points:

- *A good story helps people recognize and honor the full humanity of all persons, especially the stranger, the enemy, the powerless, and particularly the religious "other."* The parable of the Good Samaritan from the Christian scriptures relates the story of a religious outsider who assists a beaten man of unknown ethnic or religious identity who has been ignored by two religious insiders.
- *A good story helps people step away from violence and reckon with suffering and tragedy.* The Hadith tells the story

of Mohammed, who makes a nonviolent pilgrimage to a city from which he was violently banished. His journey leads to a peace treaty.

- *A good story helps people accept the paradox of their own humanity, both their tremendous gifts as well as their terrible flaws.* In the Hebrew scriptures, the prophet Nathan points out King David's adultery indirectly and through a story, inviting him to pass judgment first on a character in the story, then ultimately on himself.[10]

A good story highlights the best of a religious tradition, thereby contributing to common human flourishing.

THE NARRATIVE ASPECT OF TRANSFORMATIVE LEARNING

Theologians and philosophers are not the only ones to recognize the unique role of narrative in human meaning-making. Educational theorists emphasize *narrative reflection* as a signature pedagogy for *transformative learning*. M. Carolyn Clark argues that the "understanding of the self as narratively constituted opens up new possibilities for [transformative] learning theory."[11] In distinguishing transformative from informative learning, Robert Kegan notes the value of both, while underscoring that the former comes closer to the meaning of "education," literally, *e- + -ducare* in Latin, "leading out."[12] *Informative* learning fills in a preexisting form, while *transformative* learning creates new forms. In this way, transformative learning is always about epistemological change, challenging old ways of knowing and clearing the path to new ones.[13]

Religious literacy often focuses on informative learning, with an emphasis on knowledge about tenets, texts, and traditions. In contrast, interfaith studies offers great potential for transformative learning. Encountering the stories of religious others, a person or community is prompted to construct narrative meaning in new ways.[14]

Narrative reflection is the process of analyzing one's own narrative in order to make sense of new experience. Because of the role narrative plays in the construction of identity, stories offer enormous potential for personal change. Identifying with a powerful story makes sense of experience in new ways and leads to action.[15] The intentional process of constructing a personal narrative reveals discrepancies and creates disorienting dilemmas, internal and personal crises that disrupt the established story.[16] Whether dramatic or subtle, these dilemmas offer the opportunity to retell that story, exploring and clarifying past experiences. By "re-storying" that narrative, one develops a new, more truthful story.[17] The life of Malcolm X embodies this process of disorientation and reorientation. Disillusioned with a newly perceived "racism" in the Nation of Islam's teachings, he makes the hajj. The pilgrimage inserts him into the stories of Mohammed, Hagar, and Abraham, reorienting him to the "sincere and true brotherhood practiced by all colors together."[18] Thus, he re-stories his life as a Muslim.

NARRATIVE AS A SIGNATURE PEDAGOGY IN THE INTERFAITH CLASSROOM

Carolyn Clark and Marsha Rossiter describe three modes of narrative learning: learning journals, autobiographical writing, and instructional case studies.[19] Learning journals permit students to create a conversation between themselves and the material, both cognitively and affectively. Reading and writing spiritual autobiographies invite dialogue between the story of self and others for mutual illumination. Finally, instructional case studies give students the opportunity to engage in a real or fictional incident that has the possibility of multiple endings. Case studies make the participants part of the story through both listening and creating. To achieve transformation, we scaffold these three modes of narrative learning into the required sequence of religion courses.

The task of the interfaith educator is to discern which narratives might best be used at various curricular levels of students' academic journeys in order to maximize their transformative potential. Entering students need to discover they have a story to tell. They journal their way into the whole process of storytelling, and they learn from examples of spiritual or religious autobiographies. Upper-division undergraduates are ready to dig more deeply into the stories of the world's religions; they can engage in comparative narrative reflection and storytelling.

Finally, graduating seniors have accumulated stories from their own experience, and they are eager to examine the interreligious dimensions of these encounters through case studies. Taken together, these levels of narrative align with courses required for entering, upper-division, and graduating students to offer transformative learning with the goal of creating interfaith competence.

The Introductory Course

Students, particularly in their first year, often need to be convinced they have a story to tell. They need encouragement to see themselves as "storied" people, already bearing unique gifts. We have found that the best way to offer that encouragement is to give them biographies and autobiographies of people wrestling with the same big questions they have. Interacting with these stories in learning journals then empowers them to author their own stories.

The first required course in religion, Religion, Vocation, and the Search for Meaning, covers Judaism, Christianity, and Islam, focusing on how each describes the problem of the human condition by acquainting students with the central stories that address that problem. We have found it helpful to display these great traditions as lived realities, assigning a spiritual autobiography written by someone inside each tradition. For Judaism, we have used Robert Schoen's *What I Wish My Christian Friends Knew About Judaism*; for Christianity, Nadia Bolz-Weber's *Pastrix*; and for Islam, Eboo Patel's *Acts of Faith*.[20]

Two strategies can be used to invite students into dialogue with the narratives. Learning journals demand that students intentionally engage material as they experience it. For example, an assignment called "Letters to the Class" invites students to write a series of letters addressed to their classmates. Sometimes the prompt for this assignment concerns themes unique to a particular reading; sometimes the prompt simply invites students to share something that they found interesting, insightful, or challenging. Always the prompt requires students to articulate how the reading intersects with their own life stories in some way. Students write to their classmates, and this exercise launches small group and plenary discussions.

Spiritual autobiography invites students to tell their own stories. A second signature assignment, "Roots and Wings," focuses on Eboo Patel's *Acts of Faith*. Rubrics for this assignment reference one of the book's key insights: "The tradition you are born into is your home, Brother Wayne told me, but as Gandhi once wrote, it should be a home with the windows open so that the winds of other traditions can blow through and bring their unique oxygen. 'It's good to have wings,' he said, 'but you should have roots too.'"[21]

Students are asked to reflect on the sources of Patel's beliefs and values. What are his "root" experiences? How do they shape the "wings" of his commitment to interfaith work? What obstacles has he encountered, and how did he overcome them?

Finally, students are asked to pose these same questions to their own emerging life stories. What are the "root" experiences in their own lives? In reading their own life stories alongside Patel's life story, students gain a sense that they too have a story to tell. More importantly, they begin to author it. Claiming agency or authorship of one's own narrative is a crucial step toward transformative learning.

The Upper-Division Course

Stories of self are crowded, peopled stories. Parker Palmer relates his teacher's wisdom that, because there is no selfhood outside relationship, "the ancient human question 'Who am I?' leads inevitably to the equally important question 'Whose am I?'"[22] For better and for worse, individuals shape and are shaped by many different communities, including families, neighborhoods, religious traditions, and political parties. Communities can call out an individual's gifts and confirm them. Communities can also overlook an individual's gifts and stifle them, particularly if they don't fit that community's leadership profiles or stereotypes.

Students enter college knowing a lot or very little about the tradition or traditions in which they were raised. They may or may not feel they belong to these communal stories. Some students were not raised in a religious tradition at all, and they claim affiliation with the "nones." Whatever their upbringing, students form commitments. With modeling and invitation, they learn to narrate the stories of how their values came into being.

After students are clearer about their own stories and how communities may have shaped or misshaped them, they listen more closely to stories of people from different religious traditions. Because they have a critical appreciation for the role of communities in shaping selves, they can hear stories from other religious traditions not simply as stories of "them" but as stories of "us."

Students continue to explore the themes of vocation and the search for meaning in a second required religion course, which often explores Eastern and Western religions, as well as perspectives from Native American, shamanist, and atheist and agnostic thinkers. One course in particular, Ethics and World Religions, demonstrates how narrative reflection can be used to further students' understandings of these worldviews, of their own worldviews, and the impact of these stories on how they show up in the world, propelling them toward seeing themselves as interfaith leaders.

A series of assignments move students to engage in a more advanced form of autobiographical writing, comparative narrative reflection and storytelling. An initial assignment asks students to write a reflection on the poem "Where I'm From" by George Ella Lyon. They respond by composing a poem-essay describing places, experience, people, and events that have shaped their identities and made meaning for them. Students are then asked in small groups to share all or part of their work, as they are comfortable. The more students risk sharing across their differences, the more potential there is for transformative interfaith learning.

In one class, Maryam, a Muslim student, was in a group with Carlos, a Catholic, Amber, the daughter of a Lutheran pastor, and Adam, who identified as agnostic or atheist. After sharing their work, they reflected on two questions: What commonalities did you find in your stories? What did you find unique in the other person's story? Maryam was surprised to learn that they all highlighted how a grandparent shaped their belief systems. Adam delighted in hearing that Amber shared his love of the Boundary Waters Canoe Area. While the BWCA deepened Amber's connection to God, for Adam it deepened a connection to all living things. Carlos asked Maryam how fasting during Ramadan could be a rich spiritual practice. Comparative storytelling enriched the narrative of each, a deepened mutual understanding.

This strategy gives students an appreciative understanding of their own belief systems, as well as the worldviews of others. While creating a common environment, it also invites students to explore difference. This opening exercise sets the stage for students to then learn from exemplars in different traditions, all of whom have been agents of change. Later in the course, students come back to this assignment, thinking about how they have re-storied their own narratives through the personal narratives of these exemplars.

A final assignment asks students to engage in a twofold reflection process. First, they place in dialogue two exemplars from different traditions, comparing "where they are from" in terms of the exemplars' core commitments, examining both the commonalities and differences. Then students reflect on how the lives of these exemplars challenge them to think differently about their own sense of what it means to live ethically. Which of their own beliefs have been reinforced or challenged? In the finally analysis, these assignments invite students into the process of re-storying, opening them up to new ways of knowing and being.

The Keystone Course

As students prepare to graduate, they return to the central theme of the introductory courses in religion, "vocation and the search for meaning." These courses have become increasingly interdisciplinary, pairing religion faculty with faculty in departments ranging from business to the natural sciences. The students integrate curricular and co-curricular elements of their undergraduate experience, reflecting on incidents they have witnessed on campus or in the workplace.

Case studies provide a helpful framework for reflection. They invite students to retell the story of an interfaith encounter, focusing more analytically on the narrative trajectory of an incident. This final narrative strategy in our curricular design explores the path from "is" to "ought to be," what happened and what might have happened. The distance between these two worlds generates change, as students draw on a usable past to acknowledge a broken present and point to a more hopeful future. Stories of past struggle can animate change in the present.[23] In her chapter for this volume, Pluralism Project's research director Ellie Pierce explores case studies in more depth. Here we signal how they might work in a rudimentary way in a course such as Augsburg's Senior Keystone.[24]

As Pierce notes, case studies move students "beyond storytelling" into an imagined public realm. If the Augsburg introductory course gives students an agency of authorship and the upper-division course gives students an agency of comparative analysis, the Senior Keystone course gives students civic agency, placing them in actual situations of interreligious conflict. A case study in the Senior Keystone course involves a threefold rubric: description, information, and resolution.

A first *descriptive phase* aims at a thick description of an actual situation of interfaith encounter. It is important to signal to students that these incidents need not be solely conflictual, but could be positive and trust-building. After reading over the case study, this descriptive assessment asks several questions.

- What is going on—and for whom? This question raises the structural dimensions of the case, race, gender, and class but focuses on religion. Students are invited to see the situation from various points of view, imagining themselves in different roles.
- What are the issues—and for whom? This question challenges students to inhabit multiple roles in the case.

A second, *information-gathering phase* demands that students attend to context and identify any additional information they need about any of the various dimensions identified in the descriptive phase. It also requires that students stop to gather information instead of rushing to judgment or action.

- Who are the stakeholders? This question asks students to look at the broad context, signaling that the various actors are also part of larger communities.
- Are there rules, policies, or standards at play that warrant investigation?

Finally, a *resolution phase* examines potential outcomes of taking particular actions. Students are also asked to regard doing nothing as a form of agency, often one with high stakes.

- What are possible courses of action and/or resolution?
- What might be potential outcomes of these courses of action or inaction?
- What are your takeaways from this case?

Having read and discussed several interfaith cases, students then write their own rudimentary case studies. They describe an incident they have experienced that involved religious diversity in a community they know personally. It can be a workplace, a school, an athletic team, a neighborhood, or a place of worship. Defining "community" broadly signals the range of arenas in which interfaith leadership might be needed. Students are then asked to follow the same threefold rubrics they used to analyze other case studies. Finally, they must examine how leadership was or was not exercised in the incident.

As students craft their own case studies, they wrestle with the task of thick description, the difficulty of objectivity, the importance of context, and potential outcomes and their consequences. They then present these case studies in class. Discussion focuses on the interreligious factors in the case study, attempting to disentangle them from other dimensions.

One case study involved an incident at a mall, a setting the student described as "public yet privately owned." Seeking a less-crowded space to pray, a Somali Muslim woman laid out her prayer rug in front of an unmarked closed door and began to pray. The door turned out to access an office in the mall, which became apparent when an employee sought entrance. The employee interrupted the prayer and asked the woman to move. When the woman continued praying, the employee sought a security guard, who surveyed the situation and decided to wait until the prayer was complete. After the prayer the woman rolled up her rug, and the employee gained access. The next day the incident was reported to mall management, which decided to inform all mall tenants to allow people to worship wherever, however, and whenever they needed—without challenge and above all without creating a scene.

The student described the case as objectively as he could, then collected information on the population of Muslims in Minnesota, different cultural assumptions about public space and private property, and religious difference. In his leadership analysis, he noted that the management exercised minimal leadership, acting solely to avoid conflict, and "did nothing to help the larger community address the root issues of this conflict." An interfaith leader, he concluded, would have convened a conversation between involved parties to achieve "greater awareness of how to blend conflicting ideas and assumptions." In short, this student understood that interfaith leadership moves beyond merely avoiding conflict into the messy realm of building trust.

CONCLUSION

In our classrooms, we have found that narrative reflection helps students to gain appreciative understanding of themselves through another's religious or nonreligious worldview. We have argued that different kinds of stories are appropriate at different levels of the undergraduate curriculum: spiritual autobiographies in the introductory course, comparative storytelling and story-listening in the upper-division course, and instructional case studies in the Senior Keystone course. Scaffolded into the arc of a student's learning, these narrative pedagogies offer the possibility of transformative learning in the interfaith classroom.

We write from the academy, but we are not ivory tower scholars. We know we are training professionals, parents, and citizens, and we hope to equip them with tools for the workplace, home, school, and public square.

Interfaith work is neither a luxury nor an ivory tower endeavor.[25] People need interfaith awareness to be professionals, as they encounter workplaces that are increasingly religiously diverse. They need interfaith awareness to be parents, as they teach their children to engage with, rather than merely observe, religious diversity. Most important, they need interfaith awareness to be citizens, as they move into public spaces where religion can either create conflict or trigger transformation. Mutual witness sparks transformation, and witness happens when all parties risk speaking their truths, trusting that they will be heard.[26] Stories change minds and hearts more readily than arguments. Stories matter.

A PEDAGOGY OF LISTENING

Teaching the Qur'an to Non-Muslims

Michael Birkel

In a small faculty one can teach widely. Though I was not formally trained in Islamic studies, the gross and intentional misrepresentation of Islam and of Muslims in US society compelled me to study the tradition of Islam so that I might teach a course on it with integrity. I did not, however, find the classic historical-critical method to be sufficient in this endeavor. As such, this essay builds upon my experience developing a course with a new pedagogical frame in mind: asking students to study Islam and the Qur'an *on Muslims' own terms*. This pedagogical shift, I propose, is transformational for student learning and is in keeping with the overarching goals of interfaith studies as a developing field.[1]

For a non-Muslim unacquainted with Islam's holy book, the Qur'an presents challenges. It is not arranged chronologically or thematically. My initial attempts at reading the Qur'an brought to mind the biblical book of Jeremiah. If the uninitiated were parachuted down into the thick of Jeremiah, they would encounter divine address to the prophet, assurances of coming judgment, condemnation of idolatry, demands for social justice, words of consolation, and more—but not much in the way of a sustained argument, a narrative that could be followed, or, frequently, the identity of the rulers under castigation or other specificities as to context. A beginner would need help in order to grasp just what this text meant at the time of its composition, why it is in the scriptural canon, and what it means to current believers who read it. Like Jeremiah, the Qur'an needs introduction and accompaniment for the newcomer.

LISTENING TO THE TEXT, LISTENING TO CRITICAL SCHOLARSHIP

So I turned to scholarly works on the Qur'an, most of them written by Western non-Muslims. And I was thrilled. In my years in seminary and graduate school, the historical-critical method was dominant, and I was captivated. A number of my peers in graduate school went on to participate in the famous Jesus Seminar, and although I did not ultimately find the work of that group methodologically satisfying, I continue to be excited by biblical studies.[2] So naturally I looked to scholarship on the Qur'an that mirrored the careful historical approach of biblical scholars. In my teaching of the Qur'an, I find it essential to address the historical context of the seventh century, to talk about what Christians and Jews were doing and thinking in that era, and to reflect on possible interactions and influences. I am intrigued, for example, by the work of the scholar Fred Donner, who proposes that the community founded by Mohammed was not the familiar Islam with firm boundaries, which he argues took many years to develop, but instead was a movement of devout monotheists from various religious traditions who took the ethical and pious demands of their faith very earnestly and who looked forward to a coming judgment. Similarly, I delight in the scholarly work of Angelika Neuwirth, whose approach combines a willingness to consider traditional Muslim understandings of the Qur'an and its origins with precise and insightful perceptions about the literary character of the Qur'anic text.

But while I enjoy reading and teaching this material, I must admit that this approach to the Qur'an largely reinforces my own predispositions as a scholar of religious texts. And while I maintain that such approaches constitute an immensely valuable approach to the understanding of a text as a concretely historical phenomenon, I have come to realize that they contribute little toward assisting my students in coming to understand their Muslim neighbors. Slowly but surely I came to the conclusion that it was just as important—no, make that more important—to introduce to my students the manner in which devoted Muslims read the Qur'an: as a living, sacred scripture, not primarily as a historical document. If one goal of education is to prepare students for life in a civil society, then the teaching of Islam should take into consideration the expressions of Islam that they are most likely to encounter.

LISTENING TO CONTEMPORARY MUSLIMS

So I felt compelled to move beyond what is done in many college and seminary settings, where the default approach to teaching the holy texts of another religious community is to import secular Western historical-critical methods. My purposes were different. Yes, I wanted my students to realize that the study of the Qur'an is, like everything else in contemporary Western scholarship, full of contention regarding the emergence and integrity of the text, and full of skepticism on every religious claim made about the text. But, because one of my primary goals was to promote understanding of living Muslims, an equally important focus of my pedagogy was on contemporary Muslims as interpreters of their own sacred book, with attention to the great variety and vitality of interpretive voices.

The difficulty lay in the fact that I could not find a book that felt right. I wanted one that attested to the wide spectrum of Muslim voices in North America. At the same time, I wanted a volume that American Muslims could read and then recognize as theirs the Islam that was portrayed. I wanted a resource that demonstrated what interfaith theorist and activist Eboo Patel calls "appreciative knowledge" that invites a positive attitude toward another religious tradition.[3]

Ultimately, I ended up producing such a book, with significant help from my conversation partners in the project. It was my privilege to meet with twenty-five Muslim religious leaders and scholars, women and men, Sunni and Shi'i.[4] Some were experts in religious jurisprudence, accustomed to reading the Qur'an and looking for guidance with regard to a legal ruling. Others—and the two are by no means mutually exclusive—came with a pronounced mystical approach, seeking a deeper meaning for the mystery of the inward life and one's relationship with the ultimate. All of my conversation partners extended a welcome to join them in a careful consideration of a passage from their sacred scripture.[5]

I frequently tell my students that, whatever they think Islam is, it is wider than that. No single voice speaks for the entire community. Here is a sample of some of what I heard from my conversation partners, my Muslim teachers:

> The purpose of the human life is to identify, understand, and emulate the divine attributes of God, to know God in order to live a godlike life. Muhammad as the final prophet is the model that manifest[s] these divine attributes on earth.

> The Qur'anic call for justice is a call to resist patriarchy, hegemony, racism, sexism, homophobia, and the unjust class system. The Qur'an itself is the basis for the reform and transformation of the law and the culture of Muslims toward more equality and reciprocity.

> The basic rule governing the relationship between Muslims and non-Muslims is that of peaceful coexistence, justice, and compassion, irrespective of their religious choices.

> We certainly live in a world where individuals, groups, and governments commit various forms of violence and terror, committed in the name of ideology, narrow forms of nationalism, and religion. Counteracting violence with more devastating violence enhances that vicious cycle. Little attention has been paid to finding out the root causes of violence, such as gross injustice and dehumanization of others. While religion has been abused to justify senseless and unnecessary violence, it can be constructively invoked to stem the tide of violence. The common values of revealed religions, in particular, can contribute immensely in that endeavor. It is the duty of religious leaders and scholars to clarify these values and clarify misinterpretations of scriptures not only to others but also for their own religious communities. Intrafaith dialogue is as much needed as interfaith dialogue.

Heaven and hell are not two physical places in the afterlife. Rather, heaven and hell are conditions or states that people find themselves in. When one is close to God, not physically but spiritually—having developed the divine attributes within oneself—one is in a heaven-like state. When one is detached from God, which is the meaning of sin, one is in a state of hell. Hell is not for punishment, but for reformation. God lifts up people from hell, out of that spiritual condition, when they are ready to progress to the next stage. Likewise the joys of paradise are also symbolic or metaphorical. There is no gratifying of physical desires with virgins.

When the Qur'an speaks of good versus evil, or about the God-conscious versus the hypocrites, the point is not to identify the good team and the bad team. All people have the potential for goodness and for evil. The struggle between good and evil is not an external, physical battle but a conflict within each human heart.[6]

Not all held all these views. Students discover that there is considerable difference of opinion among Muslims. Diversity in opinion is a long-standing feature of Islamic jurisprudence and was considered a divine mercy among classical Muslim scholars.

As important as the content of the Qur'an is the experience of what it feels like when believing Muslims read it.

When reading the Qur'an, one feels a sense of the overwhelming presence of God, and when one feels that, then in those moments everything else becomes irrelevant and meaningless, unimportant. On the one hand, you don't want to turn back to creation, to anything that is less than divine, so there is a sense of profound *sakeena* or tranquility. You're at rest; you don't want to be anywhere else. You feel a sense of delight which is like nothing else. . . . That's one feeling. There is also a feeling of incredible compassion toward everything else. You don't want anything from anyone. . . . When one opens the Qur'an and reads the *basmala*, "In the name of Allah who is most merciful and ever merciful," if one does not feel that divine mercy, then one is not reading the Qur'an.[7]

LISTENING TO STUDENTS AS THEY LISTEN

One of the great joys of producing and teaching *Qur'an in Conversation* was the opportunity to listen closely to my students as they encountered the foundational text of another community.

As in many places, the student body where I teach has a pronounced commitment to social justice. Students therefore appreciated one scholar's bold engagement with the so-called wife-beating verse (4:34), as well as another's candid discussion of racism inside and outside of the boundaries of the Muslim community. After the media's frequent images of Muslims bent in prayer, they are surprised to read one scholar's statement that the ritual of prayer is only a means, not an end. The goal is social justice, care for the marginalized, and common kindness. These are sacred duties. Prayer is to remind believers of what they need to take from the time of prayer into a lived life. Otherwise, outward ritual observance is only show.

Students are surprised and delighted that compassion or mercy (*rahma* in Arabic) emerges as a central theme, both within the Qur'an itself and among its commentators. This entry point in turn helps them to read with greater sympathy Muslims who might not be so readily labeled as progressive—and eventually to see that such labels can obscure as much as they reveal. There can be more than one way to live out a dedication to justice.

Consistently students identify the mystical commentary on the story of Moses and his encounter with the mysterious figure Khidr as one of their favorite stories.[8] Khidr baffles Moses with his bizarre actions, which include making a hole in a boat in which they are traveling and nearly sinking it, killing a young boy whom they meet, and repairing a dilapidated wall to a town that had been inhospitable to them. Moses, the great lawgiver, is confounded by Khidr, who operates from an utterly different species of divinely inspired wisdom. To read this story in the company of Muslim scholar Maria Dakake, who was my conversation partner and guide to this passage from the Qur'an, was to read with the great spiritual masters of Islam across the centuries because she is so steeped in their wisdom.[9] She successfully invited students into another realm of reading and seeing.

Most of my students had never heard voices of African American Muslims, who have respect for classical tradition but point out that Middle Eastern Muslims have no monopoly on interpretation, especially with regard to the lived social reality of the black community in the US. Students tend to want to be independent thinkers, but, more than that, they come to see how important it is for believers to live in that dual faithfulness to their holy text and their social reality rather than choosing one or the other. Students come to see how the Qur'an is a resource for justice. Many did not enter the course with that perspective, because the media often centers its attention on a portrayal of Muslims as backward, trapped by a time-bound scripture.

Students grappled with what it is like to be a guest of the Qur'an. How does one come to appreciative knowledge, to an inward place of openness to change while still maintaining a commitment to one's own religious identity or secular life stance? It can be daunting to come into the presence of a text that has such power and that makes demands on its readers. This can be unnerving. The temptation is to read it as a text comfortably locked in the past rather than one that empowers readers that are committed to it as truth.

Part of the challenge for students is that many of them, as "nones" or spiritual but not religious, lack a sense of a firm religious identity of their own from which to encounter the Qur'an.[10] Here my role as an educator is to assure them that if they are making an effort to engage in deep self-honesty and to use the best tools that their culture offers them, they are on firm ground. I affirm whatever life stance to which they profess adherence. At the same time I encourage them to be open to opportunities for inward growth. Dialogue is not conversion. It begins with self-knowledge.

This experience deepened my commitment to a pedagogy of listening: listening to the text, listening to interpreters, and listening to ourselves as we respond. The Qur'an gives life to Muslims. It comes to life among Muslims as they read and interpret it. Can it come to life and be life-giving to those outside the historical community of the prophet Mohammed? My experience, both as a reader and as a teacher, is that it can. For some people, this may violate their sense of propriety: a professional academic must, in their eyes, always maintain a proper emotional distance from the object of study. I feel that permitting myself to be moved by the beauty of a text is not a betrayal of my commitment to my faith or to my identity as a scholar.

LISTENING TO MY OWN EXPERIENCE: ADVICE TO TEACHERS

Some of my questions are similar to those of my students. How do I engage the Qur'an with integrity, without projecting my own values upon it? Can I offer the Qur'an the same compassion that it so frequently invokes and requires of its readers and hearers?

Reading another's scripture can be an exercise in hospitality, which is an exchange. At its best, the giving and receiving are reciprocal and travel in both directions. Of course, I never expected to be more than a guest. I was not shopping for another religion. Boundaries between religious communities are to be honored. They don't just keep out. They also hold together. If religion were left to majority rule, my little group called the Quakers would have been voted off the island long ago. That, I feel, would have been a loss to the human spiritual legacy.

I return to my scriptures with the echoes of the Qur'an in my ears. The stories of Joseph, of Moses, and of Mary are not the same. The Qur'an has come to inhabit my biblical world in ways that enrich my community's texts. When someone has traveled to another land and culture and lived there for a time, the culture shock is often greater upon return to one's once-familiar surroundings than it is upon arrival in the foreign land. The known seems less so. Narratives familiar to readers of the Bible can appear "cleaned up" in the Qur'an. Jacob is wiser, not so deceptive, more confident of providence, less self-protective. On one level I had known this before, but after a sustained period of time as a guest of the Qur'an, the messiness of Genesis strikes me more forcefully. I find myself responding to it differently, even as I continue to count the familiar landscape of the biblical account as my home.

What does it mean to acknowledge and appreciate the beauty of another's faith? Is the beautiful also the true if God is the source and author of both? I do not feel threatened by the Qur'an's claim to truth, but neither did I ever feel drawn to commit to it through conversion. I feel fully a member of my own religious community but (mostly) not because mine is superior. The histories of both Muslim and Christian communities are riddled with contradictions, with failures to embody their ideals. The scriptures of both contain passages that I find deeply troubling with regard to women, slavery, and apparent divine condoning of violence and cruelty.

Instead, I feel fully within my tradition and community because that is the way that I know how to get to what I sense and admire in their tradition. This is not necessarily relativism, whether new or old. Here I recall the late Roman non-Christian Symmachus, who urged toleration for his religious heritage in the face of anticipated persecution by the early Christian empire with his famous utterance that surely by one path alone it is not possible to arrive at so great a mystery.[11]

Is it all the same grand mystery toward which we strive to seek a path? The fact that it is a mystery, beyond the powers of human utterance, compels me to admit that I cannot be sure that I know. Still, the power of mutual recognition suggests to me that it is the same mystery that beckons us all. Here I am thinking of an occasion when a Muslim said to me, "I can see your *noor*," which is the Arabic word for light. Muslim spirituality speaks of an inward *noor*, which is a manifestation of divine presence. His light beheld my light in mutual recognition. My experiences among these generous Muslims gives rise to a desire to continue and deepen the engagement, to perceive the beauty and *noor*, and to be further transformed.

There is a sacred hadith: "I was a hidden treasure and desired to be known." Is that a deep desire, imprinted into the fabric of the universe? If so, then our coming to know one another is a holy task, a participation in divine purpose.

Here, I tell my students, is where they come in. The work that resulted in *Qur'an in Conversation* is not the work of a trained scholar of Islam. I went and spoke with Muslims—and admittedly a very special group of them. I tell my non-Muslim students that they can do the same. I say to them, "Go and talk with your Muslim neighbors. You will experience the same depth of hospitality. It will change your life for the better."

MEETING OTHERS, SEEING MYSELF

Experiential Pedagogies in Interfaith Studies

Wakoh Shannon Hickey
and Margarita M. W. Suárez

A Muslim undergraduate chokes back tears as she tells a group of twenty classmates, faculty, and staff about being verbally and physically attacked while wearing a hijab. Her hair now falls around her shoulders because she feels unsafe covering it in public. She explains how painful it is to be afraid to do something that had felt to her like *home*, and how painful it is to face criticism within her Muslim community for *not* wearing the hijab.[1] She is heartbroken, and, as we listen quietly, our hearts break open in sympathy for her.

Experiences like these, alongside the escalation of religiously moti-vated hate crimes since the 2016 presidential election, fuel our sense of urgency to promote a culture of pluralism, in which social differences are not feared and hated but valued as resources for solving human problems.[2] Diversity is a fact of American life, and, as educators in religious studies, we believe that equipping young people to engage con-structively and collaboratively with those who differ from them is the only realistic way forward.

When we began our teaching careers we adopted the traditional stance of our academic discipline: we focused on teaching *about* unfamil-iar religious ideas, practices, objects, and stories, with a neutral attitude toward particular religious norms and truth claims. Students can develop this sort of *religious literacy* at arm's length and from the neck up, within the confines of a classroom. But we changed our approach after we each completed a weeklong faculty-development seminar titled "Teaching Interfaith Understanding," cosponsored by the Council of Independent Colleges and Interfaith Youth Core. We were inspired by the emerging field of interfaith studies, which promotes both religious and *interfaith literacy*. The latter involves not just knowledge but also *attitudes* necessary to engage positively with religious others. The basic difference between a religious studies approach and an interfaith studies approach is that the latter is more embodied, engaged, affective, and integrative. It asks students to encounter "others" directly, both individually and at unfamiliar religious sites; to be moved emotionally by these encounters; to strive not just to understand others on their own terms but also to use concepts and resources from other religions to think with; and to connect the world of the classroom with the worlds outside it, both on and off campus. Interfaith studies has the explicit goal of promoting pluralism as a social norm. Thus, in our classrooms, we profess that religious differences are not merely to be learned but also *appreciated* or *valued*.

GOALS OF THE INTERFAITH STUDIES CLASSROOM

Reflexivity, Empathy, and Humility

Interfaith studies promotes not merely "objective" knowledge but also the dispositions of reflexivity, empathy, and humility. In social research, "reflexivity" means recognizing that *who* does the research affects which questions are asked, how they are explored, and how results are interpreted. It is particularly salient in ethnography, where the researcher becomes closely involved in the society and culture studied.[3] Our tacit assumptions usually go unnoticed until we encounter contexts in which they no longer apply. Reflexivity requires one first to describe one's "social location"—for example, race, sex, gender, age, socioeconomic class, education level, religious background (or lack thereof), ethnic and cultural heritages, and regional upbringing. Then one considers how these factors shape one's perceptions of others. Finally, reflexivity requires authentic encounters between researchers and informants, in which researchers share themselves and their findings with informants, who are considered valuable collaborators in the research and writing process. We know, having been influenced by feminist and postcolonial studies, that there is no fully objective "view from nowhere" from which to study cultural phenomena such as religions.[4] We are all situated somewhere, and we each approach our studies from particular perspectives. We know too that the personal is political, so our teaching praxis attends to the ways that different forms of power and privilege affect relationships within and between groups.

We ask students to reflect on their own social locations and the ways their backgrounds shape the perspectives and assumptions they bring to class. We demonstrate reflexivity by situating ourselves amid the complexities of postmodern religion in North America. Suárez was raised Catholic, ordained as a minister in the United Church of Christ, and later embraced Reform Judaism. Hickey was raised in mainline Protestant churches, briefly embraced fundamentalist Pentecostalism, and is now ordained as a priest of Sōtō Zen Buddhism, which she has practiced for more than thirty years. Our students are diverse in multiple ways (race, class, sexual orientation, and so on), though the majority are Christians of various denominations.

In addition to teaching reflexivity, we work to foster *empathy*. This entails imagining oneself in the place of others in order to understand them more fully, which first requires one to awaken to one's tendency to assume that one's own truths apply universally. Empathy enables us to understand accurately the viewpoints and reasoning of others, and, in the words of Linda Elder and Richard Paul, "to reason from premises, assumptions, and ideas other than our own."[5] It is associated with humility: remembering and accepting that we can be wrong, even though we want to believe we are right.

Intellectual and cultural humility means recognizing that one's own perspective or knowledge is limited: developing what Elder and Paul describe as "sensitivity to circumstances in which one's native egocentrism is likely to function self-deceptively" and acknowledging honestly one's own biases, prejudices, and limitations. "Intellectual humility depends on recognizing that one should not claim more than one actually knows. It does not imply spinelessness or submissiveness. It implies the lack of intellectual pretentiousness, boastfulness, or conceit, combined with insight into the logical foundations, or lack of such foundations, of one's beliefs."[6]

Reflexivity, empathy, and humility must temper critical inquiry. We want students to challenge others' assumptions, to question biases in various sources of information, and to notice whose interests are being served in particular situations and whose are not. But critique can be destructive when it lacks self-awareness or is not modulated by kindness. At its best, interfaith studies can help us learn to "get over ourselves"—that is, to transcend our egocentricity and small-mindedness for the sake of meaningful relationships. A capacity for self-forgetting frees us to be more fully present with others and open to them.

Pluralism

These dispositions foster pluralism. In *Sacred Ground*, Eboo Patel, drawing on the work of Diana Eck and Harvard's Pluralism Project, observes, "Where diversity is a fact, pluralism is an achievement . . . it means building strong bonds between people from different backgrounds." A pluralistic society is one "characterized by respect for people's religious (and other) identities, positive relationships between people of different religious backgrounds, and common action for the common good."[7] These goals seem to us consistent with the goals and values of education in the liberal arts and sciences. Yet liberal education and *liberating* education are not exactly the same. The liberal arts and sciences teach students how to think as historians, scientists, sociologists, and religionists. A liberating education trains students not only to be able to think within the frameworks of different disciplines but also to be transformed—by seeing the world from the perspectives of others, especially those who are marginalized.

Some of our students will begin and complete our courses holding exclusivist religious beliefs, and they are free to do so. But we hope to nudge all of our students toward the understanding that each person's position is but one position, not *the only possible position* one might adopt. We also want to persuade students that people who differ from us have something useful to teach: not just about themselves but about ourselves. We must allow ourselves to be changed by encounters with religious others, by hearing their stories, practicing dialogue, and being pragmatic about the fact that that we will encounter challenges and difficulties as we forge new relationships.

TOOLS FOR THE INTERFAITH STUDIES CLASSROOM

We used the following three activities to engage students in cultivating reflexivity, empathy, and humility as they also develop their capacity for critical analysis. The first is an individual, contemplative exercise involving a Buddhist moral precept; the second is a contemplative dialogue; the third involves one or more visits to an unfamiliar religious site.

Precept Exercise

The precept exercise is most appropriate for courses on Buddhism, but it could be adapted for any course in which the ethical systems of major Asian religions are discussed.[8] Most forms of Buddhism emphasize five fundamental moral prohibitions against killing, taking what is not given (stealing), engaging in false speech, misusing sexuality, and using intoxicants. The number of precepts undertaken by ordained Buddhists varies by school, but these five are broadly applicable to ordained and lay people in most traditions. In the meditation-oriented schools, moral conduct (*śila*) is considered the foundation for meditation (*samadhi*), which leads to liberating wisdom (*prajñā*).

Hickey introduces these precepts in the context of the Buddha's Four Noble Truths and Eightfold Path, then invites the class to discuss both literal and metaphoric meanings they can have. For example, although the traditional meaning of "not killing" is to not murder, might there be other ways we "kill" people? Could one regard gossip as a form of stealing, as taking and sharing information not freely given? In what ways do people engage in false speech? Can video games and cell phones be considered intoxicants?

Students choose one of the five precepts and commit to observing their lives through the lens of that precept for a week. Hickey finds that sustained focus on a single precept prompts deeper inquiry and reflection than would be possible if trying to practice more than one.[9] The assignment instructions say:

> This is an exercise not just in thinking *about* Buddhist . . . ideas and practices; it is an exercise in using them to think *with*. You do not need to accept any Buddhist doctrine to do this exercise; you simply need to be aware of your own thoughts and actions. The goals . . . are to understand Buddhist ethical practices better, and to become more aware of your thoughts, feelings, and behavior, and their effects on other beings. You need not change your behavior, but simply observe it. Increased awareness is part of liberal education, and you can achieve it whether or not you actually modify your conduct.

The instructions propose questions for students to consider. For example:

> Avoid killing or harming sentient beings.
>
> Have you harmed any sentient being, by aggressive behavior or avoidance? By things you say or your facial expressions or body language? Intentionally or unintentionally? By laughter? In the past 24 hours have you eaten anything? What? How did it get on your plate? Do you know or have you considered who planted or cultivated it, harvested or butchered it, cleaned and cooked it?

Students keep a daily journal and begin to notice their habits of mind, speech, and action more clearly and pay more attention to the consequences of their choices. They develop new insights about themselves and about Buddhist methods for cultivating the virtues of harmlessness, beneficence, and equanimity. In their reflection paper on this activity, they are asked to discuss the following: "How do meditation and moral conduct produce Buddhist wisdom? How have these practices helped you to understand how religious disciplines work in people's lives? If [possible], say something about how these have helped you to understand or to think differently about your 'self' and your relationships with 'others.'"

Some students, contemplating the precept of refraining from killing or harming sentient beings, reflect upon their perfectionism and habit of constantly criticizing themselves and others. Others grapple with their love of hunting or their impulses to squash insects found inside their homes. Some reflect on the origins of consumer products and food in ways they have not done before.

These reflections are confidential unless someone discloses something suggesting imminent harm to themselves or others. (This has occurred only once, thus far.) Hickey offers feedback but does not judge what authors say they did or didn't do. She simply assigns a "check," "check-plus," or "check-minus," according to how seriously students seem to take the assignment, how clearly and well they write about it, and how thoughtfully they engage with relevant course readings. These papers are enjoyable to read and open opportunities to communicate with students more personally than is typical in the classroom. The exercise also helps students use Buddhism to think with and to develop a more visceral and appreciative understanding of religious ethics, important elements of an interfaith studies approach.

Careful Conversation

A "Careful Conversation" is a structured, contemplative dialogue of about one hour, between a student and someone who differs in religious orientation.[10] The exercise, designed by Sid Brown of the University of the South (Sewanee), can be adapted for use in any comparative course, but conversation partners should identify with different religions, not different subgroups of the same religion. Those who are nonreligious should find partners who are devoutly religious, in order to emphasize the difference between them. Participants are frequently surprised by how much they have in common with people they perceive as religious others. Students write reflective papers before and after this encounter, which help them to both clarify and appreciate their own positions more deeply and to appreciate other possibilities.

Hickey sometimes invites students to find their own partners. In other cases she has paired English-speaking students in her university's undergraduate college with international students in its English Language Institute. This gives international students an opportunity to practice conversation skills and builds relationships across the two academic units. Hickey's students write a preliminary, two-page reflection addressing questions such as "What do you expect? What do you want to remember to do during the conversation? What are you most excited about? What are you most anxious about?" They are asked to review all their notes and identify something specific that "interests, intrigues, delights" them about any of the religions covered in the course to that point.

The Careful Conversation itself is an intensive, contemplative dyad. In an environment free of distractions, the partners read the instructions aloud to each other and take turns answering questions about early memories of their religion, worldview, or ethical system, both pleasant and painful; the first time they became aware of religious difference; what they appreciate most about their own tradition or values; something they appreciate in another religion or ethical system; and what they would like "never said again" about their religion or worldview. Participants are encouraged to give mindful attention to their breathing, physical sensations, and emotions; to maintain steady eye contact; to refrain from interrupting; to answer "*from your emotions*, not your intellect" [emphasis in original]—usually with the first thing that comes to mind; to safeguard each other's confidentiality; and to wait patiently through periods of silence, even awkward, extended ones. Each participant is free to answer in whatever way she wants and to decline to answer any question. "Whether you think what the person is saying is wrong, right, hateful, or weird, whether you think the person's experience is just like yours or completely different from yours, whether you feel enthusiastic or saddened, *your whole job as listener is to listen deeply and seek to understand and empathize, without interrupting.*"[11]

Directions for the four-page, post-conversation reflection paper ask students to discuss what made the exercise memorable and worthwhile and how it relates to other material we have been discussing in class.

In one case, a devout American Catholic woman met with a Muslim international student. The Catholic student had earlier made an in-class presentation about the hajj (pilgrimage to Mecca) and the holiday Eid al-Adha (the Feast of Sacrifice). During her research for that project, she found a survey by the Pew Research Center showing that "40% of Americans think that a great deal or a fair amount of Muslim Americans are extremists. In addition, while 48% of Muslims report that they feel Americans are friendly toward them, still 28% say that people act suspicious of them, and 22% have been called offensive names." She reported that her conversation partner "made a point to keep telling me over and over" that

> just because there are a few violent people does not mean that the whole religion is bad. . . . "Our religion is good, but there are bad people, too." She then said that many people refer to Muslims as terrorists. What hurt my heart the most was the fact that she was struggling to find that word. . . . I had to aid her in saying "terrorist," and as it came off of my tongue, I felt a pain in my chest. I did not want to say that word to her, because I did not want to bring her any of the pain that I knew must come from hearing it.[12]

The student's attention to her own emotions and the physical sensations associated with them, as well as her intellectual understanding of research data about Islamophobia, is precisely the sort of integrative, embodied approach to learning that interfaith studies entails. Her willingness to remain emotionally present in the conversation despite her own discomfort, in order to forge a meaningful connection, is what makes this exercise a contemplative practice rather than a merely informational interview. The partners found agreement in wishing "people would understand that in our respective traditions, women *are* honored and valued."[13] Months later, in a public forum, the Catholic student said the exercise helped her to appreciate Islam better but also her own Catholicism, by prompting her to think about what she loves best in it.

The Careful Conversation is similar to an exercise Suárez leads in Anthropology of Religion, called "Representing Others." Its purposes are to help students learn to listen closely and ethically and to present their partners to others in such a way that the people being described can recognize themselves in the descriptions. "Honesty" and "responsibility" are the watchwords, as students interpret their partners' spoken stories, translate them into writing, and evaluate what seems to be most important to relay to their classmates.

Ethnographic Fieldwork

Suárez's courses World Religions, Anthropology of Religion, and Women, Religion, and Ethnography all require some level of ethnographic field research. In introductory classes, Suárez wants students to get a taste of ethnography, so they must visit a religious site that is not their own. Suárez sets up all the field-site options in advance, engaging contacts who will answer students' questions. Students consider the following points and write a "First Impressions" paper.

- What did you observe? What did you hear? What did you smell?
- How did you feel?
- How were your expectations different from what you actually experienced? What excited you? Made you anxious?
- As you walked in, what did you notice [about] the space: its decorations, art, interior design, furniture or lack thereof, religious symbols? Was it inviting? Off-putting? Neutral? Were you greeted as you entered? Were there signs to make it easy to find things? Did it feel that visitors were welcome? Or are only practitioners able to function in the space?
- What was the neighborhood like? (Race/class/ethnicity evident in the neighborhood)
- *If you are a visual art major*: What kind of architecture is the building/space? How did you feel about the space, before you

entered it? Was it inviting, off-putting, or neutral? Why do
you think you felt this way?

- How did leave-taking occur? Was there a fellowship time
  after the ritual/worship? Were you easily able to introduce
  yourself to the leader(s)? How accessible did they appear to
  be? Can you make an appointment to meet with them?
- Was the worshiping community amiable or distant? Did
  you feel that returning would be welcomed? Resented? Received neutrally?
- What are you learning about this tradition's practices that
  you couldn't have gotten just from reading books about it?*
- What was the theme of the religious leader's talk/teaching/
  sermon?* (at least half a page)
- How did you decide to pick this religious tradition to study?*[14]

Questions marked with an asterisk were required to be discussed in
the paper.

In Anthropology of Religion, an undergraduate class, students make
several visits to a religious site outside their own experience and write three
papers. Each has a particular focus: rituals, teachings, and community-
building practices in the chosen congregation. Each student decides
which religious community she wants to visit and makes her own contacts before attending for the first time. The anthropologist Ruth Behar's
work on being a "vulnerable observer" has most influenced Suárez's
own ethnography and her creation of assignments that move students
beyond *describing* "others" to *engaging* both themselves and others,
seeking similarities, learning to respect differences, and learning about
themselves through such encounters.[15]

Ethnographic work requires not only book learning but also active engagement with others. Studying textbooks can help students understand intellectually the specific requirements for participating in a
particular ritual, for example, but it is through presence in a religious
service—of any tradition—that student ethnographers truly begin to
appreciate the power of religious experience. One can read about the
Ummah (community of Muslims), but when one sees people standing

shoulder to shoulder in a mosque, with no distinctions on the basis of race or socioeconomic status, and praying with their entire bodies, one gains a more visceral understanding of what the Ummah means to Muslims. It doesn't matter whether one is able to join the prayer line or simply observes. After describing a particular ritual in detail, students compare it to another with which they are more familiar, either from their own religious tradition or from American civil religion (e.g., oaths of office, public memorial rites, military ceremonies).

For the second paper, students study the chosen community's ethical and philosophical or theological teachings and discuss them with religious leaders at the field site. Again, they compare these concepts to those that are more personally familiar. Through comparison, students often begin to see similar ethical imperatives across traditions. For example, the "greater jihad" of Islam—that is, the spiritual struggle against *shirk* (hubris)—can be compared to the expectation in Judaism that humans will live God's *mitzvoth*.[16] Both traditions stress human free will, the goodness of human nature, and our finitude and imperfection compared to God's eternality and perfection. Such comparisons help students to develop and demonstrate the key dispositions of intellectual humility and empathy.

In the third paper, students explain how the religious groups they are exploring understand the nature of community and how they create spaces in which community can flourish. How does a Buddhist sangha help its members to cultivate greater wisdom and compassion together? How is the Mormon practice of wearing sacred undergarments similar to the Sikh practice of wearing the "Five Ks"—*kesh* (uncut hair, sometimes wrapped in a turban), *kara* (a steel bracelet), *kanga* (a wooden comb), *kaccha* (cotton undergarment, also spelled "*kachh*" or "*kachera*"), and *kirpan* (a steel sword)? How do these physical practices reinforce communal identity and commitment?

Through these papers, students begin work on a final project in which they explain how this experiential approach to learning promotes pluralism and interfaith cooperation. The learning outcome, to "demonstrate appreciative understanding of religious others," is achieved holistically through a combination of textual study and ethnographic research.

Reflexivity and humility help to form a vulnerable observer, who can see and appreciate parts of herself that she first perceived in others.

Assessment

One might wonder how to assess the dispositions of reflexivity, empathy, and humility. Which behaviors demonstrate these qualities? Three of the "VALUE rubrics" (Valid Assessment of Learning in Undergraduate Education) developed by the Association of American Colleges and Universities can be helpful. The Intercultural Knowledge and Competence rubric establishes benchmarks for cultural self-awareness, empathy, and openness. The Integrative Learning rubric measures how students connect experience and knowledge, make connections across disciplines or perspectives, and transfer learning from one context to another. The Global Learning rubric measures self-awareness, perspective-taking, and the application of knowledge to complex problems.[17]

Another way to assess these dispositions might be to create an initial survey with open-ended questions to measure "flexibility, open-mindedness, appreciation of difference, and a tolerance for ambiguity."[18] Students can then keep course blogs or journals, in which they reflect upon their changing dispositions, their challenges, and new discoveries. Student participation in interfaith organizations and activities can be observed directly. Case studies, used effectively in most business schools, can enable interfaith studies instructors to see how students reason, develop solutions to problems, and demonstrate the qualities we want them to cultivate. Richard Paul and Linda Elder's work on "critical thinking competency standards" suggests ways to develop learning outcomes that measure both intellectual humility and empathy.[19]

CONCLUSION

Liberal arts education has come under attack in recent years by those who argue that colleges should provide practical training in skills that will net graduates high-paying jobs. Whatever jobs our students do assume, they will work alongside people whose cultures, values, and assumptions differ from their own, and they must be able to forge productive working relationships amid such differences. We have seen the integrative, embodied pedagogical strategies we describe here transform students not just into better thinkers and writers but also into more compassionate, wise human beings. We believe this is what business-minded people would call a "value-added" approach to learning. We do want our students to be able to demonstrate basic religious literacy and to understand and apply the theories and methods of our academic discipline. Because the majority of our students do not go on to become religious studies majors, however, we want even more for them to become better citizens: to question religious rhetoric, to challenge toxic theologies, to forge meaningful connections across lines of difference, to stand in solidarity with minorities when they are targeted, to interrupt hate speech and violence. We hope the interfaith studies classrooms we are creating will empower students to uphold our country's founding principle of liberty and justice for all.

III

CHALLENGES AND CHOICES

SIX ISSUES THAT COMPLICATE INTERRELIGIOUS STUDIES AND ENGAGEMENT

Rachel S. Mikva

At first glance, key objectives of interreligious studies and engagement might seem straightforward: develop literacy in and appreciation for diverse life stances, explore the history of interaction and cultivate fruitful relationship between people who orient around religion differently, and work together for the common good.[1] As the field develops within a constantly shifting religious landscape, however, there is growing awareness of issues that complicate the interreligious project. This chapter briefly explores six issues as they play out in a US context, along with strategies to address them. They impact both the academic field of interreligious studies and community-based interreligious engagement—a synergistic distinction I will return to at the end.

"Live and learn." The idiom suggests that if you pay attention, you will avoid previous mistakes, but I have repeated my share. Having been involved in interreligious teaching and activism for many years now, I cannot think of one endeavor that completely avoided the trouble spots. Instead, we learn to notice them, name them, work at them, and try to turn deficits into assets through the relationship-building capacity of a shared struggle. Although we can often point to missteps, most of the problems emerge from the context of interreligious work itself.

The rabbis of late antiquity often introduced anecdotes to illuminate a matter, beginning with the phrase, "*Ma'aseh shehaya*—It once happened." I suspect that the warp and woof of memory reshaped details for pedagogic purposes, but the tales have become part of the fabric of learning—premodern case studies. The story was generally a simple one, plainly told, while its unpacking revealed complex matrices of interrelated questions, none with a simple answer. Since narrative can address both theory and praxis, it is a good vehicle to explore this interdisciplinary field that (like urban studies and gender studies) has a practical application and commitment to social transformation alongside its academic focus.

Thus *it once happened* that I was invited to participate in a multifaith academic consortium titled "Just Peace," and my experience sheds light on the issues addressed in this chapter, in ways both pedestrian and profound.

POLITICS OF REPRESENTATION

The Just Peace consortium gathered Muslim, Christian, and Jewish scholars to talk together about the textual and theological roots of just peace practices as well as real-world implications. Upon arriving, I scanned the room to see who was there. What life stances were represented, in what proportions? Was there intrareligious diversity in terms of denominations or movements? What about race, ethnicity, gender, and sexuality? What place did participants occupy within their traditions? There is no perfect recipe.

For a time, interfaith work in the United States was generally populated by white male clergy who explained their religions to each other.[2] While the lacunae of this model are clear, the politics of representation have grown more complicated. The common focus on Judaism, Christianity, and Islam is not adequate to address the burgeoning religious diversity of the American context—including not only Eastern traditions but also new religious movements, historically marginalized religious and ethnic communities (for example, Dalit, Yazidi, and Romani), and indigenous cultures that are still overlooked. Secular humanism is increasingly recognized as part of the conversation, but the field still linguistically accounts for secular life stances by what they are not (that is, nonreligious), and they must fight for funding and inclusion in campus spiritual life, as well as moral authority in the public square. With a growing number of individuals who identify as spiritual but not religious or as interspiritual (alternatively, of multiple religious belonging), it is misleading to presume that everyone identifies with a defined faith community.

It also matters a great deal who is present from each community. At Chicago Theological Seminary, the historically Protestant but increasingly diverse school where I teach, we encourage students to speak *from* a particular life stance rather than *for* it. Nonetheless, the perspective of those we meet from other traditions invariably shapes how we view the life stance in general. Relying too much on a single story distorts our understanding.

Representation raises questions beyond who is invited to the table in interreligious encounter or how one organizes the field in the academy. Who determines the boundaries of a religious community, and who has a voice? Should Roman Catholic Womenpriests be counted as Catholics even though they have been excommunicated by the Vatican? Why don't Ethiopian Israelite and Black Hebrew movements get explored in discussions of Jewish diversity? Which form(s) of Yoruba tradition are considered authentic? Theology, history, ethnicity, and status all impact the make-up of interreligious space. We might wish to resolve all these queries in inclusive fashion or favor people's self-definition, but boundaries are designed not merely to exclude—they also help to define and support.

Power dynamics integral to such questions are complex. The dominant academic culture privileges historical critical study of sacred texts, for instance, but few Muslim scholars view the Qur'an through this lens. If the perspectives of those who do are favored in interreligious scholarship, some will raise concerns of the "native informant"—marginalized individuals drawn to support marginalizing ideologies because of cultural oppression.[3] Others will counter that such a term denigrates those who dare to articulate internally unpopular opinions, imposing a restrictive definition of the subjugated group's "interest." How are these voices registered in academic discourse and community encounter?

The field of interreligious studies has itself developed a dominant culture, in which progressive religious outlooks may exclude or silence some voices. Commitment to "active seeking of understanding across lines of difference" does not necessarily require *theological* pluralism (affirming the religious value and sufficiency of diverse faiths), but many religious conservatives have been reluctant to become involved in interfaith studies and engagement.[4] As this gap closes, new issues arise. Questions of gender and sexuality become more fraught, as does the matter of proselytization. The latter has generally been out of bounds for interfaith engagement in Western contexts; if groups join the conversation without being able to bracket that part of their identity, it can become problematic for others to "sit at the table."[5]

Nonetheless, this more multivocal perspective on the interreligious project also brings critical balance. Scholars, students, and community participants must learn to advocate their position regarding religious pluralism without the presumption that it upholds an objective standard. Rather, it represents a subjective voice within a coformative public discourse.[6]

CHRISTIAN PRIVILEGE

Hosted by a United Methodist theological school, the two-day meeting drew scholars from around the country. My friend on the planning committee noted that the first draft of the schedule began with a cocktail reception. No, she politely insisted, we cannot do that. Some of the Muslim participants cannot be present if alcohol is served.

It simply seemed normal to the organizers to begin that way and even struck some as gauche to *not* offer spirits in a social setting. The cultural assumptions that informed the norm were most closely tied to the Christian cohort. While it was simple to excise the alcohol in this case, it flagged other issues of Christian privilege. Like so many interreligious efforts in North America today, the hosting organization was Christian. What symbols and structures does that impose, and, more importantly, what power does that convey? It impacts who controls the agenda, who gets funding from foundations, who is best represented, and whose opinion carries weight. Whether in seminary, college, or community contexts, Christian voices frequently dominate interreligious space, Christian questions shape comparative religious discourse, and Christian experience stands at the center.[7]

The just peace paradigm and the just war theory to which it poses a contrary vision, for example, were developed by Christian scholars, with Christian theological frameworks. Similarly, the "theology of religions" integral to much interreligious discourse frequently still revolves around a threefold pluralist-inclusivist-exclusivist model flowing from Christian questions about salvation.[8] Subsequent revisions do not yet account for life stances that have alternative concerns or that have no need for a theological explanation of religious difference.

When entire interfaith degree programs are housed in historically Christian institutions, there are significant ramifications for theological education—even if the student body ceases to be predominantly Christian. Many master of divinity programs became multifaith without fully reckoning with the extent to which the degree is embedded in Christian history and culture. What do secular humanists or others without a scripture do about the emphasis on sacred texts? Will a classically trained Christian practical theologian appreciate how pastoral care (note the language) changes in a Zen Buddhist context? Schools may adapt requirements and have multifaith faculty, but Christian privilege abides, from the institutional calendar to rhythms of worship to curricular standards and cultural assumptions. Not all Christians experience it in the same way, of course. Evangelicals often feel profoundly marginalized within diverse Christian spaces, yet they still benefit from its "invisible package of unearned assets."[9]

The secular academy is not immune. Having moved beyond nineteenth-century history of religions (*Religionsgeschichte*), in which faiths were seen to have value to the extent that they paralleled the Christian "norm," there is still a tendency to focus on traditions that are theistic, scriptural, and global, communities that have recognizable hierarchies, clergy, and organizational structures.[10] Some knowledge is still subjugated—obscured or discredited by what people expect "religion" to mean.[11] Historical Christian bias continues to impact scholarship and pedagogy—old anti-Jewish tropes sneak into discussions of universalism and particularism, law and grace, spirit and letter—and feminist theology's assault on perceived gender discrimination in Islam revives Orientalist stereotypes.[12] Within shifting shapes of privilege, one sees the suppleness of social power.

Given the self-critical capacities of the academy and the traditions themselves, much work is being done to address these issues. There are no neutral spaces in which interreligious conversation and study can occur, however, because the broader context still systematically advantages Christians. In 2003, psychologist Lewis Schlosser broached this "sacred taboo" with a list of twenty-eight signs of religious privilege. These include seeing people of your tradition in leadership and show business, not having everything you do ascribed to your religious identity, and avoiding discrimination in employment, social settings, adoption, media, and housing because of your faith.[13] Our context inevitably impacts the interreligious project.

ACCOUNTABILITY

For an opening ritual, one member from each tradition was asked to share an object of religious significance. A Christian presenter discussed a jar of soil from a sacred spot. A Jewish presenter explicated the intricate symbolism wrapped in the tzitzit *(fringes) of the prayer shawl. A Muslim presenter explained that Muslims cannot equate any object with Allah, because it is* shirk—*a serious violation of Islamic theological commitments. I remember thinking that it might be a brilliant cover for forgetting his assignment and having no object in hand, but it also implicated the other presenters. Had he just suggested, by accident of course, that their words bordered on idolatry? He could have brought prayer beads, a* mihrab *that points the way to Mecca, or another Muslim ritual object—since no one had equated their items with God.*

In theorizing difference, we may easily avoid the trap of equating it with inequality, but our own religious stories always implicate each other. Sacred texts often portray religious others, not always in the best light, and there is a temptation to discuss our own tradition in its ideal form while in "mixed" company even if other people admit the lived messiness of their own communities. Power intervenes again here; it is easier for privileged religious voices to admit the ugly stuff. Also, every detail we elect to share suggests something about what other religions are or are not. Comparison is a continuous activity, explicit and implicit, conscious and subconscious, shaping the way we think about our own life stance as well as those of others. What does it mean to be accountable in the coformative space of interreligious encounter?[14]

Leonard Swidler's early work in interfaith dialogue tried to establish ground rules for accountability. His "Dialogue Decalogue" included the requirement that adherents be allowed to define for themselves what it means to belong to a particular tradition and to indicate whether their partners' understanding of it is recognizable.[15] When studying another religion, I require my students to present their learning to a person who stands inside it. How does it make the adherent *feel*? Why did the observers emphasize what they did, and how will their choices impact what others think? What happens when the roles are reversed? Students are required to engage these questions together, learning what it means to be accountable.

Interreligious engagement provides transformative capacity to see our own life stance in new ways.[16] While experience shows that encounters generally deepen and clarify our commitment rather than attenuate it, we must resist meeting religious difference for the sole purpose of enriching our own spiritual capacities. Problems of erasure were deeply embedded in early exploration of Jesus as a Jew, for example. Although it kindled learning about Judaism and had potential to counter centuries of anti-Jewish teaching, many scholars and lay people were primarily interested in what it could reveal of Christian origins. Judaism was an object, while accountability requires an intersubjective lens for learning.

Accountability also raises questions about appropriation and ownership. Krister Stendahl spoke of "holy envy," acknowledging a profound appreciation for rituals of other traditions without attempting to adapt or adopt them.[17] While a history of mutual influence is evident in the ongoing formation of traditions, his caution remains fundamentally important. As interspiritual movements challenge our easy assumptions about who owns traditions (and why), navigating the waters between appreciation and appropriation becomes ever more challenging.

Determining a response when we encounter something offensive in interreligious space can be especially perplexing. Diana Eck offers a strategy that recognizes the diverse registers of our voice. Commenting on a prayer guide published by Southern Baptists that described Hindus as lost in total darkness, she wrote:

> As a scholar of Hinduism, I must say you have seriously misrepresented the Hindu tradition . . . and I would be happy to speak with you about where I think your portrayal is misleading. As an American and fellow citizen, however, I will defend your right to believe and practice Christianity as you do, to believe the worst about our Hindu neighbors, to believe they are all going to hell, and to say so, both privately and publicly. But as a Christian, let me challenge you here, for I believe that your views of our neighbors are not well grounded in the Gospel of Christ, as I understand it.[18]

Careful deployment of our multiple voices can help us discern how our stories impact others, negotiating difficult conversations while being accountable to one another.

RESISTING ESSENTIALIZATION

Despite the experience and sophistication of the assembled scholars, we repeatedly resorted to expressions such as "Judaism says," "Christianity teaches," and "Islam believes"—as if these multivocal, fertile traditions were singular and static entities for which we could speak unilaterally. Since the objective of the conference was to explore peace within the three faiths, we also knowingly oversimplified complex histories and teachings that have much to say about peace but have also justified war, conquest, and oppression.

One challenge of interreligious literacy is the tendency to essential-ize, downplaying intragroup diversity and ignoring the ways in which lived tradition is not fully represented in texts and formal religious teachings. It is difficult to introduce students to unfamiliar life stances without broad generalizations, and every syllabus must exclude more than it can cover. Even the foundational terms "interfaith" and "inter-religious" falsely imply that there are agreed-upon definitions of fixed things called religions and that we study the relationship between them. The reality is more porous, polymorphous, and provisional—a growing web of relationships within and among internally diverse spiritualities. What tools are there for more robust encounters with the multiplicity of spiritual living and learning?

Speaking in plurals helps to reinforce internal diversity: Judaisms, Christianities, and so forth. We can also complicate ideas about what constitutes religion. Robert Orsi offers the example of "Lourdes" water that mysteriously began flowing outside a church in the Bronx. His stu-dents regularly resist treating the folk veneration as religious praxis, and he presses them to reconsider.[19] Remembering that study of religion in the West tends to package spiritual beliefs, practices, and communities in familiar ways, we can problematize its imposition on life stances that do not fit the mold—as when diverse Hindu cultures and traditions are reduced to yield Hindu*ism*. Recognizing that perceptions of difference are themselves constructed, we can examine the impact of media, his-tory, and politics on how we view the varieties of religious experience.[20]

Diverse pedagogies are important. Textual learning provides focus and what one hopes is reliable information. Experiential learning adds actual encounter, resisting reification. When an individual adherent's perspective differs from the "official" version, I remind students or par-ticipants that while a certain text (academic or sacred) states one thing, some adherents may remember or receive it differently. One is a textual "truth," and the other is an embodied "truth."

Religious studies has long acknowledged these complexities. Wil-fred Cantwell Smith's 1962 controversial but now classic book, *The Meaning and End of Religion*, argued that religion was a modern Eu-ropean invention that did not sufficiently account for diversity. Ninian

Smart spoke of doctrinal, mythological, ethical, ritual, experiential, institutional, and later material "dimensions" of religion. He also highlighted "religion on the ground," and scholars continue to do critical work on lived religion.[21]

Yet the immediacy of interreligious encounter can press against theoretical complications. What is the minimum one needs to know to engage respectfully? How is what we understand limited by who we meet? Frequently, the normative value of religious tolerance overemphasizes commonalities and idealizes traditions—even though conversations about differences and shortcomings can be invaluable. During the formation of the interfaith just peace paradigm, for example, participants broke through a stubborn roadblock by agreeing to bring each other their "worst" scriptural text. It not only illuminated dimensions of their scriptures that had been neglected in conversation; it also built trust because self-critical capacities facilitate openness in intergroup settings.[22] The promise of interreligious studies is its stress on learning in the presence of the other, weaving the supple cloth of sophisticated study in real relationship.[23]

THE WORLD WEIGHS HEAVY

One of the Jewish participants protested that the Israeli-Palestinian conflict dominated theoretical and practical discussions at the conference, as it always does in peace-oriented conversations among Jews, Christians, and Muslims. Given the number of conflicts around the world that involve or address religion, and the number of people impacted, he felt there should be more balanced attention.

The world impinges upon the work of interreligious studies and engagement in countless ways. Current events such as the continuing scourge of Islamophobia or the rise of ISIS occupy the space of interreligious encounter even if they are not on the agenda or the syllabus. Current movements such as women's empowerment, LGBTQ equality, and postcolonial critique raise particular kinds of questions. Events need not be ripped from the headlines to have an impact. As Faulkner wrote, "The past is never dead. It's not even past."[24] The near genocide of

Native American tribes, echoes of Crusades or La Convivencia, and images of the other in sacred texts are but a few of the historical developments that continue to shape interreligious perspectives and encounter.

In community engagement efforts, hot-button issues often become the proverbial elephant in the room. If the group declines to discuss them, some will claim the encounter is inauthentic, and others will stay away; they cannot agree to bracket a matter so urgent or cannot sit down with people who do not stand with them. When groups decide to address an issue they have trouble avoiding, it often consumes all the air in the room. Participants may not have adequate information, perspective, skills, or time to deal with the complexities. If there is no container for the problem, it can derail entire projects and undermine the building of relationship or trust.

Often people walk right into the elephant without meaning to. In a case study compiled by the Pluralism Project, students worked for months planning an interfaith *iftar* in the synagogue—and then noticed the "We Stand with Israel" sign out front.[25] They wanted to cover the sign as a gesture of hospitality, but would the rabbi agree? How would synagogue members respond? Would an incident of violence overseas inflame passions on both sides? The case-study model is useful because its established methodology for analysis includes attention to context, background, and multiple stakeholders. It shows how the world intrudes.

Judith Plaskow notes that the academy, despite its ivory tower reputation, "participates in the same tensions and contradictions, challenges and possibilities as the society in which it is situated, and is often a microcosm of wider cultural conflicts. Moreover—and this is the important point—our scholarship and teaching are broadened and deepened to the extent that they are in touch with and responsive to larger cultural currents."[26] Interreligious studies emphasizes this intersection. While comparative religion seeks an ostensibly "objective historical or phenomenological account of similarities . . . between religious traditions," according to Paul Hedges, interreligious studies "is more expressly focused on the dynamic encounter between religious traditions and persons."[27]

Consequently, the field can be powerfully buffeted by political winds. The enormous scholarly output about religious violence and historical traditions of religious tolerance, for example, is a response to current tensions and governmental focus on "countering violent extremism." So is the recent proliferation of university chairs in Islamic studies. With appropriate interdisciplinary rigor, the influence of politics, history, media, and science on interreligious studies at least becomes visible.

INTERSECTIONALITY

An African American colleague confided that she always feels her racial identity more powerfully than her religious identity at such gatherings. She is often the only black person in interreligious space and finds that race is generally obliterated as a difference of substance—as if it had no impact in religious circles.

We simultaneously bear notions of race, class, gender, sexual orientation, and nationality in shifting balances and contexts; we never come to the table as only one thing. Our diverse identities also press upon each other, as evident in religious teachings about gender and sexuality, or particular histories of religious communities regarding race. While the diversity of life stances is the central category of analysis in interreligious studies, the discipline cannot afford to ignore other types of difference.

Efforts to challenge discrimination and resolve conflict can be successful only if we engage the intersectionality of identities and oppressions. Interreligious studies must grapple with the unique ways that aspects of identity combine in our social context. Just as a woman has historically been viewed differently depending on her skin color, so too are religious experiences often different depending on other dimensions of our being.[28] While intersectional analysis runs the risk of multiplying the tensions of identity politics exponentially, it enables participants to encounter each other in their full humanity, with a complex story to tell, still being written.

The academy has been crucial in excavating intersectionality—as it continues to be in addressing all the issues raised in this chapter. Its theoretical analyses provide insight for interreligious engagement, cultivating greater self-awareness and sensitivity. Community-based efforts, in turn, comprise "praxis labs" that also generate new understandings, funneled back into the academy. Thus the realms of interreligious studies and interreligious engagement are interdependent, and they also overlap. Both arenas equip people to navigate a complex multifaith world, and some so equipped will become interfaith leaders. Both can generate research into best practices, metrics assessing impact, and standards for literacy. Campus contexts, which often furnish individuals' most intense encounter with diversity, involve curricular and cocurricular elements.

As evidenced in the above discussion of "six issues that complicate interreligious studies and engagement," it is difficult to tease apart the academic field and the activist movement. The Just Peace conference itself straddled the imaginary border as it both researched the interfaith paradigms and embodied the challenges of religious diversity. It is important to restate that the conference was *not* an example of failed engagement. It facilitated learning of substance and deepened relationships around shared commitments. The tales merely elucidate the most consistently useful strategy for addressing the complicating factors in interreligious studies and engagement—honest, careful attention to the trouble spots. We may find that the irritating grains of sand are polished into pearls.

THE PROMISING PRACTICE OF ANTIRACIST APPROACHES TO INTERFAITH STUDIES

Jeannine Hill Fletcher

As a socially engaged project, interfaith studies might be conceptualized as a discipline dedicated to positively shaping our world by increasing knowledge of diverse faiths and encouraging cooperation among people of different convictions. These particular aims are relevant to both public and private education as the North American citizenry in which this field emerges is among the most religiously diverse in the world.[1] But in order for our project to find a home among other interdisciplinary efforts of critical pedagogy, we must see clearly the structural transformations that are necessary to create the conditions for the possibility of interfaith solidarity.[2] That is, we must recognize the weight of America's history as a White Christian nation as it continues to privilege some persons and disadvantage others. This chapter invites us to attend closely to our nation's legal history that provided an advantage for White Christians and to consider how those advantages persist today. It is only with a clear sense of how religio-racial projects constructed the US as a White Christian nation that interfaith studies can contribute to religio-racial projects that today will be transformative for the thriving of *all* persons in a multiracial, multireligious America.

To see our work as part of this moment's religio-racial project, we need a sense of what such a project is (theoretically) and how it has worked historically. The idea of a religio-racial project is adapted from the work of sociologists and critical race theorists Michael Omi and Howard Winant in their investigation of America's racial projects.[3] With Omi and Winant, we might see race as a functional fiction and racial projects as the means by which race is constructed, assigned, applied, and enforced. At any given moment in our nation's history, we can look at how the categories of "the races" were proposed ("White," "Black," "Indian," "Hispanic," and more), how persons were sorted into them (on the basis of skin color, country of origin, an imagined blood line, and so forth), and the material benefits that a person was granted or denied on the basis of them (citizenship, education, ownership, and more).[4] Naming this dynamic as racial "projects," these sociologists help us to see how ideas about race were generated in a given time and place and how legislation was enacted on the basis of these imagined races. But we can also study how racial projects were challenged and how they changed. As scholars have shown, the dynamic racial projects of any given time were manufactured through political speech, popular press, education systems, legislation, and other vehicles by which ideas about "the races" gained currency. The laws enacted both contributed to and reflected what was in the air at the time. By extending the sociologists' work to the idea of a religio-racial project, we can train our eyes to see the way *religion* functioned—for example, in sermons, religious tracts, and actions of religious bodies—within a given racial project, as well as how it functions today. A chronicle of America's dominant religio-racial project as a White Christian nation can function simultaneously as illuminating the theoretical concept and as an impetus for transforming our nation with new religio-racial projects of diversity.

The original religio-racial project of what would become the United States was fostered at a time when European racial discourse was emerging in the service of colonization and when, in the words of James W. Perkinson, "Christian supremacy gave birth to white supremacy."[5] The rules of engagement for the exploring nations of Europe was that if the land they "discovered" was inhabited by a Christian nation, then they had no right to it, but if the land was inhabited by a non-Christian nation, Christians had the right to lay claim to the land either through economic negotiations or military action. This protocol is reflected in writings like Pope Alexander VI's *Inter Caetera* in which Christian rulers and religious leaders collaborated in expanding Christendom. Subsequently, as European nations began settling colonies in what would become the United States, religious ideologies of Christian supremacy directed land grants to "all Christian peoples."[6] Governing authority of the land was rooted in reasoning found in Christian scripture.[7] In this era, a growing sense of the resistance of Native peoples to Christian rule caused missionaries to construct them as a different race of humanity. Seeing resistance as entailing a "pagan" mind-set, missionaries saw Native peoples as misunderstanding God's directive to subdue and cultivate the land. Tracing this back to religious ideologies, the racial project named Native peoples "red" on account of the body paint they wore on sacred occasions.[8] Thus named as different from the White Christian colonizers, the humanity of Native peoples could be further called into question. The original religio-racial project in the land that would become the United States was to claim priority for Christians and to racialize others on account of their divergent religious ways and practices.

As colonial education systems expanded, educators (often religiously affiliated) fueled religio-racial projects where a White Christian nation was seen as part of God's design. Historian Craig Wilder recounts: "In a 1783 sermon celebrating the American Revolution, Yale president Ezra Stiles lauded the rise of the 'whites' whose numerical growth alone proved divine favoritism toward the children of Europe. God intended the Americas for 'a new enlargement of Japhet,' the minister began, invoking the curse of Ham, and Europe's children were quickly filling the continents."[9]

This religio-racial project of White Christian supremacy was written into law when citizenship was restricted to "free White persons" and Christians were privileged in the system of landownership. The latter was made possible legally through the case of *Johnson v. M'Intosh* (1823), which ruled that Native peoples' "right to occupancy"—as non-Christian "pagans"—was superseded by Christian nations' "right to title."[10] Claims about the supremacy of Christianity translated into economic advantage that gave title and prosperity to Christians as land ownership formed the basis for the accumulation of wealth. As law scholar Eric Kades describes, "The rule of *Johnson v. M'Intosh* ensured that Europeans would not transfer wealth to the tribes in the process of competing against each other to buy land."[11] Without economic and political power, Native peoples were at a disadvantage to the White Christian nation as it pursued "Manifest Destiny," passed legislation to remove Indians from lands east of the Mississippi in the nineteenth century, and moved the original inhabitants to smaller and smaller sites of land "reserved" for them. The "doctrine of discovery" still disempowers indigenous peoples in their struggles for sovereignty today.[12] Yet, throughout this history, we also see religio-racial projects of resistance to White supremacy in the Ghost Dance of the nineteenth century, the American Indian Movement of the twentieth century, and the water protectors of today.

Simultaneous to the dispossession of non-Christian Native peoples and the racialization of indigenous populations drawn from their religious expressions, the disempowerment and disadvantage of African peoples was similarly rooted in a religiously grounded racialization. Like the land theft that brought the United States of America into being, the labor theft of enslavement was employed to build the nation. This social and economic reality was fueled by a religio-racial project that marked Black skin as a sign of (the Christian) God's curse and African practices (including Islam) as inferior to Christian ones. As David Whitford explains, the logic of "the curse of Ham" was a set of "interlocking tropes that gave the slave trade not only justification but a veneer of nobleness to the slave trader and owner." He describes:

> The Matrix consisted of three fundamental elements: 1) that black skin is the result of God's curse and is therefore a signal and sign of the African's cursedness to slavery; 2) that Africans embodied this cursed nature through hypersexuality and libidinousness; and 3) that these sinful and cursed Africans were also uncivilized brutes and heathens who

were helped by slavery because they were exposed to culture and the saving Gospel of Jesus Christ. . . . This Matrix was then used for more than two centuries to repel any attack against the practice of African slavery in the English colonies of America.[13]

As the new nation borrowed ideologies from European Christian thinking, legislation was put in place to cement the dispossession of non-White others based on their non-Christian heritage. In 1682, legislation in Virginia named as slaves virtually "all servants . . . who and whose parentage and native country are not Christian at the time of their first purchase."[14] It was on the basis of religious and racial superiority that White Christians argued over hundreds of years that enslavement was justified. It is important to see that it was not simply uneducated slave owners who mobilized these arguments. Rather, this was mainstream Christian theology manufactured by and disseminated from scholarly and pastoral systems.[15] Such Christian theological production endured even into the nineteenth century, as the nation's dominant religio-racial project offered religious justification for enslavement that also eliminated religious diversity as it imposed a Christian hegemony.[16] While such reasoning supported legislation right up to emancipation in 1863, we remember also the religion of resistance that was another thread among the nation's religio-racial projects. The dominant refrain of America as a White Christian nation has *always* been challenged through the voices of courageous people such as Frederick Douglass, Sojourner Truth, and countless others.

The project of a White Christian nation was not only focused on the dispossession and disempowerment of Native peoples, Africans, and African Americans, it was mobilized to exclude some people altogether even while it used their lives to build the nation's future. In the late nineteenth century, people shaped by Asian religious traditions had already arrived in large numbers on the US West Coast. They helped to settle the land only recently acquired through a military conflict with Mexico, and their labors connected this new part of the nation to the old through the transcontinental railroad. Yet, in 1873, on the floor of the US Senate, Senator A. A. Sargent rolled out a plan to ban immigration to the US from China. His argument was that by their customs, their way of life, and their religion, the Chinese were inassimilable to a White Christian nation. His plan was that Christian missionaries should travel to China, "wash their robes and make them white in the blood of the Lamb."[17] Then being fit for citizenship, the Chinese might apply to immigrate. Sargent's religio-racial project of America as a White Christian nation was made reasonable by the many diverse scholarly and pastoral productions of figures like Jesuit priest James Bouchard and Methodist minister Otis Gibson, who publicly debated the possibility of the Chinese assimilating and then disseminated widely a published account of their exchange. While Bouchard, the son of a Delaware man and a captive French woman adopted into the Delaware people, mobilized his argument to oppose the citizenship of "the immoral, vicious, pagan Chinese," Gibson supported their citizenship but nonetheless upheld the notion of America as a Christian nation. In his words, "All invidious legislation should be repealed, and Christian men and women must multiply their efforts to uplift and Christianize these people."[18] Such efforts by Christian ministers toward non-White, non-Christian others was grounded in the ideology and theology of White Christian supremacy that was in the national discourse at this time, circulating even at the origins of the modern interfaith movement in Chicago at the 1893 World's Parliament of Religions. There Rev. Alexander McKenzie invited the international delegates to see clearly the exceptional nature of the United States, where Christian citizens in their churches and schools had been "manufacturing a republic—taking the black material of humanity and building it up into noble men and women; taking the red material, wild with every savage instinct, and making it into respectable men."[19] In popular writings of the time we see a wider public sharing the same sentiment that it was the duty of white Christians to uplift non-White others.[20]

The religio-racial project of America as a white Christian nation was legislated further with an immigration ban on the Asiatic Zone (1917) and with restrictive quotas (1924).[21] Thus, from 1924 to 1965 immigration policies curtailed the arrival of persons deemed unassimilable to the culture of the White Christian nation, including African, Asian, southern European, and eastern European immigrants.[22]

Though today's efforts to promote religious diversity arise from within systems of immigration and naturalization that were transformed by the Hart-Celler Act of 1965, the residual effects of an ideology of America as a White Christian nation remains. Islamophobia, backlash against the civil rights gains for African Americans, and resistance to immigration give evidence of what's popular in today's religio-racial projects.[23] But what exists structurally is even more insidious. The structural reality that White Christians still enjoy material benefits from earlier exclusions must be part of our analysis of systems in need of transformation. A crucial component of our nation's historical religio-racial project of a White Christian supremacy was to assign material benefits on the basis of a Whiteness that had been deeply entwined with Christianness. Native peoples were denied the material benefits of land ownership, which was granted to Whites. African Americans were denied the generational benefits of education, fair employment, and full enfranchisement, which were defended for White citizens. Asian populations were denied the foundational benefit of citizenship. And the underlying ideology of America as a country for "free White persons" persists. Through many acts of legislation, material well-being for White populations was secured, but the same well-being was denied to America's non-White, non-Christian others. The generational effect of these decisions is a structural reality of White supremacy, where White Christians continue to hold greater economic resources and positions of influence.[24] Situated in the context of the United States and its project of White Christian supremacy, interfaith studies has the capacity to contribute to a new religio-racial project in a multireligious, multiracial nation, but we must recognize this imbalance to effectively do our work.

Interfaith studies might aim at transforming systems through which a religio-racial project of multiracial, multireligious America might thrive. Given our roles as educators, we might think of our work as transforming the very system of education with new content and pedagogies that affirm the importance of the many religious ideologies and communities within our nation. Given the ways in which Christian religious education has functioned historically to produce and disseminate a religio-racial project of White Christian supremacy, special attention might be given to the transformation of religious education in this country. Additionally, because of the ways in which historical dispossessions have disadvantaged people of color in the United States, the structures and systems we aim to transform might include reparations and reforms so that more people of color and diverse faiths might be part of the educational process within our classrooms. Finally, given the close association we've seen between the institution of citizenship and the ideology of White Christian supremacy, we need to be vigilant in our attention to the intersection of our role in the systems of education, including religious education, with other systems of enfranchisement, including, but not limited to, immigration, naturalization, and voting rights.

INTERFAITH STUDIES AS ANTIRACIST PRACTICE IN A WHITE CHRISTIAN NATION

As we learn from history to see the actors whose choices created the conditions of privileging some persons in a White Christian nation, we are empowered to understand the uneven playing field that is our inheritance. But we might also find tools to analyze the flow of power and to understand who are the actors (including ourselves) who might re-create our religio-racial project for the flourishing of all. In the field of interfaith studies, we are scholars and educators, researchers and teachers, not lawmakers. Yet the knowledge that we produce *does* impact the wider sphere of national ideology and ultimately the rights and privileges conferred.

Historian Craig Wilder shows how the ideology of White Christian supremacy, which underwrote legislation prioritizing White Christian well-being, was manufactured in the educational systems of America's first colleges.[25] It was the ideologies and theologies of White Christian supremacy, manufactured in America's educational systems, that made legislation dispossessing people of other faiths appear reasonable. In that same spirit, scholars in interfaith studies may be empowered to do our work cognizant of the way we might contribute to a new national discourse. By asking questions about who holds resources (both symbolic and material) and who is afforded power and control of those resources, we might see ourselves as agents of social change. Seeing more clearly the flow of power and the role of decision-makers in systems of power, educators in the field of interfaith studies can be more aware of their own gatekeeper function, whereby we hold power to provide access or limit access for people of color and people of all faiths.[26]

While critically aware of the legislated privileges of White Christians in America, antiracist practice asks us to see this history as impoverishing our nation. In their antiracist training, the People's Institute for Survival and Beyond promotes the sharing of culture as a positive response to this history of impoverishment. As the institute describes, "Culture is the life support of a community. If a community's culture is respected and nurtured, the community's power will grow."[27] The application of this antiracist principle in the work of interfaith studies is twofold. By fostering the growth of a community's religious culture, communities disempowered by our uneven playing field might find resources for thriving. Simultaneously, by sharing culture across communities of religious difference we create networks of appreciation that nurture the power of solidarity. From a social perspective, culture sharing fosters the power and empowerment of solidarity. From a theological perspective, the sharing (and appreciation) of religio-racial difference helps to destabilize the Christian theologies of supremacy that have underwritten legislation that has structured America as a White Christian nation.

As we together develop curricula of interfaith studies we might be guided by questions that help us remain attentive to a critical pedagogy and our role in a new religio-racial project. These questions might include the following:

- Learning from History
  - Where does your religious tradition fit within the history of America as a White Christian nation?
  - How does the history of structural dispossession and generational inheritance shape the current religio-racial landscape of your community?

- Mapping Power
  - Who holds the resources in your community? Are the anchor institutions (schools, hospitals, houses of worship, etc.) religiously affiliated? Is there diverse religious representation in legislative bodies?
  - How is your religious affiliation related to resource-holding institutions and individuals?

- Gatekeeping
  - Where do you have power to inform the knowledge production of your community?
  - Where do you have power in relation to the material resources of your community?
  - Where do you have power in relation to the political resources of your community?

- Sharing Culture
  - How does your work positively inform the creation of a multiracial, multireligious culture?
  - What are the sites of resistance to the creation of multiracial, multireligious cultures (theologically, politically, socially, practically)?

As we work to transform the systems and structures of White supremacy in our nation, interfaith studies might be a leader in critically analyzing our historic failures and forming our future in a truly multiracial, multireligious country.

THE POSSIBILITY OF SOLIDARITY

Evangelicals and the Field of Interfaith Studies

Marion H. Larson and Sara L. H. Shady

Most voices within the growing interfaith movement define their work as inclusive of all religious and nonreligious perspectives—for how else will we learn to live together amid our differences? Nonetheless, the movement isn't always as diverse as its participants might imagine it to be. As in any growing social movement, the ideals of interfaith cooperation are often challenged by the complexity and conflict that emerge in lived reality. In addition to differences between the content of our religious and nonreligious beliefs, conflict can easily arise over issues such as how faith commitments inform who we are to be in the world, how we are to interact with persons of other religious traditions, and what we believe our faiths tell us about how to respond to the social and political challenges we face. Interfaith coalitions cannot assume unanimity on any of these issues. Thus, it often seems that there is limited room for those who challenge some of the rules of interfaith engagement by retaining a commitment to proselytizing and by upholding a theologically exclusivist perspective. And while the movement advocates action for the common good of all, it is not clear that conservative political voices are always welcome. Echoing bell hooks's influential work *Feminism Is for Everybody*, we ask whether the work of interfaith cooperation can and should really be for everybody, and whether a corollary academic field of interfaith studies can serve as a corrective for these shortfalls or merely replicate them.

Academic disciplines that grow out of social movements, like gender studies and interfaith studies, must maintain at least some normative commitments in order to preserve the relationship between theory and practice. As Kate McCarthy notes in this volume, "Like other disciplines with applied dimensions," the field of interfaith studies "serves the public good by bringing its analysis to bear on practical approaches to issues in religiously diverse societies."[1] For the field of interfaith studies, one such normative commitment is fostering respect for the different ways that persons orient around religion. Another commitment is cultivating a capacity for critical examination of religious identity. Furthermore, much of the scholarship emerging from this field arises directly from practical challenges and questions raised in the context of the interfaith movement. Following from these commitments and these challenges, the field must further explore the possibility of inclusion when religious identity and commitment lead persons to divergent social and political positions. We believe, therefore, that one of the primary purposes of the emerging field is to develop further scholarship on how to fully support and actualize the goal of inclusion within the interfaith movement by analyzing and addressing the areas in which inclusion is lacking. And, given the connections between theory and praxis and scholar and practitioner, the academic field as such must also develop methods for maintaining clarity about its own core commitments as significant internal differences arise, which they undoubtedly will.

In this chapter we endeavor to begin the process of using the tools of the academy to improve the field of praxis by focusing on a practical issue arising from the interfaith movement: the surprising underrepresentation of evangelical Christians in the movement in the United States. The reasons for this underrepresentation are complex, requiring critical examination by those in interfaith studies. To this end, we explore some of the core reasons why evangelicals may be excluded or may exclude themselves from interfaith initiatives, focusing particularly on issues of identity and recognition. These two concepts, often used in political theory to promote inclusion in democracy, are applicable, we believe, to the pluralistic goals of both the interfaith movement and the field of interfaith studies. By integrating political theory into scholarship within interfaith studies, we can explore with increasing depth the challenges of cultivating solidarity. Overall, we believe that constructive strategies for cultivating solidarity amid significant differences comprise both a realistic and a necessary path for interfaith studies to pursue, both for itself and for the movement to which it is tied.

WHERE ARE THE EVANGELICALS?

In the fall of 2016, a majority of the evangelicals who voted in the presidential election cast a vote for Donald Trump, a decision that seems oppositional to the goals of both the interfaith movement and the field of interfaith studies.[2] Yet, that same fall, a group of evangelical college students partnered with a local Islamic center to send warm clothing to refugees in Syria. This was the second year of a student-led effort to provide aid to refugees beyond a simplistic social media response.[3] Motivated by Jesus's command to love all neighbors, and the work and wisdom of Christians like Dietrich Bonhoeffer and Henri Nouwen, these students believe that this interfaith partnership provides an opportunity to live out the essence of Christianity.

The juxtaposition of these two events helps to illustrate the complexity of evangelical identity—a topic well suited for further examination from scholars in interfaith studies. There is no simple answer to the question of why evangelicals are or aren't reluctant to join interfaith efforts, of course. Furthermore, individual evangelicals will vary in their reasons for lack of involvement. Some avoid interfaith engagement because they wrongly perceive that "interfaith" means seeking to find a least common denominator across all beliefs—a sort of religious United Nations, in the words of John Azumah, "whose ultimate aim is a 'United Religions' through negotiations, . . . where compromise is the watchword."[4] But if this were the only reason for their absence in the interfaith community, addressing this misperception would be all that is needed in order to make evangelicals feel welcome. Evangelical hesitation more likely centers around two interacting and potentially self-reinforcing factors: identity and misrecognition.

The Complexity of Evangelical Identity

Political theorists have long affirmed the crucial importance of identity and recognition for a healthy, inclusive democracy. This is because, notes Charles Taylor, "our identity is partly shaped by recognition or its absence, often by the *mis*recognition of others, and so a person or group can suffer real damage, real distortion, if the people or society around them mirror back to them a confining or demeaning or contemptible picture of themselves."[5] This idea is consistent with the commitments of interfaith studies, as we seek to recognize and critically examine our assumptions about religious identity. As Eboo Patel explains, one of the central aspects of interfaith leadership is "respect for identity," acknowledging that "people have a right to form their own identities regarding religion" and that both these identities and their expression "should be reasonably accommodated."[6]

Respect for identity is important in part, observes Taylor, because our sense of self develops in dialogue between self-perception and the ways in which we are perceived and understood by others. When dialogue is healthy, each person's identity is properly affirmed and recognized by others, despite their differences. But there is a correlative danger for those who aren't adequately understood and identified. Taylor calls this "misrecognition." As he puts it, "Misrecognition shows not just a lack of due respect. It can inflict a grievous wound. . . . Due recognition is not just a courtesy we owe people. It is a vital human need."[7] Within the context of the interfaith movement, Patel similarly maintains that "to respect someone else's identity does not require you to agree with it or to accept it," but it does imply "positive, constructive, warm, caring, cooperative engagement."[8]

Respecting evangelical identity starts with recognizing and seeking to understand its complexity. The term "evangelical" was initially used in the early decades of American history to indicate individuals who had experienced a "spiritual awakening" and made a conscious decision to

live out the Christian faith. For early evangelicals, such as George Whit-
field and John Wesley, the term was used to differentiate a revivalist
Christianity from what some referred to as the "dead orthodoxy" that
followed the Protestant Reformation. It wasn't until the mid- to late
twentieth century that the term "evangelical Christian" became nearly
synonymous with political conservatism. There is disagreement today
about the essential definition of evangelicalism and whether its necessary components are more rooted in theology or in political ideology.
In fact, many self-identified evangelicals increasingly contest the term.[9]

While we should be wary of any narratives that absolutize evangelical identity, it is a term often used to describe a subset of Christians in
America. Despite the differences among evangelicals, Wesley Wildman
offers a helpful summary of several common components of evangelical Christian identity: a combination of "group-defining oppositional
elements and morality-defining piety elements with a stress on spiritual
rebirth (being 'born again') and a particular understanding of the gospel."[10] This definition helps illuminate some of the apparent tensions
between evangelical Christians and many of those involved in the interfaith movement. While it is natural for all religious and social groups
to define themselves at least in part by considering the differences and
even "oppositional elements" that distinguish "us" from "them," evangelicals (particularly conservative ones) tend to "maintain the most
rigid conception of in-group Christian identity of all Christians."[11] For
a Christian with such a perspective, it can be deeply unsettling to learn
through interfaith interactions that there are many beliefs and religious
practices that various religions have in common. As Christopher Lamb
describes such an experience: "The devout 'other' believer shakes my
stereotyped version of his or her faith, and therefore of the person, pro-
vokes me to question my own practice, my particular Christian tradition, and sometimes the very basis of my faith. The uniqueness of the
Christian religion is suddenly radically relativized, and I am left with an
alarming sense of insecurity."[12] Thus, some evangelicals fear that interfaith interactions may cause them to compromise their Christian identity by acknowledging too much common ground with non-Christians

or even with more progressive Christians. In fact, note R. Khari Brown and Ronald E. Brown, evangelicals often see their beliefs as being "in conflict and competition with non-Christians."[13]

This sense of conflict and competition is complicated by the second component of Wildman's definition—"morality-defining piety elements with a stress on spiritual rebirth." For some evangelicals, the former may suggest a combative stance toward those of other faiths, whereas the latter speaks of the need for Christians' faith to lead them to become people who follow Christ's command to treat others with love rather than combativeness. Christian pastor and theologian Brian McLaren describes this sense of possible contradiction within evangelical identity as "conflicted religious identity syndrome."[14] This syndrome emerges when struggling to maintain a strong commitment to one's own faith tradition while at the same time seeking to avoid hostility toward people of other faiths. While both are important goals, the problem arises when a person assumes that strong, loyal Christianity is best demonstrated through actively opposing all other faiths. This leaves an internal tension for many evangelicals that can impede productive interfaith engagement.

Another impediment to productive interfaith engagement can be seen in Wildman's final element of evangelical identity—"a particular understanding of the gospel." This particular understanding is a religious exclusivist perspective that understands Jesus Christ to provide the only path to salvation. It could be argued that this perspective is at odds with the core commitments of the interfaith movement, particularly the commitments to openness and tolerance. Thus, in the words of Azumah, "truth claims in general and the Christian witness of the uniqueness of Christ" are seen as having "no place at the roundtable of interfaith dialogue."[15]

If religious exclusivist beliefs are incompatible with interfaith dialogue, and if religious exclusivism is central to the identity of many evangelical Christians, then it's no wonder that evangelicals feel that they can't participate. They fear that they have to sacrifice their roots "in order to branch out to others."[16] For many, this is too high a price to pay.

It is certainly possible for those who believe their religion to be the only path to God to communicate such a conviction in ways that sound judgmental and arrogant. But this isn't a necessary result of religious exclusivism. Charles Soukup and James Keaten maintain that the most significant conflict in interfaith interactions isn't that of "pluralist" versus "exclusivist." Instead, the issue is whether a person responds to religious otherness in a "dehumanizing" or in a "humanizing" way. In fact, they note, it is possible for both pluralists and exclusivists to be dehumanizing toward those with whom they disagree. By contrast, "anyone with a humanizing response, regardless of their orientation toward religious otherness, is capable of engaging in productive encounters across faiths."[17]

Recognition and Misrecognition

While conflicts within evangelical Christian identity offer one possible explanation for lack of evangelical involvement in the interfaith movement, the field of interfaith studies must pay attention to and analyze ways in which misrecognition of what it means to be evangelical by those outside of the evangelical community can also be a causal factor. In order for the interfaith movement to be fully inclusive, it must properly recognize the identities of everyone who "orients around religion differently." This means seeking to humanize those with perspectives different from our own. Without understanding the complexity of evangelical identity, it becomes too easy to stereotype and dismiss evangelical perspectives. Interfaith studies needs to analyze and understand how failing to genuinely recognize evangelicals makes it less likely for evangelicals to want to participate in the interfaith movement, thereby suggesting a path out of this problem. In order to build solidarity between evangelicals and the interfaith movement, the field of interfaith studies must draw from various academic disciplines in exploring the complexity of identities represented in, as well as potentially marginalized by, the movement. One possibility for future scholarship is to use work done in social and political philosophy to promote healthy models of inclusion and solidarity amid significant differences of identity, commitment, and values.

Iris Marion Young's work is particularly helpful on this topic. Young, best known for challenging modern democracies to a higher standard of inclusion on issues of race and gender, advocates for a deliberative model of democratic interaction. According to Young, healthy social interaction involves welcoming as many voices as possible to the dialogue, being sure to recognize and give voice to underrepresented groups and perspectives. This is essential because it moves us away from "an initial self-regarding stance" to a genuinely inclusive society where we accept our responsibility to listen to and learn from others.[18]

In our efforts to foster healthy democracies in a pluralistic context, Young discusses many reasons why we might fail to be fully inclusive. Most applicable to our discussion here is what Young describes as "internal exclusion," where the views and experiences of some individuals are dismissed, discounted, or even patronized.[19] This can happen when individuals or groups are viewed as problems to be discussed rather than persons with whom to interact, when we fail to really listen to those on the outside and fail to speak in a manner that enables them to hear and understand, and when the narratives we use perpetuate misunderstanding and stereotype. In each of these cases, members of the excluded group are dehumanized, in that they're not fully recognized, understood, and welcomed.

There are ways in which the misrecognition of evangelicals, whether intentional or unintentional, has contributed to an environment that can appear inhospitable. For decades, many evangelicals have claimed that a "liberal bias" in the media and academy works against them. As Christian Smith explains, evangelicals "often feel excluded, marginalized, or discriminated against by secular institutions and elites."[20] Writers such as Robert Wuthnow and Nicholas Kristof confirm that there is some truth to that claim. From Wuthnow's perspective, American higher education, which claims to be committed to "truth and fair-mindedness," harbors "disdain for evangelical Christians."[21] The presence of such disdain, says Kristof, "creates liberal privilege"—particularly problematic for conservative evangelicals.[22] And in such a potentially hostile environment, there is often little effort among those outside evangelicalism to try to understand it.[23]

It's true that evangelical Christians can at times be "contentiously exclusivist, self-congratulatory, and intolerant of diversity."[24] Even so, failing to interrogate and complicate this view of American evangelicalism can perpetuate a vicious cycle between evangelicals and the interfaith movement—a cycle that the field of interfaith studies can help to recognize, analyze, and avert. Given some aspects of evangelical identity discussed above—particularly the tendency to focus on differences rather than similarities between themselves and others—misrecognition can be particularly destructive. It makes evangelicals feel like unwelcome outsiders. This then can lead their participation to be more strident or defensive than it might otherwise be. It can also lead them to avoid participation altogether. Thus, misrecognition has a polarizing effect.[25]

COMBATING MISRECOGNITION OF EVANGELICALS

According to Young, combating misrecognition requires giving special attention to the greetings, rhetoric, and narratives we use. By greeting, Young means a person-to-person recognition that expresses willingness to listen to and learn from the other.[26] This doesn't require participants to agree or to have a shared conception of the good. Rather, it affirms the equal status of each in the dialogue, a desire to learn from the religious or philosophical life of the other. For example, the interfaith movement might be particularly conscious of its efforts to share positive stories about evangelicals, affirming the good things that some evangelicals have done or said—such as their charitable work, past and present. While the good that's been done by evangelicals is far from the whole story, a focus on this and on other examples of what Patel and Meyer have called "appreciative knowledge" of evangelical Christianity can help evangelicals feel more welcomed.[27]

When considering rhetoric, Young encourages us to use forms of communication and speech that are appropriate to the audience of participants.[28] Within an interfaith context, this means that each participant should be allowed to use his or her own religious language, not prioritizing a religiously neutral way of expressing a concept. So an evangelical Christian speaking in an interfaith setting ought to feel free to speak of the "incarnation of Christ" (rather than the "birth of Jesus"). Or a Muslim might speak of "Mohammed receiving the Qur'an" (rather than "Mohammed writing the Qur'an"). And there ought to be space for evangelicals in interfaith settings to express religiously exclusivist ideas, just as those with more pluralist understandings are free to express theirs.

This is a contested claim within the field of interfaith studies and an important issue for future scholarship. For example, Kate McCarthy argues that the field should be religiously neutral in order to maintain its integrity within the secular academy.[29] We believe, on the other hand, that interfaith studies should challenge the dominance of secularism within the academy. In order to remain committed to pluralism, the field ought not pretend that secular language is neutral language. If Young is correct that healthy pluralism in a democracy requires inclusion of different speech patterns, because our voices are deeply rooted in identities shaped by race, ethnicity, class, and gender, then the field of interfaith studies lives out its commitment to religious pluralism when it allows religious groups to speak in their own terms.

Third, Young implores us to use narratives that promote understanding between persons with very different experiences. This helps combat our assumptions and flawed generalities about different groups. At the same time, though, we must recognize that narratives can "manipulate irrational assent," opening up the potential for misleading and even deceptive conclusions to be made about different groups.[30] When evangelicals are only ever referred to as the "problem" or as "obstacles" in our case studies, when our narratives about them overemphasize their commitment to proselytization, and when assumptions are made about their political beliefs, we perpetuate false generalizations. These myths only further promote the vicious cycle of misrecognition that leads to perceptions that the interfaith movement and the field of interfaith studies are inhospitable. Instead, narratives could be used to help give voice to the complexity of evangelical identity, showing the diversity of perspectives within evangelical Christianity. Including more evangelical voices in various publications and presentations would be another step in the right direction.

SOLIDARITY AMID DIFFERENCE

The challenges that identity and misrecognition pose to the genuine inclusion of evangelical Christians suggest the need for creativity in imagining how to encourage partnership despite significant ideological differences. Much work in the interfaith movement has focused on bringing people together to forge common ground. At the same time, solidarity also relies on our ability to navigate conflict and disagreement as we simultaneously affirm our individual identities. Underrepresented groups are unlikely to build bridges of solidarity if they perceive that they're not welcome to be themselves.

Solidarity is essential to the field of interfaith studies if there is to be some shared commitment to a set of common goals bolstered by mutual respect and understanding. At the same time, however, solidarity doesn't require as much similarity as we might imagine. Once again Young's work on solidarity is helpful. Defining solidarity as "commitment and justice owed to people, but precisely not on the basis of a fellow feeling or mutual identification," Young emphasizes mutual respect and support in the face of significant differences. Although she developed this concept in response to the problem of spatial segregation along racial lines, "differentiated solidarity" holds potential for helping us think critically about inclusion and recognition within the field of interfaith studies.[31] Fostering a healthy, inclusive democracy requires that we learn to communicate across these differences, but neither assimilation nor a focus on our lowest common denominators provide a viable solution. Instead, differentiation alongside solidarity allows those who orient around an issue differently to group together while at the same time maintaining bridges of inclusion through a commitment to respect and affirmation. For example, the field of interfaith studies can work across religious lines to facilitate scholarship between political or theological conservatives and liberals or between religious exclusivists and inclusivists.

Young illustrates the concept of differentiated solidarity by describing a city with multiple neighborhoods, each with its own social and cultural identity. None of these neighborhoods would be entirely segregated or homogenous, however. Rather, bridges of inclusion would allow for fluid movement between neighborhoods, acknowledging that religious affiliations aren't the only meaningful way of grouping ourselves. In this city, "everyone has their homeplace, the place of their immediate residence and local community participation. No one feels that another part of the city or region is closed to him or her, however, because of the behaviour and attitude of its residents."[32]

It would be dangerous to think that solidarity in the context of interfaith studies requires assimilation to only one set of political values or theological commitments. Forming solidarity on the basis of affinity would exclude certain groups and limit our capacity for personal, intellectual, and spiritual growth. After all, if dialogue primarily consists of affirming areas of agreement, then none of us is challenged to critical reflection, a core commitment of interfaith studies. True transformation of our life together as persons who orient around religion differently requires building solidarity—not in spite of our differences but across and through our differences.

A robust field of interfaith studies will require more than mere tolerance of differences, both in theory and in practice. The type of inquiry that emerges within the model of differentiated solidarity is likely to be characterized by tension and struggle at times. Genuine respect and inclusion require that we affirm both connection and distance, in Young's words, "explicitly acknowledging social differentiations and divisions and encouraging differently situated groups to give voice to their needs, interests, and perspectives."[33] Differentiated solidarity invites us to speak openly about disagreements, even constructively acknowledging when we are offended by another's assertions, but to do so in a manner that affirms the person's right to a belief or practice that others don't share.

Martin Luther King Jr., often upheld as a model for interfaith cooperation, demonstrates what differentiated solidarity might look like. On Palm Sunday in 1959, King preached a sermon in which he presented Mohandas Gandhi as an exemplar of the work of Christ on Earth, going so far as to say "the greatest Christian of the twentieth century was not a member of the Christian church."[34] King concluded the sermon with a prayer in which he thanked God for all of God's self-revelations throughout the world, including through non-Christian religions. He then offered an evangelical "altar call," asking those present to consider accepting Christ. One of the historical heroes of work for racial justice was simultaneously committed to solidarity with other faiths and to evangelizing in the name of Christ. If a hero of the Christian faith can stand in solidarity with persons who believe differently, is there not also room for evangelical Christians to stand in solidarity with the interfaith movement? And if the field of interfaith studies can see King as an inspiring model, is there not also room for solidarity with partners in the evangelical community today?

WATER, CLIMATE, STARS, AND PLACE

Toward an Interspecies Interfaith Belonging

Lisa E. Dahill

> *We are human only in contact,*
> *and conviviality,*
> *with what is not human.*
>
> —DAVID ABRAM, *Spell of the Sensuous*

This essay's approach to interreligious engagement, like those of several others in the volume, shows a commitment to contextuality and embodiment. What distinguishes this essay, however, is its extending of such attention to embodied context beyond human communities and societies. I argue that, in a time of accelerating ecological crisis interwoven with religiously fueled alienation from the more-than-human world, the field of interreligious studies needs to orient itself deliberately within the larger web of creaturely kinship that is our shared biological reality. Such kinship is not an abstraction but the very stuff of which our bodies are composed, made from the particular animals and plants we eat. We breathe this kinship as we draw into our blood the oxygen exhaled by trees and plankton; it provides the terms of our economies, the physical and relational structuring of our lives in every particular location. Many books and essays today trace the urgency of religious traditions' retrieving their own ecological wisdom—or creating it anew—for our time. This essay builds on that work specifically in relation to the emerging field of interreligious studies, proposing that this new field incorporate a primary attention to *place* in structuring the field, so as to illuminate and empower the ecologically specific forms of interreligious vision and leadership our time demands.

INTRODUCTION

Theorists of communication—from cell biologists to cultural linguists—assert that life takes place *between*. From the membranes contouring interstitial spaces and mediating the flow of signals, nutrients, or movement between cells to the complex coding of sensory perception and feedback making possible the ongoing evolution of diverse species and cultures, life requires interaction. Biological life is a cascade of "inter" forms.

Yet a primary feature of Western economic and social models is the denial of such relationality, typically favoring conceptions of God or the heroic human individual that privilege solo existence: masculine monotheism, agro-corporate monocultures, Euro/white supremacy, and the forced subjugation of all life forms or conceptual patterns that diverge from these. Capitalism signals economic privilege by flaunting its alienation from the natural world. Buffered by buildings and pavement, cocooned within fossil-fuel-driven systems of mechanization, "virtual reality," and climate control, contemporary Westerners can live in more or less total ignorance of the creatures and bioregions literally supporting our existence, including the human beings exploited by those same systems. As a Christian on the wilder far edge of my tradition, I am all too conscious of how this ecological alienation derives from and contributes to not only forms of Christian hegemony toxic to healthy interreligious engagement but also patterns of dualism and privilege enshrined in global capitalism that consign whole populations of human beings and other species to inferior status, enslavement, or death.[1]

The interlocking ecological crises of our time announce an end to these unsustainable religious and economic models and insist that humans learn a new identity *as* humans, mobilized as effectively as possible to reverse our present course and find radically new ways to live together on Earth. How do the climate crisis and the essential recognition that we live on this planet with other forms of life—in a vast emergent universe—reshape not only particular religious traditions but also the new field of interreligious studies? How do these crises affect how we talk with each other across religious boundaries, what we teach, how we practice our faith or engage in service projects or political advocacy?[2] What are the emergent questions for this new field of interreligious studies to take on, given these crises threatening all life on Earth? Within such questions, how timely the emergence of this new field is, for we humans will learn what it means to cherish our shared home *together*—or not at all.

STANDING ROCK

On April 1, 2016, LaDonna Brave Bull Allard, an elder of the Standing Rock Sioux tribe, established the Sacred Stone Camp on her land to block the path of the proposed Dakota Access Pipeline as it approached the Missouri River south of Bismarck, North Dakota. Her grandchildren and other young tribal members stood with her, and over the course of the spring, summer, and fall indigenous people throughout North America arrived to join them, creating the largest gathering of Native tribes in the US (more than three hundred recognized tribes present) in the past one hundred years. Thousands of supporters from a number of other communities and traditions also journeyed to Standing Rock, and the success of these Water Protectors in delaying the construction of a path for the pipeline under the Missouri River drew considerable coverage on social media but also, by fall, increasingly shocking displays of violence by pipeline advocates and police. Internationally broadcast photos of nonviolent Native Americans being attacked with pepper spray, blasted with water in freezing conditions, and confronted with the overwhelming force of massed police and military power helped generate considerable pressure from beyond the camps to investigate the legality of the pipeline's use of traditional Native lands, and on December 4—one day before North Dakota governor Jack Dalrymple had ordered clearing of the camps in order for construction to resume—the US Army Corps of Engineers revoked the project's permit and called for much more extensive environmental and cultural review of the situation. The Water Protectors had won—for the time being.[3]

The larger Standing Rock experience builds on many examples of successful Native (First Nations) action across North America in protest of destructive mining, fossil-fuel extraction, or "development" plans and is galvanizing a newly stirring pan-Native identity. In such protests, Native people are—perhaps more successfully than any other single religious group—resisting the overwhelming forces of the fossil fuel industry to defend sacred land, to assert traditional religious values, and to intervene against the seemingly unstoppable global onslaught of climate change, industrial pollution of water and air, and ecocide. Those participating at Standing Rock attest that what took place there was quite explicitly not protest but *ceremony*, prayer. The local tribal leaders invited into their circle people of many other tribes and religions for an experience of chant, prayer, and enacted ritual, putting the core spiritual conviction that "water is life" into visceral and politically effective form. As confrontations with state and federal forces sharpened, the chant "*Mni wiconi!*" (Water is life) resounded at all hours in the camps, and along with daily water rites it invited participants into forms of traditional Native worldview and practice on this sacred land. Of the convictions that sparked the gatherings, Allard writes:

> Where the Cannonball River joins the Missouri River, at the site of our camp today to stop the Dakota Access pipeline, there used to be a whirlpool that created large, spherical sandstone formations. The river's true name is Inyan Wakangapi Wakpa, River that Makes the Sacred Stones, and we have named the site of our resistance on my family's land the Sacred Stone Camp. The stones are not created anymore, ever since the U.S. Army Corps of Engineers dredged the mouth of the Cannonball River and flooded the area in the late 1950s as they finished the Oahe dam. They killed a portion of our sacred river. I was a young girl when the floods came and desecrated our burial sites and Sundance grounds. Our people are in that water. . . . We must remember we are part of a larger story. . . . We are the river, and the river is us. We have no choice but to stand up.[4]

Exploring the many meanings at play at Standing Rock requires attention to matters such as the science of climate change, the interweaving of fossil fuel industry and US state power, and the history of Native exploitation. It also needs to honor Native people's religious views of water, winds, local soil and plants, the burrowing animals, hibernating amphibians, blizzards, cook fires, and blazing stars, all "relatives" needing and giving love in real relationship. By honoring these relationships, humans of all kinds come into new forms of political and religious life together. Standing Rock therefore points to the complexity of questions and relationships—not just relationships between humans—that characterize interfaith phenomena in an ecological age and that must shape their study.

How can the new field of interreligious studies adequately take account of these larger ecological connections, in which humans relate across complex and shifting religious boundaries today?[5] In addressing this question, I will first assert the significance for the study and practice of religion (including interfaith forms) of bioregional grounding in one's specific place. I assert that attention to the creatures and health of a given place brings together humans of all faiths, or none, in a context simultaneously larger, more intimate, and more tangible than most religious worlds. Next I will explore the importance, within a given place, of attending to religiously significant relationships not only within but also beyond the human community, with the plants, animals, waters, climate, forces, and landscape that make up the watershed or bioregion. Finally, I will show how attending to these relationships not only enriches interfaith engagement and interreligious study but also fosters a new capacity for shared *human* identity on Earth, toward a flourishing future together.

PLACE

Place matters. Physical, local ground, the water flowing above, below, and across that ground, its soil and climate, its native and invasive species of all kinds: these create our sense of belonging on Earth. Even as we work on pressing global problems, many are learning the wisdom of rooting deeply, of eating locally, of getting to know the neighbors, of contributing to the love and care of particular places. Linda Hogan writes, "Remembering place is significant, and that includes each visitor to a place, insect, plant, animal, or the passing shadow of a cloud in golden sunlight. All of this may be included to return the human to his or her place within the natural world, the human community, and the universe, a balance so . . . complex."[6]

For what was taken for granted just a couple of generations ago—that humans born in a place would know and love that place intimately—has become threatened or lost under immense economic pressures leading around the world to forced uprooting or migration from one's home or land—or to the land's outright destruction. Those born in cities, especially in contexts of poverty, or raised with psychic tethers to electronics and screens of all kinds, have within a few decades lost long-standing capacities for local directional, seasonal, and climatic orientation; familiarity with native plants and animals and their patterns of growth, communication, or migration; and the larger sense of relationship with these neighbors of all kinds. Asked to name edible plants native to their area in a given season or the destination of the wastewater flowing down their drains, most Americans and many inhabitants of other nations today would be as flummoxed as the students to whom I sometimes address such questions.[7] In the words of cultural philosopher Jennifer Price, we are overwhelmingly "losing track of nature."[8] In the face of such effacing of both physical landscapes and the psychic bonds connecting people with them, the language of bioregionalism has emerged, inviting participants to return perceptual attention to local bioregions. Kirkpatrick Sale defined the term "bioregion" in 1985: "*Bio* is from the Greek word for forms of life . . . and *region* is from the Latin *regere*, territory to be ruled. . . . They convey together *a life-territory*, a place defined by its life forms, its topography and its biota, rather than by human dictates; a region governed by nature, not legislature. And if the concept initially strikes us as strange, that may perhaps only be a measure of how distant we have become from the wisdom it conveys."[9]

A central assertion of this essay is that attention to the ecology and care of one's home—one's place—provides a shared interspecies "neighborhood" for humans of all religious traditions who live there. Such attention thus gives these humans literal common ground on and within which to engage their diverse faith traditions in both traditional and new interspecies forms and to come together—as the Native leaders in North Dakota have modeled for the rest of us—for action on behalf of that place for the larger common good.

RELATIONSHIPS WITHIN THE MORE-THAN-HUMAN WORLD

A primary dimension of indigenous or other animist worldviews includes the cultivation of relationship not only with other humans but also with the plants, animals, waters, winds, and other forces or features of one's home: from migratory birds and storms to sacred rock formations, from salmon and wolves to medicinal or ceremonial plants.[10] What does it mean to conceive of communicating—let alone sharing one's religious practice—with creatures of other species, with the larger animate world, or the cosmos itself? Such questions, both scientific and religious, pose an obstacle for many Westerners. How do plants and animals communicate with one another or with humans? Would relating to other beings as part of one's spiritual practice draw energy away from human or divine relationships that are more important within a given worldview? Another problem has to do with the generalizations in this very paragraph. To speak of "Westerners" needing to learn from "indigenous people" about relationality within a larger more-than-human context is impossibly oversimplified, each term an abstraction effacing distinctive variations and running the risk of demonizing or romanticizing complex communities of insight.[11] Surely even in terms of ecological wisdom, learning and teaching flow in many directions as humans who love Earth grow to respect one another's ways of honoring it religiously.

Despite these problems, I point to the question of interspecies communication precisely because it represents perhaps the most entrenched dimension of the largely but not exclusively monotheistic alienation from the natural world noted above. The anthropocentric religious imagination—oriented at best to all humans generally and in more extreme forms solely to one's own tribe in communion with God—creates a widespread incapacity to imagine in real terms that there exist other religiously significant beings around us, who live here too, who communicate, who have their own sentience and emotions and needs, and with whom humans ought to be in conscious and ethical relationship. As many have noted, the Western imagination especially since the Enlightenment has tended to think and speak of the natural world and its creatures as "it" rather than "Thou." This has made possible commodification and tremendous exploitation of the planet and its peoples, resulting in widespread perception of a disenchanted, even inert or dead Earth, a vast sink of "natural resources" humans are free to ravage, a huge toilet into which we then dump our waste—rather than an astonishing living communion of beings with whom we are privileged to live.

This imaginative and conceptual limit means that a potentially unifying dimension of human identity—namely how we each and all relate to the actual creatures, water, and land with whom we share our place, our home—does not even appear on the religious radar of billions of humans. The study of interfaith engagement needs therefore to include normative attention to interspecies questions both because such attention is a feature of some religious traditions already and thus figures in interfaith encounters and because, to the extent that religious perceptions shape broader ethical and social norms, the capacity for religious attention to the creatures and natural forces around us matters for human survival.

Developing the capacity for such attention on the part of religious practitioners, communities, or scholars is not easy. Getting to know a place and its inhabitants deeply takes a very long time and requires cultivating forms of attention and wisdom increasingly alien to populations oriented toward fast-paced digitally mediated interactions with humans and machines. It requires slow, contemplative attention of a kind known by scientists, practitioners of surviving indigenous traditions, and countless toddlers, birdwatchers, farmers, gardeners, outdoor enthusiasts, poets, and artists, even in cities.[12] Thus coming to know the complex forms and lives of a place invites sustained collaboration with a broad variety of people. Especially in North America—but also in every other place where indigenous communities survive—these conversation partners need consistently to include indigenous participation. Much wisdom has already been lost in the centuries during which Native communities have been killed, silenced, and forced from their land. It is long past time for dominant traditions to learn to listen anew to these communities and make efforts toward restoring their collective voice, traditions, and lands, for the larger common good.[13]

Interspecies relationality is an impossibly complex and multifaceted topic, involving the move beyond anthropocentric conceptions of relationship and into a biotic world alive with "Thous." Religious and interreligious movement in this direction has the potential to reanimate traditions facing decline and irrelevance, to push back against the relentless digitizing of value and collective imprisonment in human-constructed and human-programmed worlds, to invite persons to get to know the neighbors in their larger biotic neighborhoods, and thus to invite alienated humans back into communion with the larger wild world, threatened and degraded yet still powerfully alive with relationship, beauty, danger, and joy. Here in the wild—in wildness—is in fact the heart of the human experience of the sacred, without which no faith will long survive.

NEW FORMS OF IDENTITY

A tremendous gift of human engagement with nonhuman others in a given place is the dawning of new forms of identity precisely as human. As David Abram notes, "We are human only in contact, and conviviality, with what is not human." Others too have noted how the emergence of a much larger Universe Story, along with the threats to life our impact on the planet has generated, has the potential to generate a whole new perception of human identity. Not denying or effacing our differences, we can recognize a deep sense of kin, shared species-skin, with one another, in relation to the astonishing diversity of other forms of life on Earth and the endless abyss of no-space. Such new forms of identity make possible the work of coming together to enact the monumental transition to healthier forms of economy and engagement with the world. We can't afford any longer to notice only what divides us from one another or from the rest of the natural world. The massive political and economic change needed and the degree of resilience and wisdom required even in a best-case climate scenario in decades to come will require this deep sense of kinship with one another, all voices engaged. Such active kinship with one another, across boundaries, motivated by shared love of a place and in touch with the wellsprings of diverse traditions' cosmologies, is the gift of a place-based interspecies life: where "interfaith" simply means *human*.

For every human is an astonishing work of evolutionary art, and every human is part of an Earth story that demands an appropriately ecological sense of belonging, reverence, and action. Yet the new forms of identity our times demand are not only distinctively human ones. Living in intimate relation to other creatures reminds us viscerally that we, too, are animals, creatures. We are kin with all that has fur and a skeleton and eyes, all that breathes, all that photosynthesizes, all indeed that is formed from stardust. Moving beyond our tribal, religious, and species bubbles to learn to interact again with creatures beyond ourselves on their own terms—and to consider the mystery of our existence on this planet—makes possible new visions, in many religious languages, of human uniqueness and kinship with all.

CONCLUSION

With many others, I sense that returning our primary attention to the ground where we live and to its flourishing is a politically powerful and personally sustaining move. Increasingly I am realizing that such attention is the means for cultivating interspecies relationships that transcend and welcome humans across cultural and religious boundaries as well. It invites humans into forms of seeing, hearing, perceiving, and thinking with the creatures of every given place, forms that are congruent with those that indigenous traditions have never abandoned. Such attention to the flourishing of one's place and its creatures provides larger unitive scaffolding for interreligious encounter, since all share the biological and physical reality of place. In fact, Earth provides the secure rooting for all mutual respect, conversation, and collaboration; our shared dependence on healthy land, air, water and larger biotic relationships transcends all divisions. A commitment to the flourishing of one's literal common ground strengthens our collective capacity as humans to share our Earth-reality with one another and all other creatures, drawing on the best wisdom of every tradition.

If we fail to create a fully interfaith Earth allegiance and ethics, we are unlikely to hand down religious traditions worth maintaining on the increasingly barren and desolate planet we will also bequeath to our children. In contrast, the shared journey into relationship together with our common places has the potential to reawaken profoundly religious awe, joy, and humility in the face of the vast mystery of being alive on Earth. Ultimately each religious tradition—if it is to contribute fruitfully to planetary thriving—must stretch its own vision and ethics to encompass the creatures of the local watershed, the scope of human economic impact, the viability of species we can't see and of generations yet to come. The field of interreligious studies can and must help shape this larger vision: a pluralism that includes the more-than-human world, a common good that is truly good for all.

IV

APPLICATIONS BEYOND THE CLASSROOM

THE VALUE OF INTERRELIGIOUS EDUCATION FOR RELIGIOUS LEADERS

Jennifer Howe Peace and Or N. Rose

All great literature is one of two stories; a man goes on a journey or a stranger comes to town.

—LEO TOLSTOY

If we have no peace it is because we have forgotten we belong to one another.

—MOTHER TERESA

This chapter draws on multiple sources. It stems from work we have done individually as educators, activists, and writers as well as work we have shared over the last ten years as coteachers and codirectors of the Center for Interreligious and Communal Leadership Education (CIRCLE).[1] It also draws upon conversations with fellow educators, students, and communal leaders and insights and questions that have arisen from our particular experiences as a Christian and as a Jew.[2] In all of this work, we have seen firsthand the value of interreligious education in the cultivation of effective and transformative religious leaders.[3] Interreligious education attends to the relationships among individuals and communities with different religious commitments and the intersection of this dimension of identity with other elements of human experience (for example, race, class, and gender). Interreligious education includes what happens in the classroom but goes beyond this to what happens in various cocurricular contexts, including worship services, peer group gatherings, fieldwork, retreats, and travel experiences. When done well, interreligious education helps nurture religious leaders with a deep understanding of their identities in relation to others, their responsibilities to various communities to which they are accountable, and a broader sense of commitment to the well-being of our religiously diverse democracy and to the world as a whole.

As we reflect on the value of interreligious education for religious leaders, we realize that most of our strongest held pedagogic convictions are encoded in *stories*: stories of encounter in the classroom, cafeteria, clergy meetings, prayer services, and rallies. These are stories of insight, questioning, kinship, and struggle. At the core of these stories, and of our work more broadly, is an abiding commitment to cultivating and sustaining authentic relations in which people are open to learning and growing with and from one another, both in moments of agreement and disagreement. For us, respectful and honest interactions are the essential building blocks of this endeavor. Thus we have designed this chapter around three brief vignettes involving encounters among people from different walks of religious life. These anecdotes serve as the primary "raw data" as we analyze and articulate our model of interreligious education. We hope that this narrative approach provides readers with a textured understanding of our educational vision as it has grown out of our lived experiences.

THE VALUE OF INTERRELIGIOUS EDUCATION FOR PERSONAL RELIGIOUS FORMATION

Basma always sat near the back of the classroom. She had come to the United States from Egypt with her husband, who was enrolled in a PhD program at a nearby university. While taking care of their two young children, Basma was continuing her own writing as a PhD candidate at Al-Azhar University in Cairo. Fluent in Arabic, Hebrew, and English, Basma was also leading a peer group for students from both Hebrew College and Andover Newton focused on exploring attitudes toward the religious other in Jewish, Christian, and Muslim sacred texts.

Our weeklong intensive course Religious Leadership in a Multireligious Society focused on the rich and diverse religious landscape of Boston. Capping the class at thirty, we found ourselves with a lively group of Jewish, Christian, and Unitarian Universalist students along with one Muslim—Basma. Soft-spoken by nature, Basma tended to listen more than speak. But one day she raised her hand and began describing how limited her encounters with non-Muslims had been before coming to the United States and how varied and rich her experiences had been since arriving. She ended by saying: "Our experiences change who we are."

"OK," we thought, glad that she had spoken up, though the observation seemed mundane. The next day, Basma raised her hand again, and said, a bit more slowly, "Our experiences change who we are."[4]

Embedded in Basma's simple assertion are three ideas that help frame our work as religious educators with interreligious commitments: the power of interreligious *encounters*, our emphasis on *transformative* learning, and the impact of interreligious education on religious *identity formation*.

Taking each point in turn, if "our experiences change who we are," it is incumbent on us as teachers and mentors to think carefully about the kind of educational experiences—classroom-based and cocurricular—that are essential in forming and informing effective religious leaders with interreligious capacities. Like Basma, many of our students enter our classrooms with limited experiences engaging with people outside of their own religious circles or reflecting critically on these encounters.[5] To help address this, we strongly favor an educational model in which our Jewish, Christian, Unitarian Universalist, and Muslim students learn *with* and not simply *about* one another.

One pedagogical tool that has been a touchstone for us is the ancient rabbinic model of *havruta* (companion) study. In this dialogical framework peers engage in regular and ongoing discussion of both theoretical and practical matters.[6] This practice encourages students to move beyond an exclusively intellectual focus on the basic tenets of the "world religions" to a broader relational awareness of how individuals enact their beliefs and values in particular times and places. *Havruta* study helps students explore vital spiritual, ethical, and communal issues, while establishing meaningful personal connections that often have bearing well beyond their years of formal study.[7]

Basma's comment offers a second insight about the nature of our work. It is about transformation: "Our experiences *change* who we are." Reflecting on her encounters with non-Muslims since coming to the US, Basma recognized a personal shift—a shift toward greater understanding and appreciation of religious similarity *and* difference, both within and across traditions.[8] Analogous comments from students over the years have led us to think about interreligious education as a form of consciousness raising. The kind of change in awareness we see in our students is not characterized by a weakening of religious commitment but rather a more nuanced understanding of the complex relationship among religious people, ideas, and practices. In a yearlong seminar we cotaught, Jewish and Christian Dialogue and Action, one of our students described moving from a posture of "basically we are all really the same" to a recognition that simply celebrating our commonality is not enough. As he wrote in his final reflection, "What I had yet to realize was that there is even more need to understand and appreciate each other's differences . . . [for] in our difference lies our dimensionality, our depth, our richness." This insight led this student to spend more time studying the particularities of his own Baptist tradition so he could return to the "interfaith table" better equipped to articulate the distinct contributions he had to offer out of a deeper understanding of his own religious roots.

This brings us to the final point encapsulated in Basma's remark: "Our experiences change *who we are*." Basma's comment suggests that she was no longer the same person as when she first arrived from Egypt. If religious identity formation is one of the goals of seminary education, a fundamental assertion that underlies this chapter is that we are formed in *relationship*, not in isolation. Engaging with peers and mentors from different traditions provides students with the opportunity to reflect on both their core commitments and ongoing questions.[9] Further, doing so in the presence of the religious other can be very helpful to students in gaining greater skill and confidence articulating their beliefs, values, and uncertainties. We have come to describe this educational process, in which students engage in sustained learning and exploration during this time of intensive personal and professional development, as one of interreligious "coformation."[10] This reorientation of seminary education to prioritize interreligious engagement can have a profound impact on the personal formation of religious leaders in their preparation to lead and serve in the kinds of challenging situations described in subsequent sections of this chapter.

THE VALUE OF INTERRELIGIOUS EDUCATION WITHIN AND ACROSS RELIGIOUS COMMUNITIES

Hebrew College (HC) and Andover Newton Theological School (ANTS) had been building a close collaborative relationship for a few years when the staff and student fellows of CIRCLE raised the possibility of holding a joint program for Yom Ha'Shoah (Holocaust Memorial Day).

For many years (dating back to before HC moved to our shared hilltop in Newton) ANTS had held its own annual service of remembrance. Hebrew College had a tradition of joining the wider Boston Jewish community for an evening service to commemorate Yom Ha'Shoah and typically held a brief candle-lighting ceremony during school hours. It seemed to us that there was an opportunity to develop a meaningful joint program.

In discussions with the presidents and deans of our respective schools, CIRCLE was charged with coordinating a joint Holocaust memorial service. A small planning team was assembled to craft a midday program that included songs, poems, and prayers. Members of the CIRCLE team also called on Jewish and non-Jewish students and faculty to participate in facilitating the event.

While the service we led was meaningful for many people from both communities, there was more critical feedback than we expected. One HC faculty member explained: "I need a time and place to be with just my fellow Jews at HC to mourn and reflect on this horrific tragedy that decimated my family and people." A student leader from ANTS said to us, "As a Christian I feel a great deal of shame on this day, and

I need to process this and other feelings openly with other Christians."
A senior administrator from HC added, "This can't be the one time
during the year when we cancel classes and ask students and faculty to
come together."

The CIRCLE team went back to our interreligious drawing board
to reflect on and modify our approach to Holocaust Memorial Day.
We realized that we needed to think about this event not in isolation
but in relationship to our programming throughout the year and our
broader interreligious educational agenda. Several important lessons
emerged. To begin with, we came away with a deeper appreciation
of the importance of carefully gauging the interest and willingness of
one's community to participate in such events, particularly if the focus is on an emotionally charged subject. While the CIRCLE team had
held internal discussions and brought the idea for a joint remembrance
service before school administrators, we did not discuss it in advance
with a sufficient number of faculty and students. Had we done so, we
would have likely concluded that, for different reasons, each community needed an opportunity to grapple with the pain and horror of Yom
Ha'Shoah independently, whether or not the schools might also come
together for a joint gathering. In subsequent years we experimented
with this model of separate events followed by a shared gathering. We
also expanded the joint event beyond a single ritualized remembrance
to incorporate related programming the day before and the day after
the service that included time for discussion, study, multimedia presentations, and meetings with Holocaust survivors. Participants were much
more receptive to this model, as it respected the distinct needs of our
two communities.

In the wake of these experiments with different models we also recognized the need to provide a wider range of people (beyond the core
group of those who regularly chose to participate in CIRCLE programming) with a more diverse set of opportunities for interreligious engagement.[11] The HC school administrator we quoted above was right:
Holocaust Memorial Day could not be the only time when we changed
our class schedules and brought our communities together. Because the
experience of planning the Yom Ha'Shoah program brought several

complicated and painful issues to the surface, we were also reminded again of the need to tend carefully to the complex histories and power dynamics that exist between our communities. Ignoring the darker chapters in Jewish-Christian history or downplaying the asymmetries that exist between a majority and minority group run the risk of undermining our attempts at cultivating authentic relationships and transformative educational programming.

It is only by thoughtfully delving into the depths of these matters that we can move toward the kind of honest and informed interreligious engagement that we are advocating here. The differences and dilemmas are real, and the historical record is complicated. Without some understanding of this complexity, our students will have a limited understanding of their own traditions and of the various connections across our communities—both positive and negative—and they will not be easily able to think critically about how to advance their interreligious initiatives thoughtfully in light of these challenges.[12]

THE VALUE OF INTERRELIGIOUS EDUCATION FOR CIVIC LIFE

The Reverend Dan Smith of the First Church in Cambridge has been a frequent visitor to our classrooms and community events. A United Church of Christ minister in his mid-forties, he is equally passionate about leading his mainline Protestant church and working with other religious and civic leaders from across the city on various social justice issues. Dan often says that he has "one foot firmly planted in his church and the other out in the world." Among the stories Dan regularly shares with our students is one about a moment of serious challenge in the life of the Greater Boston Interfaith Organization (GBIO), an interfaith community organizing group in which he serves as a member of its strategy team.

In 2004, organization leadership played an important role in helping to reform health-care coverage in Massachusetts. Working with a number of grassroots organizations and governmental agencies, their intensive organizing led to the passage of new health-care legislation, providing seventy thousand previously uninsured people with much-needed coverage. Just as GBIO and its allies were gaining ground with the health-care campaign, the issue of same-sex marriage emerged as a hot topic throughout Massachusetts. Politicians, activists, journalists, and others were speaking, writing, and organizing with great fervor both in favor and against the introduction of a new bill to legalize same-sex marriage. Leaders within GBIO found themselves on opposite sides of the debate and the picket lines. The public discourse was intense, and it became painful for the clergy and lay leaders who had been working together so closely on health care to be so divided on this bill.

Feeling that the fabric of the organization was fraying, GBIO leaders and their constituents needed to find ways to rehumanize one another. And so, in keeping with the relational ethos of the organization, they arranged to meet with people on both sides of the issue, inviting them to tell their stories and to explain how these personal experiences informed their perspectives. In one such meeting, Hurmon Hamilton, then senior pastor of Roxbury Presbyterian Church, met with members of Temple Israel of Boston. Reverend Hamilton was lobbying against the passing of the same-sex marriage bill; the Temple Israel clergy were working for its passage. Among the assembled group that evening were LGBTQ members of Temple Israel and allies.

After an evening of heartfelt conversations that included personal storytelling, Pastor Hamilton closed his remarks by saying that when he walked into the house earlier in the evening, he'd felt as if there was a "brick wall" separating the two groups, but as he prepared to leave he felt as if that barrier had been replaced by a "glass wall."[13]

What can we learn from Hamilton's statement and from other elements of this story? First, while GBIO focuses on issues of common concern—like health-care reform—inevitably there are areas where there is disagreement, including potentially painful disagreements. We should not be surprised by this. Diversity and divergent perspectives go hand in hand. The question at such moments is how deeply one is motivated to continue to be in relationship with the person or people with whom one disagrees. This is true of personal and communal relationships. How much tension can we hold individually or collectively? There are, of course, some issues that simply cannot be overcome without severely altering or even ending relationships. In this case, however, the leaders of GBIO felt that the relationships they had cultivated were too valuable to give up. As Jonah Pesner, then a rabbi at Temple Israel and a key GBIO leader wrote, "We became a community . . . not just a coalition," and it was a community that made the choice to press forward together.[14]

Further, the GBIO leaders recognized that there was too much good work they could do together where they *did* agree on matters of substance. They understood that they had built a powerful community of change agents that had the capacity to work across lines of difference to make a real and lasting difference in the lives of tens of thousands of people. Imagine all of the people—preschool children, young mothers, out-of-work professionals, senior citizens, et cetera—who could not previously access basic health care but were finally receiving the critical medical attention they needed. If GBIO could play a constructive role in this campaign, what else could its members do together? This does not mean that the pain of their differences over the same-sex marriage bill was erased or even blunted. How could it be, as it touched on several critical issues of individual and collective identity, including biology, sexuality, religious belief, social mores, and human rights? It also did not mean that GBIO members were going to stop advocating passionately for their positions.

However, as Hamilton's comment indicates, the GBIO leaders and constituents made a genuine effort to engage one another humanely. They sought to topple the walls that allowed them to speak of the "other" at a distance without having to see their faces or hear their voices. Meeting together gave people a chance to share their stories— their pain, fear, hopes, and dreams. For Hamilton and others, the brick wall was replaced with a glass one. This relational renovation was invaluable as it helped many people within the GBIO community weather the storm of disagreement and continue their commitment to be in relationship. And as several leaders have reported, it had a direct impact on the ways in which they spoke both privately and publicly about the issues at hand and the people with whom they disagreed.

As we reflect on our commitment to interreligious education for future religious leaders, it is stories like this one that remind us what is at stake: namely, the quality of our relationships across communities and the health of our civil society. Religious leaders are often on the front lines of critical social and political struggles regarding housing, hunger, and health care. As GBIO and other organizations like it demonstrate, interreligious solidarity can create the necessary leverage to make transformative change. While not all of our graduates become community organizers, learning from such activists can help students think critically about the possibilities and challenges of working for common goals and maintaining personal and professional relationships in the face of serious theological or ideological differences.

CONCLUSION

As Mary Elizabeth Moore of the Boston University School of Theology wrote to us in 2016,

> The value of interreligious education in religious leadership formation is to touch worlds beyond your own, to discover and appreciate spiritual beauty wherever it is found, to encounter the 'other' with deeper understanding, to engage new insights and challenging questions, and to know yourself more deeply. These are all related. . . . The results cannot be guaranteed, but interreligious education can cultivate the ground for a more compassionate, just, peaceful, and ecologically sustainable world.

While both of us are strongly committed to teaching our students about the richness of our particular Jewish or Christian traditions, we believe that future religious leaders also require training as interreligious bridge-builders. Living as we do in a religiously diverse society and a highly interconnected world requires that our graduates develop the skills, knowledge, and experience to navigate the interreligious terrain thoughtfully and effectively. As the great scholar of religion Wilfred Cantwell Smith wrote several decades ago, "Unless [we] can learn to understand and to be loyal to each other across religious frontiers, unless we can build a world in which people profoundly of different faiths can live together and work together, then the prospects for our planet's future are not bright."[15] These words remain as important today as when he wrote them in 1962. While our religious identities and institutional loyalties are of vital importance, we must not forget that we are also accountable to a global community that extends far beyond our particular religious frontiers.

As we have argued in this chapter, we believe it is incumbent upon religious educators to provide ample opportunities for future religious leaders to learn *with* one another and not simply *about* the other. To be religiously literate today requires that our students not only read theological and historical texts but also expand their experiences by meeting and developing relationships with peers from diverse religious backgrounds, exploring their commonalities and differences, and having firsthand experience with what does and does not work when they collaborate on issues of common concern. The stories in this chapter serve as touchstones for us in our ongoing work as educators. Our commentary reflects our belief in the transformative power of interreligious education for the individual, for our religious communities, and for the possibility of "a more compassionate, just, peaceful, and ecologically sustainable world."

FROM PRISON RELIGION TO INTERFAITH LEADERSHIP FOR INSTITUTIONAL CHANGE

Barbara A. McGraw

In 1996, as I was nearing the end of my religion and social ethics PhD course work at the University of Southern California, Robert S. Ellwood, the professor for whom I served as a world religions teaching assistant, received a very interesting opportunity. Lawyers representing a Wiccan prison inmate, William Rouser, had sought Ellwood's expertise on new religions. Dr. Ellwood asked me if I would like to help him in his work on the inmate's behalf. I found the invitation intriguing, given my previous work as an attorney and because my doctoral work focused on religious diversity and American law. So I agreed, and that began a journey that started with advocating for religious minorities in prisons and prison chaplain volunteering but eventually led to training federal and statewide prison chaplaincy directors. Those experiences gave me invaluable insights about interfaith engagement and its transformative effect, and they instilled in me appreciation of what it takes to be an interfaith leader engaged in institutional change. Over time, through my prison religion advocacy, volunteering, and training experiences, I came to recognize interfaith leadership for institutional change as a process that requires four dimensions: (1) identifying one's cognitive-affective frame perspective (i.e., "lens" bias) and being able to suspend it; (2) religious literacy understanding; (3) collaborative, empathic, critically reflective dialogue; and (4) transforming leadership.

BACKGROUND: PRISONS AND RELIGIOUS DIVERSITY

After my work with Ellwood on Rouser's case, I started serving as a volunteer in California prisons where Rouser had started groups.[1] My thought was that if I could help prison officials and staff to accept Wiccans, it was likely that they would open their minds to other minority religions as well. But there were numerous obstacles to overcome, which involved a steep learning curve.

∞   ∞   ∞   ∞   ∞

In the US, people do not lose their religious rights when they are incarcerated.[2] However, unlike religious minorities in society at large, where people can practice their religion using their own resources, prison inmates are not able to do so without the help of the government. To get that help, inmates are required to come forward, identify themselves, and make an official request for a religious "accommodation."

In my early years as a volunteer, I noticed that minority inmate accommodation requests were routinely denied as contrary to the prison's "penological interests." Inmate accommodation requests for familiar religions weren't necessary. Either a practice was already established or, if not, the request would usually be granted without dispute. Candles and incense were "fire hazards" when used by Wiccans but not when used by Catholics. Wearing a religious medallion that included a symbol that might also be used by gang members was forbidden, unless it was a cross. Minority religion inmates wanting to practice together as a group were suspected of gang activity or of getting together to exchange contraband (cigarettes, drugs), while Protestant and Catholic groups were deemed serious adherents not likely to pose such risks.

I wondered: why do prison policies and practices favor Protestant Christianity and marginalize other religions? Early on I discovered that prisons were founded on the model of the "penitentiary" more than two centuries ago. The underlying rationale was that prisons were places for penance and restoration to right relationship with Christ.[3] Given this history and with few avenues available to challenge the assumption embedded in this history, it was not surprising that entrenched institutionalized biases about the role of religion in prisons survived into the 1990s. Officials and staff I met readily supported inmates participating in religious services with familiar forms of practice, which seemed to them to serve worthy goals in prisons. However, there was resistance to other religions, and their practices were viewed as subversive to the purpose of religious practice in prisons.

The prisons I visited had a "Protestant chapel" and a "Catholic chapel." Other groups who had won the right to practice were allowed to use the Catholic chapel or other designated rooms because in many prisons Protestants were not willing to share their spaces. California had been more progressive than most states, including as recognized groups not only Jews but also (due to litigation) Muslims and Native Americans, although their access to space, services, and support was still quite limited. The chapel schedule was filled with daily Christian services of one sort or another: Bible study, Christian counseling, volunteers bringing music or other opportunities, special preachers speaking on various topics. "Bikers for Jesus" was a favorite of the inmates in one of the prisons I visited. Volunteers brought motorcycles for inmates to ride if they listened to Christian sermons.

At the same time, nearly all prison personnel I encountered—staff at the entry gate, chaplains, security officers, correctional officers on the yard, and administration officials—were suspicious of minority religions or even hostile to them. I witnessed outright prejudice, including pernicious name-calling (Wiccans called "the Wickeds") and prison guards failing to release inmates from their housing units to attend their religious services, even though they had necessary approvals. But what disturbed me as much as outright prejudice was how much unconscious bias, based on preconceived ideas about what "real" religion entails, factored into decisions about which religious practices were allowed in prisons.

Early in my prison religion work, the head staff chaplain for one of the California prisons told me that there would not be any celebratory-type worship services unless the inmates in my group first sat in seats in rows facing the altar, listened to a sermon about their sins, and repented those sins. If the inmates adhered to this chaplain's way of doing things for several weekly services, they could then have a special celebratory service, such as for Easter and Christmas. I explained to the head chaplain that the inmates I was working with practiced in a circle with an altar in the center and that most of their services were celebratory or ended in celebration. I also explained that that they didn't listen to sermons and didn't focus their religious practices on how bad they are but instead more on healing themselves and others and on what they have to offer their community. The head chaplain said flatly that if that were the case, their services weren't really serious, did not serve any worthwhile purpose, and, therefore, weren't valid enough to accommodate in prison in the first place—a view that echoed the penitentiary model referenced above.

To say that overcoming such attitudes was an uphill battle is an understatement. Uprooting entrenched traditions, assumptions, prejudices, and privileges in any environment requires considerable effort—persistent advocacy and even, at times, court battles.[4]

Fortunately, a new federal law, enacted in 2000 and found constitutional by the US Supreme Court in 2005, created the impetus for greater recognition of minority religions in prisons, although its impact only gradually materialized over the ensuing decade. The law, which defines "religious exercise" very broadly, requires the government (when certain circumstances are met) to provide inmates with the opportunity to practice their religion and to provide the basics to do so—for example, to provide scheduled time and space.[5] And prison officials must allow inmates (when certain circumstances are met) to use items to practice their religion—for example, an altar, a statue, or a book.[6]

Taking advantage of the requirements of the new law, I began making common cause with various inmates from minority religions and their supporters, as many more started coming forward with religious accommodation requests. At the same time, I also recognized the challenges for those corrections officials and staff who were amenable to change. They had the difficult task of realigning perspectives and resources throughout the system to accommodate increasing religious diversity. However, they had not yet fully transformed their own perspectives or gained the competency required to lead their institutions to effect change, so progress was hindered.

Consequently, when in 2004 I was asked to participate in an annual chaplaincy directors training program for officials who administer federal and statewide prison religion programs, which had been started the year before in conjunction with the American Academy of Religion annual meeting, I welcomed the opportunity. In 2011, the Center for Engaged Religious Pluralism, which I direct, joined as cosponsor, and I became the main organizer of the training program and remain so today.[7] Over time, I not only came to identify myself as an interfaith leader who is continually gaining a broader perspective and leading change but also to recognize that the program was developing interfaith leadership competencies in the officials who attended the training.

FOUR DIMENSIONS OF INTERFAITH LEADERSHIP FOR INSTITUTIONAL CHANGE

Cognitive-Affective Frame Shifting: Overcoming "Lens" Bias

The chaplaincy directors program was initially developed with religious diversity literacy as the main focus. But over time it became clear that no matter how much knowledge directors gained, the acceptance of minority religion practices would not be sufficient without a change of perspective. For example, in the beginning, the first question directors would ask when confronted with a request for new religious practice was: "Do they really *need* that?" But the directors didn't seem to notice, at first, that they never asked that question for familiar religions' practices. For example, they didn't question whether Protestants, who adhere to the doctrine of the priesthood of all believers, really need weekly Sunday services. Even when attendees learned about diverse religions, they viewed them through their own frames of reference—as we all tend to do. Practices were deemed worthy only if they fit preconceived biases.

The program revealed the same in-group affective affinities and out-group alienation ("us and them" tendencies) that occur when religion is involved, just as humans often exhibit regarding race, ethnicity, and gender. As Howard J. Ross points out, discussing bias, "This phenomenon is magnified when the 'in' group is the dominant or majority culture in a particular circumstance. Because the dominant cultural group in any environment usually creates the standard and acceptable norms and behaviors for that group, people from nondominant groups often will be seen as 'different,' 'abnormal,' 'less than,' or even 'sick' or 'sinful.'"[8]

When I started working in the prisons, the privileging of the in group was clear, as the examples above illustrate. But even chaplaincy directors who were open to more inclusive policies grappled with this phenomenon. Should a Hindu inmate be allowed to use the prayer beads he had requested for his meditation practice? The requested accommodation had been denied at one director's institution because institutional personnel had decided that the inmate did not really need the beads, and in any event prison security officials had concluded that the beads could be used to hit or strangle another inmate. Some directors agreed with that decision. What they neglected to notice, however, was that Catholic inmates had been using rosary beads as long as anyone could remember. The in group's practice was seen as necessary and not worrisome as a security risk, while the out group's use of prayer beads was seen as superfluous and a potential threat.

To avoid such obvious bias, our chaplaincy directors needed to develop the ability to identify the cognitive-affective frame or "lens" though which they and their institution's constituents viewed religion. Moreover, they needed to develop the capacity to suspend or "shift" their own cognitive-affective frame of reference to make an empathic connection with the other. In so doing, they could begin to assess the circumstances by reference to the integrity of the other's own religious worldview and practices, rather than through preexisting dominant norms and assumptions.

But how is this achieved? In the chaplaincy directors program I saw that directors can come to identify assumptions and biases and develop the capacity to overcome them provided that key conditions are met: exposure over time to extensive religious diversity involving challenging cases, engagement in dialogue with empathetic peers, and guidance by a facilitator who is knowledgeable about, and empathetic to, less familiar religions and sensitive to the challenging circumstances directors confront daily.

Religious Literacy "Understanding" and Collaborative, Empathic, Critically Reflective Dialogue

Religious diversity is a significant challenge for correctional institutions. Since the change in law, a vast variety of religious adherents have increasingly come forward in prisons, well beyond what might come to mind when one thinks of religious diversity and interfaith dialogue. They include religions that are in the majority in some countries, such as Hinduism and Buddhism; offshoot sects of more widely known religions, such as Messianic Jews or the Five Percenters (an African-American Islamic derivative group); traditions rarely included in interfaith circles, such as traditional African religion Yoruba derivatives (often syncretized with Catholicism, for example, Santería and Voudon); indigenous religions, particularly Native American spiritualities; and a variety of Pagan religions (for example, Druidism, Wicca, and Asatru). And more diverse individuals and groups are coming forward all the time. Even scholars who study new religious movements have been surprised by the wide variety of religious minorities found in prisons.[9]

Considering the extent of this diversity, it became clear that gaining knowledge about all of the religions found in prisons would be a prohibitively large task. Consequently, the competency needed is not merely basic knowledge about the major world religions but also religious literacy *understanding*. That involves learning enough about a wide variety of unfamiliar religions to appreciate difference, to know what questions to ask when one is confronted with additional unfamiliar religions, and to be open enough to hear the answers.

Still, to achieve that openness to difference, religious literacy training needs to be combined with opportunities to explore assumptions and privileges through collaborative, empathic, critically reflective dialogue in a space that welcomes the vulnerability that arises when one encounters unfamiliar beliefs and practices.[10] Our program achieved that by inviting scholars of a wide diversity of religions to give brief presentations to the chaplaincy directors, followed by extensive question-and-answer sessions for further understanding. This was particularly effective for frame-shifting when the religion presented was entirely unfamiliar or the scholar's presentation revealed a surprising insight. For example, I recall the surprise—even shock—when our program included two of the foremost experts on Messianic Judaism. Apparently, several directors had thought the inmates had concocted this religion. The seriousness of the ensuing discussion led to insights not only about that religion but also about the directors' own "lens" bias, which had been the source of their skepticism.

In addition, the program included collaborative dialogue among the directors, facilitated for openness to difference, as well as acknowledgment of, and compassion for, the daily challenges the directors described and the discomfort that occurs in encounters with the unfamiliar. The facilitators employed analogies to known practices to broaden perspectives and encouraged the directors to share stories of difficult or surprising experiences. For example, one of the directors, a Mennonite, recounted his eye-opening experience attending a Wiccan ritual. Directors also were encouraged to reflect critically together on their own views, with empathy for one another's challenges within their jurisdictions' prison systems, for the inmates who were impacted by their decisions, and for those directors who held strong religious commitments of their own while accommodating the very different beliefs and practices of others. All of this broadened the boundaries of the directors' knowledge and increased their ability to transcend their particular lens.

Religious literacy competency, combined with such collaborative, empathic, critically reflective dialogue, developed the directors' capacity to interrogate their own cognitive-affective frame and identify its parameters. They developed the capacity to step outside of the bias of their own immediate assumptions about what is important or not and what is inconvenient, troublesome, or threatening or not: they were able to "frame-shift." When one has developed that capacity, one is then better positioned to lead others to effect change.

Transforming Leadership for Institutional Change

Even when directors are able to overcome their own biases and even with the law on their side, they still have to confront entrenched biases in their own institutions. That requires more than personal transformation; it requires leadership.

Leadership is the ability to influence others so that together leaders and followers can "make things happen."[11] Of the numerous approaches to leadership, I favor leadership that is collaborative, relational, and ground-up, where participants engage with one another in a process of transforming themselves, others, and their institutions.[12] That approach eschews leadership that is transactional or focused primarily on a leader's traits (or both). Rather, it is "transforming leadership" that involves dynamic collaboration, where leaders and followers inspire each other as well as new followers, who then also adopt the leader's original imperative, taking up leadership roles themselves to reach continually for positive and lasting organizational and social change that serves a common moral purpose.[13]

I see interfaith leadership as a form of transforming leadership where the moral purpose is to promote understanding and cooperation across boundaries of religious and nonreligious differences in mutual respect and equal dignity. That may involve an interfaith process (for example, religiously diverse participants working together on a project) or an interfaith outcome (for example, an interfaith event). For interfaith leadership in prisons, the moral purpose involves both a process and an outcome. Religiously diverse participants work together toward the goal of institutional change that reflects greater religious diversity understanding and willingness to accommodate diverse religious practices, while ensuring that institutional needs are met too—for instance, good order, health, security, and fair allocation of resources. They guide others to reflect on these higher order values, while engaging them in dialogue, using a methodology similar to that employed in the chaplaincy directors' program to transform their institutions' practices and policies.

Still, it is important to recognize that achieving institutional change is an ongoing process. The combination of religious literacy and collaborative, empathic, critically reflective dialogue leads to cognitive-affective frame shifting. Suspending one's "lens" prepares one to serve as an effective interfaith leader—a transforming leader who has the perspective needed to articulate the values that galvanize followers. Such a leader influences and works with others to effect desired change while also employing religious literacy training and dialogue to develop new interfaith leaders. The entire process is repeated as institutional change leads to the potential for further transformation of those involved and the institution.

But change does not only involve policy. Social and institutional cultural change occurs as well. When I last visited a California state prison, several groups were conducting services at once in the chapels and in the yard outside. The intermingling sounds of Native American drums and chanting, Christian songs, Asatru oaths, and Muslim prayers were a testament to our efforts at that institution. Similarly, I visited a federal prison where an evangelical Protestant inmate remarked to me that nowhere else would he have had the opportunity to become

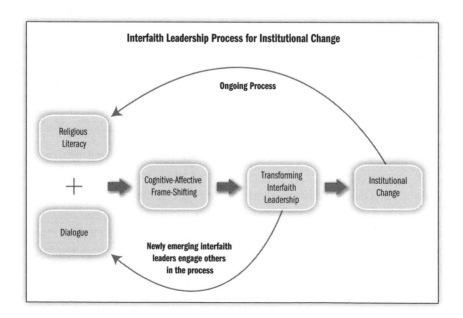

friends with such religiously diverse people, as they coordinated usage of chapel space: Catholic, Protestant, Jew, Muslim, Buddhist, Wiccan, Odinist, and Hindu. He said he had come to respect the others for their commitments to make a positive difference even though he didn't agree with their beliefs. He wanted to share his new perspective about other faiths, he said, with his family and community when he was released from prison (which wasn't far off). I expect that others will do the same, perhaps becoming bridge-builders for interfaith understanding and co-operation in the larger society as interfaith leaders in their own right.

Still, I don't want to overstate the gains. Numerous administrative grievances and legal cases across the US attest to the struggle of inmates in all religions, especially minority religions, to gain their right to fair accommodations.[14] Also, the issue of who can be hired as a staff chaplain has yet to be reconsidered in light of minority religion inmates' gains.[15] Yet it is important to recognize that progress toward greater interreligious understanding and cooperation is being made in prisons on a scale not yet seen outside the prison walls. I think there is reason to hope that it might be coming from the prisons to the larger society, too, as prison interfaith leaders become ambassadors of interreligious understanding in the larger society.

INTERFAITH LEADERSHIP FOR CHANGE IN OTHER INSTITUTIONS

The interfaith leadership process described above has implications for other governmental institutions and organizations. For example, how might developing the competencies of an interfaith leader contribute to international business goals?

The secular assumptions and values of business organizations of the West, particularly of the US, run headlong into national cultures with different deep religious values, even when such values are not identified as religious. As Indian businessman Devdutt Pattanaik notes, in the West "vision, mission, values, processes—sounds very much like the journey to the promised land with the commandments held by the leader. And if you comply, you will go to heaven." But India has its own paradigm, Pattanaik maintains. It is based on the cyclical worldview of

Hinduism, where nothing is assured except that everything and everyone returns over and over for eternity, while God sees you and you see God in a ritual of divine compassion (*darshan*). "There is no promised land." Consequently, rigid, formulaic business structures and processes developed in the West do not work in India. Rather, Indian business succeeds through the organizational dynamic of individuals in relationship, where people are resourceful outside the parameters of guidelines, working together collaboratively to get things done.[16] The Pattanaik example illustrates that the West's business leaders would benefit from understanding such differences, while employing interfaith leadership capacities to address them and perhaps being personally transformed in the process.

Another example is domestic. Similar to those in prisons, hospital staff chaplaincy services were founded on a Christian paradigm—in this case, the "pastoral care" model.[17] Although there have been efforts to modify the original mission to be more religiously inclusive, hospital staff chaplaincy programs are still caught up in a system that has not yet engaged in sufficient critical reflection to overcome historic assumptions and biases. Even when a program is identified as "interfaith," the system does not really accommodate religiously diverse patients, who are overlooked because of the way chaplaincy programs are conceived and conducted. Religious literacy and collaborative, critical, empathic dialogue are needed to overcome lens bias involving inherent privileges found in hospital chaplaincy programs. If something like pastoral care—or "ministry of presence"—is needed for those whose religious worldviews are compatible with that approach, then comparable support for patients with other perspectives is needed too. Otherwise, the motivation and justification for hospital staff chaplaincy positions become questionable as perhaps only a remnant of a distant past.

CONCLUSION

While further study of the interfaith leadership process, each of its components, and its effects are needed, my experiences in prisons over two decades have shown me how that process can be effective in shifting institutional culture, producing fairer policies and practices. If the interfaith leadership process were adopted in other social and public sectors, similar progress might be made. Then we might begin to envision a future where organizations of many kinds foster interreligious understanding, cooperation, and respect across boundaries of religious difference throughout the world. Perhaps by then the valuing of such efforts just might have become a global norm.

INTERFAITH STUDIES
AND THE PROFESSIONS

Could Heightened Religious Understanding
Seed Success within Secular Careers?

Mark E. Hanshaw with Usra Ghazi

Sectarianism, bigotry, and its horrible descendant, fanaticism, have long possessed this beautiful earth. They have filled the earth with violence, drenched it often and often with human blood, destroyed civilization and sent whole nations to despair. . . . But their time is come. And I fervently hope that the bell that tolled this morning in honor of this convention may be the death-knell of all fanaticism, of all persecutions with the sword or with the pen, and of all uncharitable feelings between persons wending their way to the same goal.

—SWAMI VIVEKANANDA,
from *The World's Parliament of Religions*

It was a prayer of hope and optimism, delivered by the Hindu teacher Swami Vivekananda, that opened the first Parliament of World Religions, held in Chicago in 1893. This gathering is often cited as the event that launched the modern interfaith movement in the United States. And while Vivekananda's dream of a world free of sectarian and religious tension may not have been fully achieved, it is clear that the ideals that motivated this interfaith gathering have not been wholly lost, even within the context of a modern society teeming with cross-cultural angst.

The modern interfaith movement was initially fueled by the optimistic belief that engagement between individuals of differing cultural and religious backgrounds would provide a seedbed from which greater social harmony might flower and hostility between members of varied religious systems might dissipate. Without a doubt, the interfaith movement has produced positive outcomes. For example, interreligious dialogue has become commonplace on campuses across America in recent decades. Furthermore, there is an emerging academic field—interfaith studies—that brings scholarly rigor to bear on questions of civic religious diversity and trains people to engage it in ways that will benefit the broader society.

As a college administrator, I am especially interested in how taking courses or earning a degree in interfaith studies might positively affect post-graduation student outcomes. To put this question in more practical terms, how might the increased understanding of and experience with varied religious systems and communities support an individual's practice of medicine? Or in a career as a classroom teacher? Or in the role of manager of human resources?

I consider these questions as a professor and dean at a liberal arts university in Texas, drawing upon national research as well as insights from students on my campus. The coauthor of this chapter, Usra Ghazi, helps to illustrate the relevance of this research by sharing her own experience as someone who sought and gained interfaith education during her undergraduate career—despite the lack of a formal field at the time. Usra now exemplifies the value of interfaith studies competencies years later as a young professional serving in the realm of US public policy.

WHY INTERFAITH STUDIES?

In his recent book *Interfaith Leadership*, Eboo Patel identifies the term "interfaith" as one that references the ways in which our interactions with individuals of differing backgrounds and perspectives affect our own religious and ethical perspectives and, further, the ways in which our own perspectives color our engagements with others.[1] Thus, one who has engaged in interfaith study would have seriously considered the ways in which the religious and ethical attitudes and assumptions of an individual or group serve to influence social behaviors and interactions across a spectrum.

With this definitional framework laid, it may well be asked how students, specifically, may benefit from engaging a robust interfaith curriculum. What are the questions that students may confront, and what marketable skills might they derive from such focused study?

In assessing the potential utility of interfaith studies, one of the best sources of information is students themselves. In that regard, I was recently made aware of the depth of some of the concerns and anxieties motivating many of the students on my own campus, concerning issues related to religious and cultural diversity. The responses of students were insightful on a variety of fronts, but the two themes that seemed to be echoed most strongly were the belief that a collective lack of social awareness about differing religious groups had often been used to perpetuate resentments and stoke fear, and the strong expectation that broader education on issues related to religious and ethnic diversity would serve to reduce levels of social anxiety.

As regards the perception that most individuals lack a sufficient level of understanding regarding other cultures, a couple of comments were particularly potent. A twenty-two-year-old African-American student observed: "I feel we all need to step back and look at what we are doing to each other by not *knowing* each other. We would be less divided if we all learned about each other's culture and values. This stuff was all happening before the [2016] election—now it's kind of more desperate that we learn. Why don't people want to understand what *privilege* is and how others live without it?"

Further, a fifty-nine-year-old white student likewise voiced her own belief that much popular misinformation regarding varied cultures is potentially rooted in systemic biases that might be reduced through education. As she observed: "I think there has still been so much racism, and prejudice against anyone who wasn't Christian, since the 1970s, but we made people be quiet about it instead of teaching them how wrong these stereotypes are. I was one of those people until I came to school here. Now politicians are using that silence and calling it 'white Christian oppression' and making people afraid of each other. It's so divisive."

These comments, taken together, indicate a strong awareness by students of the negative impacts that biases can generate within the social sphere as well as personal cravings for opportunities to learn more about other cultures and for a greater societal depth of understanding about varied religious traditions. Many other students participating in focus groups echoed these comments.

As concerns the desirability of including enhanced interfaith and cross-cultural coursework within the university's broader curriculum, a twenty-five-year-old Caucasian student offered: "I don't think taking one religion class to meet your [General Education Curriculum] prepares you for any kind of understanding of other religions or cultures. There should be a core set of classes that discuss how culture shapes religions. I guess that's where interfaith [studies] would apply."

What this comment and others like it expose is an awareness of many students that standard offerings in religious and ethnic studies may not be sufficient to provide individuals with the background needed to navigate an increasingly diverse social environment. Further, this comment additionally exposes an important level of awareness that religious philosophies and traditional perspectives play a potentially significant role in shaping the way each person interprets the surrounding cultural landscape.

While these focus group results are anecdotal, they appear to be consistent with findings from other studies. In the recently published, expansive study of student perceptions related to religious diversity, *Emerging Interfaith Trends*, respondents voiced a strong belief in the importance of interfaith engagement.[2] According to the study, which included twenty thousand student respondents across more than 120 universities in the United States, about 65 percent of those surveyed expressed a personal desire to take coursework designed to help them better understand differing religious perspectives and cultural orientations. As well, more than 80 percent of respondents expressed the opinion that many of the world's leading challenges could be "overcome" if individuals of diverse cultural and religious backgrounds worked more closely together.[3] Even more recently, a US Department of Education study linked an institutional commitment by universities to "diversity" with stronger performance by students of varied backgrounds across a variety of performance scales.[4]

Based on both anecdotal and quantitative analysis, it appears that interfaith studies is precisely the type of academic program students desire. In the next section, I hope to show that it is also the type of program they will *need* with regard to important professional competencies.

FROM INTERFAITH ENGAGEMENT TO PROFESSIONAL PREPAREDNESS

Interfaith studies as a discipline prompts students to seriously consider the relationship between religion and "culture" and their porous boundaries. For any student focused upon a career path that will require some engagement with individuals of diverse backgrounds, a primary educational goal should be to better understand the relation between faith and cultural experience and how the overlap between these categories can impact even the most mundane social interactions. Interfaith studies programs may aid in this quest.

The value placed upon intercultural competence by prospective employers of new college graduates was vividly underscored in the recent Association of American Colleges and Universities (AAC&U) study, *College Learning for the New Global Century*. In that broad survey of employers, a strong concern was voiced regarding the limited ability of many college graduates to recognize and assess important cultural differences. Indeed, one of the skill sets most desired by employers for its new hires was cultural competence. In the survey, more than 70 percent of prospective employers voiced a desire for colleges and universities to better prepare students in each of three areas: (1) understanding of "Global Issues," (2) acquisition of "Intercultural Competence," and (3) "Intercultural Knowledge."[5]

Interfaith studies programs expose students to differing religious communities and expressions with the express goal of increasing both understanding and the opportunity for positive engagement. In the recent study "Interfaith Cooperation and American Higher Education," best practices for the field were outlined. Central to this list was an emphasis upon "professional application." In that regard, report authors recommended that courses in interfaith programs focus attention upon the applicability of interfaith cooperation to a broad array of fields, including, "health care, journalism, business, ministry and social science."[6] This list may well be too narrow. The report went on to recommend that interfaith programs include experiential learning opportunities through which students might directly apply concepts gained to real-world problems.

The best practice recommendations included in this report mirror themes highlighted in the 2015 study of employer attitudes *Falling Short? College Learning and Career Success*. That study, conducted by Hart Research for AAC&U, found that many employers surveyed placed greater value on a group of core, desired skills than upon a graduate's major. Among the most desired skills highlighted was experience in solving "problems with people whose views differ from their own," with some 96 percent of employers citing this as a valuable learning outcome. Moreover, some 78 percent of respondents in the same survey indicated that "college students should gain intercultural skills and an understanding of societies and countries outside of the United States."[7] While the survey did not ask specifically about religious cultures, I believe that the goals articulated can only be accomplished if interfaith studies plays some role within the curriculum.

Professionals, meanwhile, are often required to do more than exercise a specific set of job-related skills. Such individuals are typically encouraged to play leadership roles within the community, even outside of their professional obligations. In *Falling Short?* some 86 percent of respondents indicated a belief that university education should provide students access to "the civic knowledge, skills and judgment" to help them contribute to the larger society. Interfaith studies will certainly prepare graduates for active civic engagement in the religiously diverse neighborhoods of America.

THE PROMISE OF GRADUATES IN INTERFAITH STUDIES

Our students are often stereotyped as being ambivalent regarding events transpiring in their communities. In contrast to this, the students in our focus groups were well aware of many social inequities that exist around them, and they voiced a strong desire to see change. President Barack Obama sought to describe such social passion in his 2014 address to the United Nations General Assembly, when he proclaimed, "Around the world, young people are moving forward hungry for a better world. Around the world, in small places, they're overcoming hatred and bigotry and sectarianism. And they're learning to respect each other, despite differences."[8]

Obama's assessment of the activism of youth around the globe came as part of his broader observation that many of the most divisive and destabilizing forces on both local and international levels capitalize on religious and cultural difference, and it is only through engagement across traditional societal boundaries that anxieties rooted in such differences may be mitigated. As he argued, the central question of our age is "whether we will solve our problems together," or whether our actions will be guided by "the destructive rivalries of the past."[9] And it is our youth who must be prepared to carry forward the mantle of leadership in response to the challenges and opportunities stemming from growing cultural and religious diversity.

The former president's words appear to suggest the utility of interfaith engagement and understanding within the field of diplomacy. Indeed, as he further observed, the ability to recognize and distinguish between fanaticism and religious devotion is a critical component in effective global leadership in the modern world. Yet religious misunderstandings and bias affect far more than the diplomatic realm.

Within the context of my own university, I have worked with students who desired to acquire a broader base of understanding of varied religious systems and cultures to support their career paths in such diverse areas as law, business, health professions, counseling, and elementary education. One of my former students who taught me much about the breadth of the need for enhanced interfaith education was a medical school student finishing her residency. It was this student who explained that while her medical school had trained her well to deal with health-related conditions, it had not helped her to understand how to relate to individuals of diverse cultures. For this insight, she turned to our program in comparative religious studies.

Perhaps even more telling was the experience of a recent graduate who went to work in the marketing department of an international corporation based in Texas. Shortly after arriving, the corporation began downsizing, and most people in her office were dismissed, though she was asked to stay. When she later questioned why she, a graduate with a degree in comparative religious studies, was retained even as many people with degrees in marketing and business were laid off, she was told that her ability to understand customers, no matter their background, was an asset too valuable to lose.

Interfaith studies is an emerging field in the academy important precisely because it offers students tools that they may use to respond to critical professional challenges. For current graduates to be successful in assuming leadership roles in the modern workplace, they will need to be aware of religious and cultural differences and to have strategies to respond to disagreements, as they emerge, and to encourage cooperation. Such skills will be of value in a vast array of professional settings. As Usra Ghazi will speak to in the next section, one area where such skills will be of increasing importance is diplomacy and politics.

INTERFAITH LEADERSHIP IN THE PUBLIC SQUARE

Usra Ghazi[*]

The academic discipline of interfaith studies did not exist, as it does today, when I enrolled at DePaul University in 2005. Rather than learning

---

[*] The views expressed herein are those of the author alone and in no way constitute an endorsement, expressed or implied, by the US government, including the US Department of State.

about religious and interfaith literacy and interfaith leadership in a formal program, I built my knowledge base and skill set by attending interfaith dialogues and service projects and then organizing them myself. I enrolled in peace studies classes offered by DePaul's Department of Religious Studies and befriended religiously diverse student leaders on campus. These experiences allowed me to develop a pluralism orientation. As a result of these encounters and opportunities I learned to recognize the incredible religious diversity around me and see the potential for social change if I chose to engage that diversity toward positive ends. This perspective of the world is something I have carried with me into my professional life, along with my tool kit of interfaith skills and knowledge.

I borrow the term "pluralism orientation" from scholars Alyssa N. Rockenbach and Matthew J. Mayhew, who define it as "the degree to which one is accepting of, recognizes shared values and divergent beliefs with, and meaningfully engages with others of different worldviews."[10] This orientation is made up of a number of skills I was able to practice and develop as a result of my college experiences with interfaith dialogue and religious studies. One of those skills is the ability to apply a lens of lived religion to the world around me. That is, to see that the religious diversity in any given community is made up not only of houses of worship and religious landmarks but also of the ways that religious and moral life are lived in the public square. This involves being able to identify the encounter and exchange between communities—for instance, the historic Catholic church that due to changing neighborhood demographics becomes space for Pentecostal worship and Muslim prayer at various points in the week. This lens may also allow one to see how a seemingly political demonstration or march could be a form of religious expression for some participants. This goes hand in hand with the ability to understand and speak in values-based language that strengthens relationships between diverse groups. Another critical skill is to be able to tell a compelling interfaith story that links the religious practices, values, and symbols of diverse groups in a way that builds community.

In the summer of 2013, I began working as a policy fellow at the Mayor's Office in Boston as part of a fellowship program sponsored by the Rappaport Institute for Greater Boston, at Harvard University's Kennedy School of Government. In researching this fellowship, I knew that government agencies of the Commonwealth of Massachusetts and the City of Boston had strong ties to religious communities and organizations, and I hoped to be placed in an office where I would be best equipped to apply my interfaith skills. After all, a majority of the resettlement agencies that supported the state's Office for Refugees and Immigrants at the time were religiously affiliated organizations. The "Boston Miracle" cast the city's network of Christian pastors and ministers into the national spotlight for their successful efforts to drive down youth gang violence in partnership with the city's police department in the late 1990s. Thus, I was thrilled to be assigned to work at the Mayor's Office for Immigrant Advancement (then the Office of New Bostonians) and eager to apply my interfaith skills to the field of public policy.

As the only divinity school student in my cohort of policy fellows, I assumed I would be organizing interfaith prayer breakfasts or conducting research on the city's religiously diverse communities. While there were elements of these types of projects in my work, the most meaningful opportunities to apply my interfaith skills came through in the most mundane of moments. One day, a community member walked into the office to inquire about immigration support services. Then, noticing my hijab, she asked if I knew of a place in the city where she could make her Friday prayers. Even though Boston is home to one of the largest mosques on the East Coast, the Islamic Society of Boston Cultural Center in the Roxbury neighborhood, there is no major mosque in the downtown area. It just so happened that in my first week of work at City Hall, I conducted a bit of religion landscape mapping and learned about St. Paul's Episcopal Cathedral, where the Christian community opens its doors to allow Muslims in the downtown Boston area to make their Friday prayers, as well as the Paulist Center, a Catholic community that offered their space to Muslim worshipers while the cathedral was under construction. I shared this information with the community member, who was happy to know about these interfaith partnerships. My religious literacy regarding Episcopalian, Catholic, and Muslim practice as well as outreach and dialogue skills allowed me to explore the religious landscape of my city and build relationships with these religious communities.

I ended up extending my fellowship through the next year and had the opportunity to co-organize Boston's first Ramadan event at City Hall, cohosted by Mayor Martin Walsh and Boston city councilor Tito Jackson. In addition to working on explicitly religious initiatives, I conducted outreach and held one-on-one meetings with religious leaders and religiously affiliated organizations on issues related to immigration and refugee resettlement. I worked with a senior advisor for violence prevention and public safety to launch an inaugural faith-based advisory council. My experiences with interfaith studies and organizing allowed me to think critically about various voices and communities to bring to the table. Although the Mayor's Office has historically held strong ties with the city's Catholic and Protestant communities, I organized side meetings with Muslim, Jewish, and Buddhist community members and connected my colleagues to the secular humanist community to ensure that the City of Boston's interfaith efforts were broad and inclusive.

Every now and then, during my time at the Mayor's Office, I would come across colleagues or community members who felt strongly that religion had nothing to do with public policy, that it had no place in governance and the public square. Contrarily, as a public servant I could not help but see religion everywhere. It was in the moral voice and shared values articulated by religious communities to city officials as they called for the just treatment of immigrants and refugees. It was the motivation for hospitality and social services offered to communities in need by religiously affiliated organizations. It was in the corridors of City Hall, where I encountered dark crosses on colleagues' foreheads on Ash Wednesday, appreciated Christmas holiday decorations, shared a Ramadan meal, made my daily prayers, and reflected on the city motto, the biblical verse "God be with us as He was with our fathers," etched in Hebrew and Latin on a plaque that hangs in the mezzanine—a gift to Boston from the City of Jerusalem. I found religion in the history, narratives, ethos, and activism of Boston's diverse communities. My interfaith skills allowed me to better understand these features and to engage this diversity in positive and fulfilling ways.

After completing my work and studies in Boston, I headed to Washington, DC, where I worked at the Office of Religion and Global Affairs of the US Department of State. Early in my time at this office I helped organize a pilot program called the Days of Interreligious Youth Action (DIYA), inviting young leaders and alumni of US government programs to work with their religiously diverse and nonreligious peers, and with support from their local US embassies and consulates, to organize intra- and interreligious action projects. The projects themselves ranged from interreligious sports competitions to arts events and projects addressing environmental sustainability and economic opportunity. Proposing and running this pilot program allowed me, once more, to apply my religious-literacy knowledge to explain how *diyas* (oil lamps) are considered a symbol of hope in many religious traditions and are used by Jain, Hindu, Sikh, and Zoroastrian communities, and thus "DIYA" is an apt acronym for an interreligious initiative. This initiative also affirmed for me that my interfaith experiences and leadership skills could have global applicability on a wide range of issues. The young leaders involved in the DIYA pilot program were able to use their skills to pull together diverse communities to address local challenges. They engaged in dialogue and conversation to draw out shared values and identify common ground. These are skills that are critical to community organizing and diplomacy.

Though interfaith studies did not exist as an intentional space in the academy during my undergraduate career, I have found that many of the skills and competencies that it engenders, and which I was able to cobble together for myself, have been instrumental in my professional career and success. Now, more than ever, the world needs global citizens who can understand and engage cultural and religious diversity. It is my hope that the emerging field of interfaith studies will create the curricula and academic experiences to help others meet this need.

CONCLUSION

As the AAC&U study *College Learning for the New Global Century* demonstrates, prospective employers would like to see colleges and universities prepare students for global, intercultural engagement in their professional lives. The AAC&U study *Falling Short?* draws similar conclusions, indicating that problem solving among people with different values is a key professional skill. Moreover, the desire for these types of competencies are not just voiced by employers and business leaders. The *Emerging Interfaith Trends* report shows that undergraduate students across the country wish to better understand differing religious perspectives and cultural orientations.

Recognizing these dynamics, interfaith studies has the potential to meet the stated needs of both students and their future employers. A student of interfaith studies would have seriously considered her own values and ethics, as well as how ethical attitudes or assumptions might influence social behaviors and interactions within a broader context. As mentioned above, former students of mine who occupy the distinct fields of marketing and medicine have either been more successful because of their interreligious and intercultural competencies or felt that they were unequipped for their day-to-day work because they *lacked* such skill sets.

Usra Ghazi, the coauthor of this chapter, demonstrates the value of interfaith training in the context of her career in diplomacy and politics. She managed to cobble together an interfaith knowledge base and skill set through her voluntary attendance at extracurricular interfaith events. In that, she is the exception and also a useful signal. Our society needs professionals trained in interfaith studies too much to leave such preparation to chance or the occasional exception such as Usra. We in the academy should seek to organize the kinds of knowledge and skills that she gained, combine them with the theory and rigor of research the academy is known for, and format it all into a well-designed curriculum that students can take for credit. Such an academic program will enhance not only their college experience but also serve them well throughout their careers.

TOWARD AN INTERRELIGIOUS CITY

A Case Study

*Heather Miller Rubens, Homayra Ziad,
and Benjamin E. Sax*

In 1965, Harvey Cox wrote *The Secular City* as an invitation to consider theological questions in the context of two major forces in mid-twentieth-century life: urbanization and secularization. While urbanization remains a key factor, religious and ethical diversity demands additional attention by scholars of interreligious studies and practitioners of dialogue alike. In this case study we suggest the "interreligious city" as a new framework through which to consider theological, ethical, and political questions in the twenty-first century. As Aristotle argued in *Politics*, a city is a partnership where people, indeed strangers, with different means, talents, and abilities come together and work for a shared good. The act of navigating difference cannot happen in homogenous contexts, and the city provides the opportunity to encounter difference in a sustained and meaningful way. In focusing on the city, we prioritize embodied, not hermeneutical, religious others.

With the violent death of Freddie Gray in April 2015 at the hands of police, and with the civil unrest that followed, Baltimore entered the national conversation on race, justice, and community. While the media spotlight has since shifted away from it, the work of reimagining the city continues apace, bringing with it new and pressing questions for Baltimore institutions. At the Baltimore-based Institute for Islamic,

Christian and Jewish Studies (ICJS), the unrest of 2015 raised questions about the role of interreligious learning and dialogue in urban contexts deeply divided along racial and economic lines. This chapter explores how communal crisis has changed the ways in which the ICJS approaches and structures its pedagogy of interreligious learning, with an eye to the local and contextual nature of interreligious work in the multipart initiative Imagining Justice in Baltimore.[1] How has embracing our urban context challenged and expanded the operating definition of religion, religious communities, and religious leadership in the work of interreligious learning at the ICJS? What does it mean to build an "interreligious city"?

The ICJS has flourished for thirty years at the nexus of scholarship, civic engagement, and community building. Our commitment to interreligious learning rests upon the conviction that resilient interreligious networks require both real relationships and religious literacy. We hold that it is not sufficient to bring people together for social activities, or even advocacy work, without increasing literacy about different religious beliefs. Building the interreligious city requires people to gather and learn, with intention and purpose, over a sustained period of time. ICJS fosters the creation of *interreligious learning communities* to build lasting friendships and raise religious literacy between people of different religious commitments. Grounded in our mission to "build learning communities where religious difference becomes a powerful force for good," the institute's pedagogy addresses a critical challenge: How do we embrace the particular values of our own religious communities while understanding and engaging values that may be at odds with our own? And, as part of this process, how do we come to terms with our own deeply held prejudices about other communities?[2]

OUR CITY: BALTIMORE

On April 12, 2015, a twenty-five-year-old African American man, Freddie Carlos Gray Jr., was arrested by the Baltimore City Police Department for possessing an illegal switchblade. Gray suffered injuries to his spinal cord and fell into a coma while in police custody. He died one week later. Gray's death, coupled with decades of frustration with police profiling and endemic racial injustice, sparked several days of protests and civil disorder, popularly known as "the uprising." Some of these protests turned violent. After Freddie Gray's funeral on April 27, disaffected protesters burned close to 150 cars and looted stores in parts of the city. Maryland's governor declared a state of emergency and called in the state police and Maryland National Guard. The next day, the mayor of Baltimore announced a weeklong curfew for the city.

While the media ran a continuous loop of images that framed Baltimore as an inferno, another more powerful image received less attention. In an act that echoed the great civil rights marches of the 1960s, over one hundred local clergy from different Christian, Muslim, and Jewish denominations marched arm in arm, stopping from time to time to kneel and pray. Reportedly, when the faith leaders reached a line of police in riot gear, they convinced the officers to follow them back up the street and toward the places where the violence was taking place—effectively acting as a buffer between the rioters and the police.[3] When asked about the state of emergency in Baltimore, they responded: "There has been a state of emergency way before tonight, an emergency of poverty, a lack of jobs, disenfranchisement from the political process. This is a long time coming."[4]

Baltimore is home to a little over 620,000 people, and 63 percent of the population is black. Many speak of what Morgan State University professor Lawrence Brown identified as two Baltimores, "The White L" and the "Black Butterfly."[5] "White L" describes the shape that is made when tracing a particular route on a map of Baltimore: starting from the Mount Washington neighborhood (in the northwest part of the city), traveling south (between York Road and I-83) to Wells Street, and turning east to the city line on Baltimore Street. The neighborhoods covered in the White L are the most affluent in the city. They are predominantly white. They also include the Charm City Circulator (free public transportation), Charm City Bikeshare, the city's best public schools, grocery stores, and banks. "Black Butterfly" describes a wing-shaped set of neighborhoods around the White L. These neighborhoods are among the poorest in the city. They are predominantly black and have significantly lower life expectancies, higher rates of infant mortality, less access to healthy food, poor schools, higher crime, and have been made famous via television dramas such as *The Wire*. In this segregated city, to be from Baltimore means to be from one of two Baltimores.

The city's story is painfully familiar. Many American cities are plagued by inequity and concentrated poverty bred by racial segregation. But Baltimore stands out.[6] Segregation policies in Maryland were some of the worst in the country, and Baltimore suffered from a hundred years of state, federal, and local policies that aimed to separate white from black through unjust housing and zoning laws. The inability of black families to build housing equity resulted in affluent white suburbs and impoverished black urban neighborhoods. The National Bureau of Economic Research makes a compelling case that Baltimore may be the worst large city in the country when measured by a child's chances of escaping poverty.[7]

We believe that meaningful interreligious learning must respond to local contexts and be accountable to the communities involved. Indeed, the ICJS was born as a response and remedy to social and legal discriminations against the local Jewish community in the twentieth century. From 1987 to 2013, ICJS explored the Christian-Jewish relationship, with a dual emphasis on fostering community among Jews and Christians in Baltimore and forging a serious engagement with our religious differences and troubled histories. In 2013, the board and staff unanimously decided to incorporate engagement with Islam into the life and work of the organization, another decision that reflected demographic shifts on the ground. This has led to a commitment to confront Islamophobia alongside anti-Semitism in the public square. The commitment to building interreligious learning communities grounded in real relationships has meant active outreach to our Muslim neighbors in Baltimore, and the racial, ethnic, and economic diversity of these communities has brought into stark relief several questions about the nature of interfaith and interreligious contexts. These questions are specific to the ICJS but also apply to the larger world of interfaith engagement focused on learning and dialogue: Are spaces and programs dedicated to interfaith study and dialogue racially and economically diverse? Are educational inequities replicated in interfaith learning? In the wake of Freddie Gray's death, when the racial, economic, and educational inequities of Baltimore were brought to the national spotlight, we have raised more questions: How can ICJS, true to its history, once again be responsive to the needs of our city? What does it take to build an "interreligious city"?

IMAGINING THE INTERRELIGIOUS CITY: EXPANDING NOTIONS OF RELIGIOUS LEADERSHIP

As America's religious landscape shifts, yielding nontraditional forms of community and religious leadership, the work of interreligious learning must keep pace. In her article "Black Activism, Unchurched," Emma Green points out that a growing number of activists and change-makers in Baltimore, as in many other cities, are organizing outside of religious institutions. "In an earlier generation," writes Green, "Baltimore's churches might have been the primary staging grounds for organizing protests and political action. Increasingly, though, the church is more of a backdrop."[8] Many American progressives and activists no longer see houses of worship as hubs for community organizing, nor do they seek leadership from ordained clergy. Addressing the interreligious learning needs of Baltimore after 2015 has meant expanding our notion of religious leadership beyond congregations.

Indeed, some activists assert that religious institutions and communities encourage apathy or, worse, are complicit in institutionalized violence against the disempowered. The work of theologian James Cone highlights the dangers of uncritically adopting existing religious and theological models in response to social unrest. In his classic work *God of the Oppressed*, Cone reveals the insensitivity to questions of race and power that characterized Christian responses to the Detroit riot of 1967. White theologians, he argues, fear the threat of black violence but are blind to systematic state-sanctioned violence, the violence endemic in the very systems of law and law enforcement, and the complicity of religious traditions, beliefs, and institutions in perpetuating systemic injustice. American Muslim theologian Sherman Jackson has offered critiques of immigrant Muslim communities post-1965 (and pre-9/11): legally permitted to participate in American "whiteness," many immigrants foregrounded narratives of racial equality in Islam while upholding systems of economic injustice that kept their black coreligionists from achieving the same levels of financial and social success.

Baltimore faith leaders, many of whom are veterans of the civil rights movements of the 1960s, saw themselves upholding the tradition of nonviolent resistance to systemic injustice that coalesced around the figure of Dr. Martin Luther King Jr., a tradition that in King's words "believes somehow that the universe in some form is on the side of justice."[9] In most cases, the emphasis has been on restraint, discipline, and dignity, and a holistic vision of social healing that includes both the victim and the perpetrator. But Black Lives Matter activists remind us that these inherited models of resistance require interrogation and reenvisioning in order to meet the needs of the day. They also remind us that the theology of James Cone needs the theology of Kelly Brown Douglas in Baltimore today.[10] Theories of intersectionality and questions of gender, class, sexuality, and ability are central to conversations around race and religion for today's justice activists.

While activists might not be looking to religious institutions for leadership, not all have turned their backs on religion. Indeed, for some it is impossible to conceive and create a just world without reference to a spiritual or religious framework, or without invoking religious traditions and mobilizing religious people. Many activists also fall into the category of the so-called religious nones, that now makes up about 20 percent of the country's adults and about 30 percent of Americans under forty.[11] While many nones are disaffected by religious institutions, 40 percent identify as "spiritual but not religious." The clergy landscape is also changing. There has been a recent decline in the number of graduate students seeking degrees that lead to ordination and an increase in graduate students seeking degrees in religion that do not lead to ordination.

Imagining Justice in Baltimore (IJB) was an ICJS pilot program intentionally designed to explore the possibilities of interreligious learning in response to the changing role of religious communities in urban contexts. With IJB, we began to expand the category of religious leadership and sought to bring interreligious learning to new audiences. It became evident to us that a model of participant recruitment confined to congregations and traditional forms of religious leadership would not meet the real needs of our community. At the core of IJB was a diverse group of twenty-three spiritually committed Baltimore community leaders and activists who served as yearlong fellows in a program that imagined justice in the city as refracted through Jewish, Christian, and Islamic traditions. The main participants of this program were not exclusively clergy. The group of community leaders included providers of social services, teachers, counselors, health-care workers, activists, volunteers, and artists. We used our existing networks of friends and supporters to reach out to local agencies and organizations involved in social justice. We cast a wide net, looking for early or mid-career Baltimoreans with a proven commitment to community service or social justice work. The only requirement from the community leaders regarding religion was that they would lay claim to a Jewish, Christian, or Muslim identity and be interested in participating in a program that sought to bring sustained interreligious learning into their justice work. IJB rests on the conviction that sustained and successful change is fueled by great ideas that emerge from reading, reflection, and conversation with those who both share and profoundly challenge deeply held beliefs. Our long-term goal is that Baltimore will serve as a model of how interreligious learning can shape and influence vital conversations in the public square.

BUILDING THE INTERRELIGIOUS CITY: IMAGINING JUSTICE IN BALTIMORE

IJB fellows took part in a rigorous program of learning and dialogue, attending workshops on justice with scholars of religion in the spring and facilitating community-wide conversations on religion and justice in the fall. Each of the fellows was given an honorarium for participating. The first part of IJB was a spring workshop and lecture series that featured three notable public scholars: Robert M. Franklin Jr. (the

James T. and Berta A. Laney Professor of Moral Leadership at Emory University, director of the Religion Department of the Chautauqua Institute, and former president of Morehouse College), Mark Gopin (professor and director of Center for World Religions, Diplomacy, and Conflict Resolution at George Mason University), and Najeeba Syeed (associate professor of interreligious education at the Claremont School of Theology). Each scholar led a private workshop with the community leaders, and a public lecture drew a diverse audience of over two hundred people.

IJB reflects the concerns of interfaith studies to encourage learning at the intersection of the academy and civic engagement. We imagined the workshops as a space to challenge the often stark divide between scholar and practitioner, academic and activist. Many scholars write about their subjects at a distance and, in turn, community leaders are often not afforded time to read and reflect on the theoretical frameworks that shape their work. With the recognition that there are few opportunities for scholars and community leaders to participate in a socially engaged interreligious dialogue, the workshops provided a space for the scholar and community leaders to challenge one another and for community leaders from a shared locale to have a sustained opportunity for study and reflection with one another across religious and vocational boundaries.

The second part of IJB was a four-part series of citywide learning. In advance of the series, we conducted a recruitment campaign across the city to bring together close to two hundred Baltimoreans from diverse backgrounds.[12] We invited them to commit to four two-hour conversations over the course of four months, in four different locations around the city. We required advance registration, inviting registering participants to self-identify with a religious tradition, if applicable. With this information in hand, we created "learning tables" of eight to ten people each, bringing together, as much as possible, individuals from diverse backgrounds. The participants were required to stay with the same learning table over the duration of the series, with an understanding that the consistency of a small learning community would help participants develop trust, allow for sustained conversation, and promote friendship. Small and consistent learning tables would also enable participants to delve deeper into the materials, re-creating the environment of a seminar classroom. After an introductory session, we explored one religious tradition per evening. This approach allowed participants to spend significant time wrestling with the complexities of each tradition. We also created mechanisms for participants to meet each other socially between sessions, and, to our delight, many did.

For this public initiative, ICJS scholars employed a biographical approach to interreligious learning. Each lesson and text study explored how a prominent modern or contemporary American religious leader read, interpreted, and used her or his sacred texts to challenge inequity. We chose Abraham Joshua Heschel (racial inequity), Dorothy Day (economic inequity), and Amina Wadud (gender inequity). A biographical approach allowed us to meet an ambitious set of goals in eight hours of contact time with our audience: introducing the complex lived realities of racial, economic, and gender inequities, raising religious literacy in three traditions, and demonstrating the value of diverse religious voices in the public square. The biographical entry point demonstrated that religious traditions make serious demands upon us to act, and that Jewish, Christian, and Muslim traditions can be a rich resource for our contemporary American conversation about the sins of inequality and the rigorous requirements of justice. By choosing Heschel, Day, and Wadud, we introduced Judaism, Christianity, and Islam as vibrant and dynamic American traditions and demonstrated how our religious traditions and communities can be both sources of grave injustice and provide solutions to injustice. Biography allowed participants to enter unfamiliar religious territory with greater ease than they otherwise would have, as they were drawn to the deeply human narratives of individuals wrestling with, and being empowered by, religious traditions.

The table facilitators guided the participants into study and conversation, exploring how the teaching resonated with their experience of living in Baltimore. A key component of building successful learning tables was training the community leaders to act as table facilitators. In placing the community leaders in this key role, we hoped to integrate the learning between the first and second part of IJB and offer the chance for engaged residents of Baltimore to form relationships with local activists.

To privilege new voices in a conversation also requires privileging new spaces. We sought inclusive spaces in proximity to diverse Baltimore residents that would indicate our commitment to interreligious learning that is accountable and responsive to community. We held our public lectures at the Reginald F. Lewis Museum of Maryland African American History and Culture, located in downtown Baltimore. Three out of four community conversations were held in West Baltimore, a vital hub of black culture with a long history of civil rights activism.[13] It was also the center of the uprising after the death of Freddie Gray. The locations included Saint Bernardine Roman Catholic Church (an African American church), Beth Am Congregation (a Conservative synagogue just blocks away from the Baltimore uprising), the Islamic Society of Baltimore, and historically black Coppin State University. Choosing religious spaces also provided the opportunity for religious host communities (a synagogue, church, and mosque) to welcome friends and neighbors of different faiths and commitments into their sacred spaces and fostered an embodied learning experience for participants. Congregationally located learning has been a hallmark of ICJS and is an integral part of building an interreligious city.

A key goal of IJB was to empower diverse individuals to use their religious voices in the public square. Because of our partnership with Baltimore's local National Public Radio affiliate WYPR, our community leaders were provided a unique platform to reflect on their experiences. After the conclusion of IJB, Tom Hall, the host of WYPR's program *Midday*, interviewed three community leaders in an hour-long program that also included questions from callers.[14] Hall also interviewed Franklin, Gopin, and Syeed on separate episodes of "Living Questions," a monthly series on *Midday* sponsored by the ICJS.[15] The most important media platform for this program was a blog housed by *Huffington Post*.[16] Each community leader wrote several extended reflections for this blog.

CONCLUSION: TOWARD AN INTERRELIGIOUS CITY

After the unrest in the spring of 2015, we affirmed that sustained interreligious learning is an essential part of rebuilding Baltimore. In our programs, we strive to create opportunities for strangers to become neighbors and to open doors across the city. The success of this work rests on a constructive engagement with difference, which is integral

to a healthy, pluralist democracy. Religious and ethical traditions have been resources for both understanding and challenging the injustice, violence, and suffering in Baltimore and other American cities. We argue that the public square should be full of religious idioms and imaginaries that seek to apprehend pain as well as shape ideals and suggest solutions. Yet we recognize that empowering interreligious networks to speak in those idioms, and raising interreligious literacy, is an ongoing and imperfect process. When we provide space for engagement with the different convictions and value systems, the texts and traditions that inspire individuals to become engaged citizens in the public square, we move closer to building an interreligious city—together.

ACKNOWLEDGMENTS

This volume is the result of a significant collaboration that includes many individuals, institutions, and foundations. Interfaith Youth Core hosted a planning meeting in Chicago in August 2016 for the contributing authors. This event was essential in developing a vision for a volume that would be more than the sum of its parts. The gathering was supported in part by funds contributed by Boston University School of Theology, Hebrew College, and Andover Newton Theological School, from a joint grant the three institutions received from the Arthur Vining Davis Foundations. These three Boston-area schools have been pioneers in recognizing the importance of interreligious education for religious leadership formation. The editors are grateful for their support. In addition, crucial early funding came from the Argosy Foundation to provide resources for the editors and contributing authors. We are indebted to them for their commitment to supporting the development of new resources for academics and educators involved with interreligious/interfaith studies.

The editors wish to extend a special note of appreciation and acknowledgment to Kristi Del Vecchio, academic initiatives manager at Interfaith Youth Core, for her tireless editorial and logistical support throughout the development of this book.

EDITOR BIOGRAPHIES

EBOO PATEL is a leading voice in the movement for interfaith cooperation and the founder and president of Interfaith Youth Core. He is the author of *Acts of Faith*, *Sacred Ground* and *Interfaith Leadership: A Primer*. Named by *US News & World Report* as one of "America's Best Leaders" of 2009, Patel served on President Obama's inaugural faith council. He is a regular contributor to the public conversation around religion in America and a frequent speaker on the topic of religious pluralism. He holds a doctorate in the sociology of religion from Oxford University, where he studied on a Rhodes Scholarship. For over fifteen years, Patel has worked with governments, social sector organizations, and college and university campuses to help realize a future where religion is a bridge of cooperation rather than a barrier of division.

JENNIFER HOWE PEACE is an associate professor of interfaith studies at Andover Newton Theological School (ANTS) in Newton, Massachusetts, where she codirects the Center for Interreligious and Communal Leadership Education (CIRCLE), a joint program between ANTS and the Rabbinical School at Hebrew College. She received her doctorate in the historical and cultural study of religions from the Graduate Theological Union. Peace is the founding cochair of the Interreligious and Interfaith Studies Group of the American Academy of Religion. Author of numerous articles and essays on interfaith cooperation, she coedited *My Neighbor's Faith: Stories of Interreligious Encounter, Growth, and Transformation*.

NOAH J. SILVERMAN serves as senior director of learning and partnerships at Interfaith Youth Core (IFYC). He holds an MA in religious studies from New York University and has been involved in interfaith work for over fifteen years on three continents. Prior to rejoining IFYC in 2013, he served as the associate director of the Auburn Theological Seminary Center for Multifaith Education. He has also worked for Religions for Peace at the United Nations, the Parliament of the World's Religions in Barcelona, the Interfaith Encounter Association and the Seeds of Peace Center for Coexistence in Jerusalem, and the Tony Blair Faith Foundation in London, in addition to consulting with Hillel, the JCC Association, and dozens of colleges and universities.

CONTRIBUTOR BIOGRAPHIES

AMY L. ALLOCCO is an associate professor of religious studies at Elon University, where she directs the Multifaith Scholars program. Her research focuses on vernacular Hinduism, especially ritual traditions, goddesses, and women's religious practices in contemporary South India, where she has been studying and conducting fieldwork for two decades. Allocco's current project, "Domesticating the Dead: Invitation and Installation Rituals in Tamil South India," is an ethnography of the ongoing ritual relationships some Hindus maintain with their deceased kin.

MICHAEL BIRKEL is a professor of Christian spirituality at Earlham School of Religion in Richmond, Indiana. In interfaith studies he has taught such courses as the Spirit of Islam: The Qur'an and Its Interpreters, Abrahamic Mysticism, and Islam and Film. His publications include *Silence and Witness: Quaker Spirituality*; *Genius of the Transcendent: Mystical Writings of Jakob Boehme*; and *Qur'an in Conversation*. Currently he is completing a book on Quakers and mysticism, and he has written a forthcoming article entitled "Allowing the Mystics to Initiate Interfaith Dialogue: Said Nursi and Rufus Jones."

GEOFFREY D. CLAUSSEN is the Lori and Eric Sklut Scholar in Jewish Studies and associate professor of religious studies at Elon University. His scholarship focuses on Jewish virtue ethics, and he has particular interests in questions of love and justice, war and violence, and moral education. He is the past president of the Society of Jewish Ethics and the author of *Sharing the Burden: Rabbi Simḥah Zissel Ziv and the Path of Musar.*

LISA E. DAHILL is an associate professor of religion at California Lutheran University. Dahill is the coeditor of *Eco-Reformation: Grace and Hope for a Planet in Peril*, as well as many other essays and articles on interspecies religious thinking and practice. A scholar of Dietrich Bonhoeffer and past president of the Society for the Study of Christian Spirituality, she is happiest outdoors: biking or kayaking or "rewilding Christian spirituality" in collaboration with colleagues in the Wild Church Network.

KRISTI DEL VECCHIO is academic initiatives manager at Interfaith Youth Core. In this capacity, she supports scholars and educators across the US who are building interfaith/interreligious studies curricula by stewarding grant programs, managing faculty development seminars, and curating online educational materials. Del Vecchio has published and presented on a wide range of topics related to this emerging field, including the possibilities of interreligious environmentalism, the role of atheists and humanists in interfaith contexts, and the contributions of Catholic institutions in developing interfaith leaders.

JEANNINE HILL FLETCHER is a professor of theology at Fordham University in New York City. Hill Fletcher is a constructive theologian whose research is at the intersection of Christian systematic theology and issues of diversity (including gender, race, and religious diversity). Her most recent book is *The Sin of White Supremacy: Christianity, Racism and Religious Diversity in America*. Other works include *Monopoly on Salvation? A Feminist Approach to Religious Pluralism* and *Motherhood as Metaphor: Engendering Interreligious Dialogue*.

USRA GHAZI was a strategic designer at the Collaboratory, the design and innovation hub of the US Department of State's Education and Cultural Affairs Bureau. She is now the director of policy and progress at America Indivisible. Ghazi is an interfaith leader and aspiring diplomat with over a decade of experience in interfaith youth work through US and international organizations including Interfaith Youth Core. She has served as a policy advisor and Franklin Fellow at the US Secretary of State's Office of Religion and Global Affairs and a policy fellow for the City of Boston in the Mayor's Office for Immigrant Advancement.

MARK E. HANSHAW, formerly the dean of the School of Arts and Letters at Texas Wesleyan University, is now the associate general secretary at the General Board of Higher Education and Ministry. Hanshaw is the coauthor of *From East to West: A Comparative Study of the World's Great Religions* and the author of *Muslim and American? Straddling Islamic Law and U.S. Justice.* He is a recipient of the Texas Wesleyan Board of Trustees award for scholarship, a Fulbright-Hayes Fellowship, and a Rotary International Fellowship. He was awarded a platinum Remi at the Houston International Film Festival for his work on the academic film *The Embrace of a Loving God: Encountering Sufism.*

WAKOH SHANNON HICKEY is an associate professor of religious studies at Notre Dame of Maryland University in Baltimore. Hickey specializes in American religious history, Buddhism, religion and medicine, and interreligious dialogue, with particular interests in race and gender. Her book *Mind Cure: How Meditation Became Medicine* combines these interests. Ordained as a priest of Sōtō Zen Buddhism, Hickey uses contemplative pedagogies and has served as a chaplain in both hospitals and higher education, currently as Buddhist campus minister for Johns Hopkins University.

ELIZABETH KUBEK is a professor of literature and director of the Medical Humanities Program at Benedictine University in Lisle, Illinois. Her areas of expertise include the novel and new and emerging media, as well as literary and critical theory. Kubek's current research focus is on interdisciplinary studies and hybrid visual and verbal media, especially comics and graphic narrative.

MARION H. LARSON is a professor of English at Bethel University in St. Paul, Minnesota. She has served as a visiting scholar and sat on the board of directors for the Collaboration for the Advancement of College Teaching and Learning. She also served as the arts and humanities editor for *Christian Scholars Review.* She has published articles on faculty development, hospitality as a metaphor for teaching, and interfaith dialogue. Larson's most recent work, coauthored with Sara Shady, is *From Bubble to Bridge: Educating Christians for a Multifaith World.*

MATTHEW MARUGGI is an associate professor in the Department of Religion at Augsburg University, where he teaches and researches in the areas of vocation, spirituality, the ethics of world religions, and interfaith studies and action. He also teaches liberation theology courses in Central America. Maruggi codirects the Interfaith Scholar Seminar, a curricular and cocurricular program that promotes interfaith dialogue and community engagement with students from a variety of traditions and core commitments.

KATE MCCARTHY is interim dean of undergraduate education at California State University, Chico, where she also served as chair of the Department of Comparative Religion and Humanities and developed an undergraduate certificate program in interreligious and intercultural relations, the first of its kind at an American public university. She is the author of *Interfaith Encounters in America* and coeditor, with Eric Mazur, of *God in the Details: American Religion in Popular Culture.*

BARBARA A. MCGRAW is professor of social ethics, law, and public life and the founding director of the Center for Engaged Religious Pluralism at Saint Mary's College of California. Recipient of the Mahatma Gandhi Award for Advancement of Religious Pluralism, she speaks on interfaith leadership in business, education, and government institutions and is author or editor of works on religion and public engagement, including *Rediscovering America's Sacred Ground*; *Taking Religious Pluralism Seriously*; *Many Peoples, Many Faiths*; and *The Wiley-Blackwell Companion to Religion and Politics in the U.S.*

RACHEL S. MIKVA is the Herman E. Schaalman Chair in Jewish Studies and Senior Faculty Fellow of the InterReligious Institute at Chicago Theological Seminary. The institute and the seminary work at the cutting edge of theological education, training religious leaders who can build bridges across cultural and religious difference for the critical work of social transformation. With a passion for justice and academic expertise in the history of scriptural interpretation, Mikva addresses a range of Jewish and comparative studies, with a special interest in the intersections of sacred texts, culture, and ethics.

KEVIN MINISTER is an assistant professor of religion at Shenandoah University in Winchester, Virginia, where he teaches courses in religious diversity, religion and politics, and religion and ecology. He is also a steering committee member of the Valley Interfaith Council, a local affiliate of the Virginia Interfaith Center for Public Policy. His contribution to this volume reflects his teaching, research, and activism concerning how religious communities cooperate to create sustainable societies.

BRIAN K. PENNINGTON is the director of the Center for the Study of Religion, Culture, and Society and a professor of religious studies at Elon University. A scholar of modern Hinduism, he is the author of *Was Hinduism Invented? Britons, Indians, and the Colonial Construction of Religion*, editor of *Teaching Religion and Violence*, and, with Amy L. Allocco, coeditor of *Ritual Innovation: Strategic Interventions in South Asian Religion*. His book in progress, *God's Fifth Abode: Entrepreneurial Hinduism in the Indian Himalayas*, is a study of the pilgrimage city of Uttarkashi.

ELLIE PIERCE is the research director for the Pluralism Project at Harvard University. She began working for the Pluralism Project as a student field researcher in San Francisco. She was a section editor for *On Common Ground: World Religions in America* and coeditor of *World Religions in Boston: A Guide to Communities and Resources*, with Diana Eck. Pierce coproduced and codirected the documentary film *Fremont, U.S.A.* with Rachel Antell. She is the author of over fifteen decision-based case studies, which can be found on the Pluralism Project's website, with more in development.

OR N. ROSE is the founding director of the Miller Center for Interreligious Learning and Leadership at Hebrew College. Rose previously served Hebrew College as director of the former Center for Global Judaism and as associate dean and director of informal education at the Rabbinical School, where he still teaches. He is the coeditor of *Jewish Mysticism and the Spiritual Life: Classical Texts*; *Contemporary Reflections*; and *My Neighbor's Faith: Stories of Interreligious Encounter, Growth, and Transformation*.

HEATHER MILLER RUBENS is the executive director and Roman Catholic scholar of the Institute for Islamic, Christian, and Jewish Studies in Baltimore. Rubens develops educational initiatives that foster interreligious learning for the public in the Baltimore-Washington corridor. The questions that animate Rubens's work in interreligious literacy include when, where, and how religious communities can understand an affinity between themselves as well as constructively engage their differences. Her current project focuses on the theoretical, theological, and ethical implications of building an interreligious city.

BENJAMIN E. SAX is the Jewish Scholar at the Institute for Islamic, Christian, and Jewish Studies. Sax has published on Jewish-Christian relations, Jewish atheism, Jewish aesthetics, the Holocaust, German-Jewish history and culture, Jewish philosophy, and contemporary Jewish theology. His current research project is focused on the theoretical and theological implications of the interreligious city, tentatively titled *The Interreligious City: A Theory of Religious Pluralism*. He also is currently finishing a book titled *The Life of Quotation and Modern Jewish Thought*.

SARA L. H. SHADY is a professor of philosophy at Bethel University. With coauthor Marion Larson, she published *From Bubble to Bridge: Educating Christians for a Multifaith World*. Her writing is featured in several articles on interfaith engagement and in the books *Faith, Film and Philosophy: Big Ideas on the Big Screen*; *The Pietist Vision of Christian Higher Education: Forming Whole and Holy Persons*; and *Walking Together: Christian Thinking and Public Life in South Africa*. Her interests include constructing inclusive communities and political societies, the role of religion in politics, and existentialism.

MARTHA E. STORTZ is the Bernhard M. Christensen Professor of Religion and Vocation at Augsburg University. Stortz is a Christian theologian whose scholarship includes work in historical and systematic theology, ethics, and biblical studies. In addition to her many published articles, she is the author of *A World According to God: Practices for Putting Faith at the Center of Your Life*; *Blessed to Follow: The Beatitudes as a Compass for Discipleship*; and *Called to Follow: Journeys in John's Gospel*.

MARGARITA M. W. SUÁREZ is a professor of religious and ethical studies at Meredith College, a women's college in Raleigh, North Carolina. Trained in global contextual theologies and ethnographic methodologies, she focuses her scholarhip on religions in Cuba and interfaith leadership. She teaches courses under the broad rubric of religion and culture and interfaith studies: Anthropology of Religion; Women, Religion, and Ethnography; World Religions; Religion and Globalization in the Americas; and Introduction to Interfaith Leadership.

DEANNA FERREE WOMACK is an assistant professor of history of religions and multifaith relations at Emory University's Candler School of Theology and the director of the Leadership and Multifaith Program (LAMP), a collaboration between Candler and Georgia Tech. Her teaching and scholarship combine commitments to Christian-Muslim dialogue and American-Arab relations. Her forthcoming book, *Protestants, Gender, and the Arab Renaissance in Late Ottoman Syria*, explores encounters between American missionaries and Arab residents of Ottoman Syria in the pre–World War I period.

HOMAYRA ZIAD is a scholar-activist and writer. She has served as assistant professor of Islam at Trinity College and currently leads the integration of Islam and Muslim communities at the Institute for Islamic, Christian, and Jewish Studies (ICJS) in Baltimore. At ICJS, she creates programs for activists and emerging religious leaders at the intersection of religion and social justice. Homayra is cochair of the American Academy of Religion's Interreligious and Interfaith Studies Group and serves on the board of the American Civil Liberties Union (ACLU) of Maryland. She is coeditor of the forthcoming volume *Words to Live By: Sacred Sources for Interreligious Engagement*.

NOTES

INTRODUCTION

1. Eboo Patel, "Toward a Field of Interfaith Studies," *Liberal Education* 99 (2013): 38.
2. For greater elaboration on this point, see Eboo Patel, *Interfaith Leadership: A Primer* (Boston: Beacon Press, 2016), 97–100.
3. Patel, "Toward a Field of Interfaith Studies," 38–43.
4. This estimate comes from the organizational metrics and tracking of Interfaith Youth Core's (IFYC), which are largely taken from its grant programs that support the development of interfaith-focused courses and academic programs. IFYC's tracking in this regard is almost certainly incomplete, and we imagine that these estimates are conservative.
5. IFYC's records indicate that more than twenty undergraduate institutions have launched programs in interfaith and interreligious studies. Information about graduate programs can be found through the Jay Phillips Center for Interfaith Learning, University of St. Thomas, https://www.stthomas.edu/jpc/resources/academicprograms/graduateandseminaryprograms.
6. Boston University School of Theology, in collaboration with Hebrew College and Andover Newton Theological School, cosponsored this gathering of authors thanks to a grant from the Arthur Vining Davis Foundations.

(INTER)RELIGIOUS STUDIES

1. Patel, "Toward a Field of Interfaith Studies," 38.
2. James Simpson and Sean Kelly, *The Teaching of the Arts and Humanities at Harvard College: Mapping the Future*, Harvard University Arts and Humanities Division (2013), http://artsandhumanities.fas.harvard.edu/files/humanities/files/mapping_the_future_31_may_2013.pdf.
3. Jennifer Doody, "Building a Discussion Around the Memorial Church," *Harvard Gazette*, April 4, 2016, http://news.harvard.edu/gazette/story/2016/04/building-a-discussion-around-the-memorial-church.
4. Pew Forum on Religion and Public Life, *"Nones" on the Rise: One-in-Five Adults Have No Religious Affiliation* (Pew Research Center, 2012), http://www.pewforum.org/2012/10/09/nones-on-the-rise.
5. This includes a recently endowed chair for the study of "atheism, humanism and secular ethics" at the University of Miami. See Laurie Goodstein, "University of Miami Establishes Chair for Study of Atheism," *New York Times*, May 21, 2016.
6. See, for example, Michael Hout and Claude S. Fischer, *Explaining Why More Americans Have No Religious Preference: Political Backlash and Generational Succession, 1987–2012* (New York: NYU Population Center, 2014); Robert D. Putnam

and David E. Campbell, *American Grace: How Religion Divides and Unites Us* (New York: Simon and Schuster, 2010); and James Allen Cheyne, "The Rise of the Nones and the Growth of Religious Indifference," *Skeptic* 15 (2010): 56–60.

7. See, for example, Buster G. Smith and Joseph A. Baker, "Atheism, Agnosticism and Irreligion," in *Emerging Trends in the Behavioral and Social Sciences: An Interdisciplinary, Searchable, and Linkable Resource*, ed. Robert A. Scott, Marlis C. Buchmann, and Stephen M. Kosslyn (Hoboken, NJ: John Wiley & Sons, 2015), 1–9; Chaeyoon Lim, Carol Ann MacGregor, and Robert D. Putnam, "Secular and Liminal: Discovering Heterogeneity Among Religious Nones," *Journal for the Scientific Study of Religion* 49 (2010): 596–618; and Linda A. Mercadante, *Belief Without Borders: Inside the Minds of the Spiritual but Not Religious* (New York: Oxford University Press, 2014).

8. Interfaith and interreligious studies programs reviewed were offered by Augustana College, Barton College, Benedictine University (Illinois), California State University, Chico, California Lutheran University, Concordia College (Minnesota), Dominican University (Illinois), Drew University, Earlham College, Elon University, Elizabethtown College, Loyola University Chicago, Nazareth College, Oklahoma City University, Saint Mary's College of California, University of La Verne, and University of Toledo. Religious studies programs reviewed were offered by Brandeis University; Brown University; California State University, Chico; California State University, Humboldt; California State University, San Diego; George Mason University; Grinnell College; Hamilton College; Illinois Wesleyan University; Indiana University Bloomington; Michigan State University; New York University; Randolph-Macon College; Stanford University; University of California, Riverside; University of Alabama; University of Arizona; University of Colorado Boulder; University of Houston; University of Iowa; University of Kansas; University of Missouri; University of North Carolina at Chapel Hill; University of Oklahoma; University of Pennsylvania; University of Tennessee, Knoxville; University of Wisconsin–Madison; University of Texas at Austin; Utah State University; Vanderbilt University; and Wesleyan University. They were selected for analysis based on availability of program descriptions, mission or goals statements (or both); balance of public and private institutions; and breadth of geographic representation. Interfaith/interreligious studies program descriptions were based on a list of all known programs provided by Interfaith Youth Core (IFYC), which has supported the development of such course sequences through grants and conferences. This list included institutions associated with IFYC initiatives as well as others. Interfaith/interreligious studies programs reviewed here are those that had adequately developed program descriptions to allow for meaningful comparison.

9. D. G. Hart, *The University Gets Religion: Religious Studies in American Higher Education* (Baltimore: Johns Hopkins University Press, 1999), 191.

10. Douglas Jacobsen and Rhonda Hustedt Jacobsen, *No Longer Invisible: Religion in University Education* (New York: Oxford University Press, 2012), 24–25.

11. School Dist. of Abington Tp. v. Schempp, 374 U.S. 203, 225 (1963).

12. Bruce Lincoln, "Theses on Method," *Method and Theory in the Study of Religion* 8 (1996): 225–27.

13. Leonard Swidler, "Sorting Out Meanings: 'Religion,' 'Spiritual,' 'Interreligious,' 'Interfaith,' Etc.," *Journal of Ecumenical Studies* 49 (2014): 380.

14. Wilfred Cantwell Smith, "Comparative Religion: Whither—and Why?" in *The History of Religions: Essays in Methodology*, ed. Mircea Eliade and Joseph M. Kitagawa (Chicago: University of Chicago Press, 1959), 42; Russell McCutcheon, *Critics Not Caretakers: Redescribing the Public Study of Religion* (Albany: State University of New York Press, 2001), xi.

15. Anne Hege Grung, "Inter-religious or Trans-religious: Exploring the Term 'Inter-religious' in a Feminist Postcolonial Perspective," *Journal of Interreligious Studies* 13 (2014): 11. Emphasis in original.
16. See, for example, Michelle Voss Roberts, "Religious Belonging and the Multiple," *Journal of Feminist Studies in Religion* 26 (2010): 43–62; Jeannine Hill Fletcher, "Shifting Identity: The Contribution of Feminist Thought to Theologies of Religious Pluralism," *Journal of Feminist Studies in Religion* (2003): 5–24; and Kwok Pui-Lan, *Postcolonial Imagination and Feminist Theology* (Louisville, KY: Westminster John Knox, 2005).
17. Lucia Hulsether, "Out of Incorporation, Pluralism," *Journal of Interreligious Studies* 17 (2015): 8. See also Courtney Bender and Pamela E. Klassen, eds., *After Pluralism: Rethinking Religious Engagement* (New York: Columbia University Press, 2010); and Peter Gardella, "Pluralisms in the United States and in the American Empire," *Religious Studies Review* 29, no. 3 (2003).
18. Bruce Grelle, "Promoting Religious and Civic Literacy in Public Schools: The California 3 Rs Project," in *Religion in the Public Schools: Negotiating the New Commons,* ed. Michael D. Waggoner (Lanham, MD: Rowman and Littlefield, 2013), 103.
19. Ibid.

FROM THE HISTORY OF RELIGIONS TO INTERFAITH STUDIES

1. Patel, "Toward a Field of Interfaith Studies," 38.
2. Ibid.
3. See my section "From Theologies of Exclusion to Interfaith Engagement" for examples of such initiatives in multifaith education. Of the 66,464 students in member institutions of the Association of Theological Schools in the US, only 491 designated non-Christian affiliations in 2017 (76 Jewish, 84 Buddhist, 147 Muslim, and 184 "other"). See "Church/Denominational Affiliation of Students Currently Enrolled, 2016," 2016–2017 Annual Data Tables, Table 2.16, Association of Theological Schools, Commission on Accrediting, https://www.ats.edu/resources/institutional -data/annual-data-tables.
4. See my treatment of seminary programs below and Kate McCarthy's survey of religious studies and interfaith/interreligious studies programs in her chapter in this volume, "(Inter)Religious Studies: Making a Home in the Secular Academy."
5. Adam Becker, *Revival and Awakening: American Evangelical Missionaries in Iran and the Origins of Assyrian Nationalism* (Chicago: University of Chicago Press, 2015), 14–15. See also Ninian Smart, *Religion and the Western Mind: Drummond Lectures* (Albany: State University of New York Press, 1987), 1.
6. Daniel L. Pals, *Nine Theories of Religion,* 3rd ed. (Oxford, UK: Oxford University Press, 2015).
7. Defined by Eric Sharpe as "the historical, critical and comparative study of the religions of the world," the discipline of comparative religion is sometimes treated interchangeably with the history of religions. See E. J. Sharpe, *Understanding Religion* (New York: St. Martin's Press, 1983), vii.
8. Richard D. Hecht, "The Study of Religions in America and the Department of Religious Studies at the University of California, Santa Barbara," *Pantheon* 8 (2013): 4.
9. Amy Kittelstrom, "The International Social Turn: Unity and Brotherhood at the World's Parliament of Religions, Chicago, 1893," *Religion and American Culture: A Journal of Interpretation* 19 (2009): 245.
10. Justin Nordstrom, "Utopians at the Parliament," *Journal of Religious History* 33 (September 2009): 352.

11. Richard Hughes Seager, *The World's Parliament of Religions: The East/West Encounter, Chicago, 1893* (Bloomington: Indiana University Press, 1995).

12. Eric J. Sharpe, *Comparative Religion: A History*, 2nd ed. (London: Duckworth, 1986), 1.

13. Tomoko Masuzawa, *The Invention of World Religions: Or, How European Universalism Was Preserved in the Language of Pluralism* (Chicago: University of Chicago Press, 2005), xi–xii.

14. Ibid., xiv.

15. Seager, *World's Parliament of Religions*, xxii; D. Keith Naylor, "The Black Presence at the World's Parliament of Religions, 1893," *Religion* 26 (1996): 252.

16. Donald Wiebe, "Promise and Disappointment," in *Modern Societies and the Science of Religions: Studies in Honour of Lammert Leertouwer*, ed. Gerard A. Wiegers and Jan Platvoet (Leiden: Brill, 2002), 189–90. See also Hecht, "The Study of Religions in America," 3–16; Joseph M. Kitagawa, "The History of Religions in America," in *The History of Religions* ed. Eliade and Kitagawa, 1–30.

17. Ninian Smart, "The Future of the Academy," *Journal of the American Academy of Religion (JAAR)* 69 (2001): 542. See also Hecht, "The Study of Religions in America," 6, 9.

18. Smart, "Future of the Academy," 545; Hecht, "The Study of Religions in America," 4. Exceptions within theological schools included the University of Chicago Divinity School, where Eustace Haydon (1880–1975), Mircea Eliade (1907–86), and Joseph Kitagawa (1915–92) advanced the history of religions as an academic discipline that moved away from apologetic approaches of comparative religion. See A. Eustace Haydon, "From Comparative Religion to History of Religions," *Journal of Religion* 2 (1922): 581–82.

19. Geoman K. George, "Early 20th Century British Missionaries and Fulfillment Theology: Comparison of the Approaches of William Temple Gairdner to Islam in Egypt, and John Nicol Farquhar to Hinduism in India," in *Christian Witness Between Continuity and New Beginnings: Modern Historical Missions in the Middle East*, ed. Martin Tamcke and Michael Marten (Berlin: Lit Verlag, 2006), 15. See also W. H. T. Gairdner, *The Reproach of Islam* (London: Young People's Missionary Movement, 1909).

20. Jan Van Lim, *Shaking the Fundamentals: Religious Plurality and Ecumenical Movement* (Amsterdam: Rodopi, 2002), 94. On the limitations of the interreligious approach at the Jerusalem conference, see Deanna Ferree Womack, "A View from the Arabic Press, 1928: The International Missionary Conference in Jerusalem," *Exchange: Journal of Missiological and Ecumenical Research* 46 (2017): 180–205.

21. Charles Carroll Bonney, "Address of President Charles Carroll Bonney of the 'World's Congress Auxiliary,'" in *The World's Parliament of Religions: An Illustrated and Popular Study of the World's First Parliament of Religions, Held in Chicago in Conjunction with the Columbian Exposition of 1893*, vol. 1, ed. John Henry Barrows (Toronto: Hunter and Rose, 1893), 72.

22. Catriona Laing, "A Provocation to Mission: Constance Padwick's Study of Muslim Devotion," *Islam and Christian-Muslim Relations* 24 (2013): 30, 33.

23. Certain approaches to religious studies also promote such interreligious awareness. For example, Ninian Smart upheld the notion of "informed empathy" as a way of learning from and about the "other." See Smart, "The Future of the Academy," 648. See also Oddbjørn Leirvik, "Interreligious Studies: A Relational Approach to the Study of Religion," *Journal of Inter-Religious Dialogue* 13 (2014): 15–19.

24. "Reaching Beyond Ourselves: ATS Schools' Response to Multifaith Context," *Colloquy: The Magazine of the Association of Theological Schools* 20 (2011): 3. The Auburn study analyzed in this ATS publication is Lucinda Mosher and Justus Baird, *Beyond World Religions: The State of Multifaith Education in American Theological Schools* (New York: Auburn Theological Seminary, 2009). The new accreditation requirements for multifaith education instituted by the Association of Theological Schools in 2012 means that such emphases will only increase within American theological education. Justus Baird, "Multifaith Education in American Theological Schools: Looking Back, Looking Ahead," *Teaching Theology and Religion* 16 (2013): 309.
25. See Paul Knitter, "Doing Theology Interreligiously: Union and the Legacy of Paul Tillich," *Crosscurrents* (2011): 117–32; Richard Fox Young, "Obliged by Grace: Edward Jurji's Legacy in the History of Religions at Princeton Theological Seminary, 1939–77," *Theology Today* 69 (2012): 333–43; Diana Eck, *A New Religious America: How a "Christian Country" Has Become the World's Most Religiously Diverse Nation* (New York: HarperCollins, 2001); John B. Carman and Kathryn Dodgson, *Community and Colloquy: The Center for the Study of World Religions, 1958–2003* (Cambridge, MA: Center for the Study of World Religions, 2006).
26. "Reaching Beyond Ourselves," 5, 7; Scott C. Alexander, "Catholic-Muslim Studies at Catholic Theological Union in Chicago," *Religious Studies News* (2016): 13–17.
27. "Reaching Beyond Ourselves," 7–8; Feryal Salem, "Fulfilling the Need for Muslim Chaplains," *Religious Studies News* (April 2016): 11. On Andover Newton, see Jennifer Howe Peace and Or N. Rose's chapter in this volume, "The Value of Interreligious Education for Religious Leaders."
28. For further thoughts on the distinctions between interfaith/interreligious studies and theological studies and religious studies, see Hans Gustafson, "Interreligious and Interfaith Studies in Relation to Religious Studies and Theological Studies," *State of Formation*, January 6, 2015, http://www.stateofformation.org/2015/01/interreligious-and-interfaith-studies-in-relation-to-religious-studies-and-theological-studies.
29. Knitter, "Doing Theology Interreligiously," 124.
30. Russell T. McCutcheon, "The Study of Religion as a Cross-Disciplinary Exercise," introduction to *The Insider/Outsider Problem in the Study of Religion*, ed. Russell T. McCutcheon (London: Cassell, 1999), 17; Kenneth L. Pike, "Etic and Emic Standpoints for the Description of Behavior," in McCutcheon, *The Insider/Outsider Problem in the Study of Religion*, 28–36.

COMMON GROUND

1. Kenji Yoshino, *Covering: The Hidden Assault on Our Civil Rights* (New York: Random House, 2006).
2. Allen F. Repko and Rick Szostak, *Interdisciplinary Research: Process and Theory*, 3rd ed. (Los Angeles: Sage, 2017), 3–6.
3. Alice E. Ginsberg, *The Evolution of American Women's Studies: Reflections on Triumphs, Controversies, and Change* (London: Palgrave, 2008), 10–12.
4. Repko and Szostak, *Interdisciplinary Research*, 268–320.
5. Tracie McMillan, *The American Way of Eating: Undercover at Walmart, Applebee's, Farm Fields and the Dinner Table* (New York: Scribner, 2012), 236.
6. Repko and Szostak, *Interdisciplinary Research*, 25.
7. J. Courtney Bourns, *Do Nothing About Me Without Me: An Action Guide for Engaging Stakeholders* (Cambridge, MA: Grantmakers for Effective Organizations, 2010), http://www.d5coalition.org/wp-content/uploads/2013/07/Do_Nothing_About_Me_Without_Me.pdf.
8. Paulo Friere, *Pedagogy of the Oppressed* (New York: Bloomsbury, 2000), 50.

9. Catherine M. Orr, "Women's Studies as Civic Engagement: Research and Recommendations," Teagle Foundation white paper, prepared on behalf of the Teagle Working Group on Women's Studies and Civic Engagement and the National Women's Studies Association, September 2011, http://www.nwsa.org/Files/Resources/WomensStudiesasCivicEngagement2011Revised_Finalpdf-1.pdf.

10. Noam Scheiber, "The Pop-Up Employer: Build a Team, Do the Job, Say Goodbye," *New York Times* July 12, 2017.

CONSTRUCTING INTERRELIGIOUS STUDIES

1. On the importance of this critique and debate, see Elizabeth Kubek's preceding chapter in this volume, "Common Ground: Imagining Interfaith Studies as an Inclusive, Interdisciplinary Field."

2. David Nirenberg, *Anti-Judaism: The Western Tradition* (New York: W. W. Norton, 2013), 6.

3. Ibid., 11.

4. David Pinault, "The Field Trip and Its Role in Teaching Ritual," in *Teaching Ritual*, ed. Catherine Bell (New York: Oxford University Press, 2007), 59. On site visits, see also "Spotlight on Teaching: Teaching with Site Visits," ed. Joyce Burkhalter Flueckiger, special issue, *Spotlight on Teaching* (American Academy of Religion) 19, no. 4 (October 2004), http://rsnonline.org/images/pdfs/oct04sot.pdf.

5. Eck, *A New Religious America*; Talal Asad, *Genealogies of Religion: Discipline and Reasons of Power in Christianity and Islam* (Baltimore: Johns Hopkins University Press, 2003); McCutcheon, *Critics Not Caretakers*.

6. Wendy Brown, *Regulating Aversion: Tolerance in the Age of Identity and Empire* (Princeton, NJ: Princeton University Press, 2006).

7. Winnifred Fallers Sullivan, "Religion Naturalized: The New Establishment," in Bender and Klassen, *After Pluralism*, 82–97.

8. Chandan Reddy, *Freedom with Violence: Race, Sexuality, and the US State* (Durham: Duke University Press, 2011).

9. Lucia Hulsether, "Out of Incorporation, Pluralism," *Journal of Interreligious Studies* 17 (2015), http://irstudies.org/journal/out-of-incorporation-pluralism-by-lucia-hulsether.

10. Roderick A. Ferguson, *The Reorder of Things: The University and Its Pedagogies of Minority Difference* (Minneapolis: University of Minnesota Press, 2012).

11. Tracy Leavelle, "The Perils of Pluralism: Colonization and Decolonization in American Indian Religious History," in Bender and Klassen, *After Pluralism*, 156–77.

12. Gardella, "Pluralisms in the United States and in the American Empire," 255–59.

13. We are grateful to our colleagues Jennifer Hart, Lynn Huber, Ariela Marcus-Sells, Toddie Peters, Michael Pregill, Jeffrey Pugh, L. D. Russell, and Pamela Winfield for discussions that informed this essay and the shape of Elon's interreligious studies minor.

LEARNING FROM THE FIELD

1. Patel, "Toward a Field of Interfaith Studies," 38–43.

2. Ibid., 38.

3. IFYC is grateful to have received funding from the Teagle Foundation, Henry Luce Foundation, and Arthur Vining Davis Foundations to support our faculty-focused programming.

4. Patel, *Interfaith Leadership*, 39.

5. See Margarita M. W. Suárez and Wakoh Shannon Hickey's chapter in this volume, "Meeting Others, Seeing Myself: Experiential Pedagogies in Interfaith Studies."

6. See Ellie Pierce's chapter in this volume, "Using the Case Method in Interfaith Studies Classrooms."

7. See Amy L. Allocco, Geoffrey D. Claussen, and Brian K. Pennington's chapter in this volume, "Constructing Interreligious Studies: Thinking Critically about Interfaith Studies and the Interfaith Movement."

8. IFYC has elsewhere promoted the examples and activities in this chapter, with permission from the individuals mentioned. See "Experiential and Engaged Learning in Interfaith and Interreligious Studies Courses," Interfaith Youth Core, 2017, http://ifyc.org/resources/experiential-learning.

9. The full description of Rose Aslan's "Park 51 Role Playing Activity" is accessible on the IFYC website: https://www.ifyc.org/resources/cic-resources/park-51-role-playing -activity.

10. The full description of Hans Gustafson's "Interfaith Service Learning Assignment" is accessible on the IFYC website: https://www.ifyc.org/resources/cic-resources /interfaith-service-learning-assignment.

11. See Elizabeth Kubek's chapter in this volume, "Common Ground: Imagining Interfaith Studies as an Inclusive, Interdisciplinary Field."

12. See Mark Hanshaw and Usra Ghazi's chapter in this volume, "Interfaith Studies and the Professions: Could Heightened Religious Understanding Seed Success Within Secular Careers?"

13. See Rachel Mikva's section on intersectionality within her chapter in this volume, "Six Issues That Complicate Interreligious Studies and Engagement." See also Kubek's section on gender identity in her chapter, "Common Ground," and Jeannine Hill Fletcher's chapter for a more thorough discussion on race, "The Promising Practice of Antiracist Approaches to Interfaith Studies."

14. See, for example, Dan Schawbel, "Liberal Arts Majors Are Screwed," *Business Insider*, May 20, 2014, http://www.businessinsider.com/liberal-arts-majors-are -screwed-2014-5.

15. One example of this is the "Careful Conversation" activity, which Hickey and Suárez describe in their chapter in this volume, "Meeting Others, Seeing Myself."

16. The full syllabus for Nancy Klancher's "Spiritual Autobiographies: Many Paths, One World" course is available on the IFYC website: https://www.ifyc.org /resources/cic-resources/manypathsoneworld.

17. We are defining religious literacy as "the ability to understand and use in one's day-to-day life the basic building blocks of religious traditions—their key terms, symbols, doctrines, practices, sayings, characters, metaphors, and narratives." See Stephen Prothero, *Religious Literacy: What Every American Needs to Know—and Doesn't* (New York: HarperOne, 2008), 15.

TRANSFORMING INTRODUCTORY COURSES IN RELIGION

1. Tomoko Masuzawa, *The Invention of World Religions*, 1.

2. Ibid., 20.

3. Ibid.

4. Roland Robertson, "Glocalization: Time-Space and Homogeneity-Heterogeneity," in *Global Modernities*, ed. Mike Featherstone, Scott M. Lash, and Roland Robertson (London: Sage Publications, 1995), 40.

5. The commitment to study religious traditions glocally reflects the growing collection of scholarship on the history, presence, and interrelation of "world religions" in the United States, including Eck, *A New Religious America*; Stephen Prothero, *A Nation of Religions: The Politics of Pluralism in Multireligious America* (Chapel Hill: University of North Carolina Press, 2006); and William Hutchinson, *Religious*

Pluralism in America: The Contentious History of a Founding Ideal (New Haven, CT: Yale University Press, 2003).

6. The commitment to encounter lived religion closely reflects the humanistic method for the study of religion advanced by Tyler Roberts in conversation with the works of Robert Orsi and Saba Mahmood. See Tyler Roberts, *Encountering Religion: Responsibility and Criticism After Secularism* (New York: Columbia University Press, 2013), 114–18.

7. For a more thorough description of these four models, see Patel, *Interfaith Leadership*, 72–82.

8. This model's presence in the world religions classroom has been most affected by Huston Smith. See Huston Smith, *The World's Religions: Our Great Wisdom Traditions* (New York: HarperSanFrancisco, 1991), 73.

9. Stephen Prothero, *God Is Not One: The Eight Rival Religions That Run the World* (New York: HarperOne, 2010), 11–12.

10. Will Herberg, *Protestant-Catholic-Jew: An Essay in American Religious Sociology* (Chicago: University of Chicago Press, 1955).

11. Robert Bellah et al., *Habits of the Heart: Individualism and Commitment in American Life* (Berkeley: University of California Press, 1985), 221.

12. In this model, I seek to redress Jonathan Z. Smith's critique that the study of religion has had "an ideological emphasis on purity of lineage" that fails to accurately represent the intermingling of religious ways of being in the world. See Jonathan Z. Smith, *Relating Religion: Essays in the Study of Religion* (Chicago: University of Chicago Press, 2004), 171. Instead, I emphasize the multiplicity of religious ways of being, shaped by the intersection of social difference, including race and gender, and constituted through the interaction of religious traditions. See, for example, Devaka Premawardhana, "The Unremarkable Hybrid: Aloysius Pieris and the Redundancy of Multiple Religious Belonging," *Journal of Ecumenical Studies* 46 (2011); Jeannine Hill Fletcher, "We Are All Hybrids," chapter 4 in *Monopoly on Salvation? A Feminist Approach to Religious Pluralism* (New York: Continuum, 2005); and Michelle Voss Roberts, "Religious Belonging and the Multiple," *Journal of Feminist Studies in Religion* 26 (2010): 43–62.

13. I regularly use four real-life case studies of interreligious conflict produced by the Pluralism Project at Harvard University and the Interfaith Youth Core. These include Karla R. Suomala, "Chalking Mohammad," in "Case Studies for Exploring Interfaith Cooperation: Classroom Tools," Interfaith Youth Core (2013), 5–8, https://www.ifyc.org/resources/case-studies-exploring-interfaith-cooperation-classroom-tools; Ellie Pierce, "Fliers at the Peace Parade," Harvard University (2009); Ellie Pierce and Emily Sigalow, "A Question of Membership," Harvard University (2012); and Ellie Pierce, "A Sign of Division" Harvard University (2008), Pluralism Project, http://pluralism.org/casestudy/selected-case-studies.

14. Jennifer Howe Peace, Or N. Rose, and Gregory Mobley, eds., *My Neighbor's Faith: Stories of Interreligious Encounter, Growth and Transformation* (Maryknoll, NY: Orbis, 2012).

USING THE CASE METHOD IN INTERFAITH STUDIES CLASSROOMS

1. Elinor Pierce, "A Mosque in Palos Heights," Pluralism Project case study (2006).

2. "Questions for Class Discussions," Harvard Business School: Christensen Center for Teaching and Learning (2008), http://www.hbs.edu/teaching/Documents/Questions_for_Class_Discussions_rev.pdf.

3. Diana Eck, interview with the author, July 25, 2016.

4. "What Is Pluralism?," Pluralism Project, http://pluralism.org/what-is-pluralism.

5. "Inside HBS," Harvard Business School, http://www.hbs.edu/teaching/inside-hbs.
6. David A. Garvin, "Making the Case," *Harvard Magazine*, February 26, 2010, http://harvardmagazine.com/2003/09/making-the-case-html.
7. Louise A. Mauffette-Leenders, James A. Erskine, and Michiel R. Leenders, *Learning with Cases* (London, Ontario: Richard Ivey School of Business, 2005), 5–6.
8. John Boehrer and Marty Linsky, "Teaching with Cases: Learning to Question," *New Directions for Teaching and Learning* 42 (1990): 41–57.
9. Benson P. Shapiro, "Introduction to the Case Method," Harvard Business School Publishing (1975), http://www.hbs.edu/faculty/Pages/item.aspx?num=17156.
10. Mauffette-Leenders, Erskine, and Leenders, *Learning with Cases*, 2.
11. Boehrer and Linsky, "Teaching with Cases," 41–57.
12. Extensive resources related to writing and teaching cases are available for free to educators through Harvard Business Publishing, https://cb.hbsp.harvard.edu/cbmp/pages/home.
13. Diana Eck, email interview with the author, July 29, 2016. All quotations below are from this interview.
14. Jennifer Peace, interview with the author, July 10, 2016. All quotations below are from this interview.
15. Marcia Sietstra, interview with the author, January 6, 2017. All quotations below are from this interview.
16. Matthew Hoffman, interview with the author, January 5, 2017. All quotations below are from this interview.
17. Brendan Randall, interview with the author, December 21, 2016. All quotations below are from this interview.
18. Brendan Randall made significant contributions to the Pluralism Project's case initiative as a student, teacher, researcher, and fellow. He passed away while this chapter was still being written. For more of Randall's research and reflections on the case method, see Brendan W. Randall and Whittney Barth, "The Case Study Method as a Means of Teaching About Pluralism," in *Teaching Interreligious Encounters*, ed. Marc Pugliese et al. (New York: Oxford University Press, 2017); and his unpublished Harvard dissertation, "Religious Belief, Free Expression, and 'Lightning Rod' Issues: Agonistic Pluralism and Civic Education in a Religiously Diverse Democracy."
19. Richard Fossey and Gary M. Crow, "The Elements of a Good Case," *Journal of Cases in Educational Leadership* 14 (2011): 4–10.

TEACHING THE "MOST BEAUTIFUL OF STORIES"

1. Prothero, *God Is Not One*.
2. Qur'an 12.3.
3. Patel, *Interfaith Leadership*.
4. Tariq Ramadan, *The Quest for Meaning: Developing a Philosophy of Pluralism* (New York: Penguin Books, 2010), 150.
5. Ibid., 138–39.
6. Stanley Hauerwas, *Truthfulness and Tragedy: Further Investigations into Christian Ethics* (Notre Dame: University of Notre Dame Press, 1977), 78.
7. Richard M. Gula, *Reason Informed by Faith: Foundations of Catholic Morality* (Mahwah, NJ: Paulist Press, 1989).
8. Plato, *The Republic of Plato*, trans. Allan Bloom (New York: Basic Books, 1991), 377c.
9. Russell B. Connors Jr. and Patrick T. McCormick, *Character, Choices, and Community: The Faces of Christian Ethics* (Mahwah, NJ: Paulist Press, 1998), 88–89. See also Darrell Fasching, Dell deChant, and David M. Lantigua, *Comparative*

Religious Ethics: A Narrative Approach to Global Ethics (Hoboken, NJ: Wiley-Blackwell, 2011), 3; and Hauerwas, *Truthfulness and Tragedy*, 35.

10. 2 Samuel 12:1–10.
11. M. Carolyn Clark, "Off the Beaten Path: Some Creative Approaches to Adult Learning," *New Directions for Adult and Continuing Education* 126 (2010): 7.
12. Robert Kegan, "What 'Form' Transforms? A Constructive-Developmental Approach to Transformative Learning," in *Learning as Transformation: Critical Perspectives on a Theory in Progress*, ed. Jack Mezirow (San Francisco: Jossey-Bass, 2000), 35–69.
13. Jack Mezirow, "Learning to Think Like an Adult," in Mezirow, *Learning as Transformation*, 3–34.
14. Peace, Rose, and Mobley, eds., *My Neighbor's Faith*.
15. Jerome S. Bruner, *Making Stories: Law, Literature, Life* (New York: Farrar, Straus, & Giroux: 2002).
16. Jack Mezirow, *Transformative Dimensions of Adult Learning* (San Francisco: Jossey-Bass, 1991).
17. Gary M. Kenyon and William L. Randall, *Restorying Our Lives: Personal Growth Through Autobiographical Reflection* (Westport, CT: Praeger, 1997).
18. Fasching, deChant, and Lantigua, *Comparative Religious Ethics*, 283.
19. M. Carolyn Clark and Marsha Rossiter, "Narrative Learning in Adulthood," *New Directions for Adult and Continuing Education* 119 (2008): 61–70.
20. Robert Schoen, *What I Wish My Christian Friends Knew About Judaism* (Chicago: Loyola Press, 2014); Nadia Bolz-Weber, *Pastrix: The Cranky, Beautiful Faith of a Sinner and Saint* (New York: Jericho Books, 2013); Eboo Patel, *Acts of Faith: The Story of an American Muslim and the Struggle for the Soul of a Generation* (Boston: Beacon Press, 2007).
21. Patel, *Acts of Faith*, 70.
22. Parker Palmer, *Let Your Life Speak: Listening for the Voice of Vocation* (San Francisco: Jossey-Bass, 2000), 17.
23. Van Wyck Brooks, *America's Coming-of-Age*, rev. ed. (New York: Amereon House, 1990).
24. Ellie Pierce, "'What Is at Stake?' Exploring the Problems of Pluralism Through the Case Method," *Interreligious Studies* 17: (2015), http://irdialogue.org/wp-content/uploads/2015/08/FINAL-What-is-at-Stake.pdf.
25. Martha E. Stortz, "Why Interfaith Work Is Not a Luxury: Lutherans as Neighboring Neighbors," *Intersections* 44 (2016): 9–20.
26. Matthew Maruggi, "The Promise and Peril of the Interfaith Classroom," *Intersections* 44 (2016): 21–23.

A PEDAGOGY OF LISTENING

1. This essay is particular in its focus on Islam and the Qur'an, but the approach proposed here can be used in teaching many religions.
2. The Jesus Seminar was an ongoing gathering of scholars who first met in the 1980s and continued early into the twenty-first century to assess the historical reliability of the New Testament Gospels. Eventually the seminar concluded that less than 20 percent of the words and deeds attributed to Jesus were authentic. Numerous studies emerged from this group, such as Robert. W. Funk, *The Gospel of Jesus: According to the Jesus Seminar* (Santa Rosa, CA: Polebridge Press, 1999); and Robert W. Funk, *The Acts of Jesus: The Search for the Authentic Deeds of Jesus* (San Francisco: Harper, 1998).
3. See, for example, Eboo Patel, "His Holiness and the Art and Science of Interfaith Cooperation," *Huffington Post*, July 18, 2011, http://www.huffingtonpost.com

/eboo-patel/dalai-lama-interfaith-cooperation_b_901392.html. In *Sacred Ground: Pluralism, Prejudice, and the Promise of America* (Boston: Beacon Press, 2012), Eboo Patel speaks of three elements of an interfaith triangle that mutually reinforce one another: positive attitudes, appreciative knowledge, and positive behaviors and relationships.

4. Michael Birkel, *Qur'an in Conversation* (Waco, TX: Baylor University Press, 2014).

5. Since the publication of *Qur'an in Conversation*, other studies of contemporary interpretation have appeared. See, for example, Suha Taji-Farouki, ed., *The Qur'an and Its Readers Worldwide: Contemporary Commentaries and Translations* (New York: Oxford University Press, in association with Institute of Ismaili Studies in London, 2015); Abdullah Saeed, *Reading the Qur'an in the Twenty-First Century: A Contextualist Approach* (London: Routledge, 2014); and Asma Lamrabet, *Women in the Qur'an: An Emancipatory Reading*, trans. Myriam François-Cerrah (Markfield, UK: Square View, 2016).

6. These sentiments are found in Birkel, *Qur'an in Conversation*, 203, 84, 155–57, 98.

7. Ibid., 13.

8. This story is found in Sura 18:60–82.

9. Maria Dakake is a professor at George Mason University and an editor of *The Study Qur'an: A New Translation and Commentary* (New York: HarperOne, 2015).

10. There has been much recent study of "nones" and the spiritual but not religious. See, for example, Mercadante, *Belief Without Borders*; Elizabeth Drescher, *Choosing Our Religion: The Spiritual Lives of America's Nones* (New York: Oxford University Press, 2016); Corinna Nicolaou, *A None's Story: Searching for Meaning Inside Christianity, Judaism, Buddhism, and Islam* (New York: Columbia, 2016).

11. "Uno itinere non potest perveniri ad tam grande secretum." Quintus Aurelius Symmachus, "Relatio III De ara Victoriae," Bibliotheca Augustana, http://www.hs -augsburg.de/~harsch/Chronologia/Lspost04/Symmachus/sym_re03.html.

MEETING OTHERS, SEEING MYSELF

1. "An Interfaith Conversation about Womanhood," event sponsored by students in Dr. Hickey's Women in World Religions course, Notre Dame of Maryland University, Baltimore, September 11, 2016.

2. "Hate Crimes," Federal Bureau of Investigation, https://www.fbi.gov/investigate /civil-rights/hate-crimes.

3. Charlotte Aull Davies, *Reflexive Ethnography: A Guide to Researching Selves and Others*, 2nd ed. (New York: Routledge, 2008), 4.

4. See Elizabeth Kubek's chapter in this volume, "Common Ground: Imagining Interfaith Studies as an Inclusive, Interdisciplinary Field."

5. Linda Elder and Richard Paul, *The Thinker's Guide to Intellectual Standards: The Words That Name Them and the Criteria That Define Them* (Foundation for Critical Thinking, 2008), 63, https://www.criticalthinking.org/store/get_file.php?inventories _id=338&inventories_files_id=349.

6. Ibid., 62.

7. Patel, *Sacred Ground*, 71.

8. For example, Jain tradition stresses nonviolence (ahimsa), nonattachment (*aparigraha*), and non-absolutism (*anekantwad*). The Eight Limbs of Yoga include social disciplines (*yamas*: nonviolence, non-deception, non-stealing, sexual restraint, non-greed) and personal disciplines (*niyamas*: purity, contentment, discipline, studiousness, and surrender/humility). Any of these virtues or practices might make a useful focus for this exercise.

9. Andrew O. Fort, "Awareness Practices in an Undergraduate Buddhism Course," in *Meditation and the Classroom: Contemplative Pedagogy for Religious Studies*, ed.

Judith Simmer-Brown and Fran Grace (Albany: State University of New York Press, 2011), 179–85.
10. Sid Brown, *A Buddhist in the Classroom* (Albany: State University of New York Press, 2008), 121–26.
11. Ibid., 123. Emphases in original.
12. Emily Schreiber, "Careful Conversation Reflection," unpublished manuscript, November 24, 2014.
13. Ibid.
14. "Research Guidelines," Pluralism Project at Harvard University, http://pluralism.org /research-guidelines/.
15. Ruth Behar, *Vulnerable Observer: Anthropology That Breaks Your Heart* (Boston: Beacon Press, 1997).
16. The 613 Commandments.
17. "Value Rubrics," Association of American Colleges and Universities, https://www .aacu.org/value-rubrics.
18. James Shiveley and Thomas Misco, "'But How Do I Know About Their Attitudes and Beliefs?' A Four-Step Process for Integrating and Assessing Dispositions in Teacher Education," *Clearing House: A Journal of Educational Strategies, Issues and Ideas* 83 (2010): 9–14.
19. Richard Paul and Linda Elder, *A Guide for Educators to Critical Thinking Competency Standards* (Foundation for Critical Thinking, 2007), http://www.critical thinking.org/files/SAM_Comp%20Stand_07opt.pdf.

SIX ISSUES THAT COMPLICATE INTERRELIGIOUS STUDIES AND ENGAGEMENT

1. Harry Stopes-Roe uses "life stance" to include secular perspectives in religious/ interreligious discourse, focusing on relationship with that which is deemed of ultimate importance and its implications for living. Stopes-Roe, "Humanism as a Life Stance," *New Humanist* 103 (1988): 21.
2. For a genealogy of interreligious studies and engagement, see Rachel Mikva, "Reflections in the Waves," in *Experiments in Empathy for our Time: Critical Reflection on Interreligious Learning*, ed. Najeeba Syeed (Brill, forthcoming).
3. Gayatri Chakravorty Spivak discusses the native informant in *Critique of Postcolonial Reason: Toward a History of the Vanishing Present* (Cambridge, MA: Harvard University Press, 1999), ix.
4. The definition comes from the Pluralism Project, http://pluralism.org/what-is -pluralism. See also Marion H. Larson and Sara L. H. Shady's chapter in this volume, "The Possibility of Solidarity: Evangelicals and the Field of Interfaith Studies."
5. For example, after the US Council of Catholic Bishops issued "A Note on Ambiguities Contained in Covenant and Mission" (2009), asserting that Christians are always giving witness in a way that invites others to join, several Jewish organizations responded, "Once Jewish-Christian dialogue has been formally characterized as an invitation, whether explicit or implicit, to apostatize, then Jewish participation becomes untenable." "Christian Conversion of Jews? National Jewish Interfaith Letter on USCCB 'Note on Ambiguities,'" Council of Centers on Jewish-Christian Relations, August 18, 2009, http://www.ccjr.us/dialogika-resources/themes-in -todays-dialogue/conversion/574-njil09aug18.
6. See Janet Jakobsen, "Ethics After Pluralism," in Bender and Klassen, *After Pluralism*, 31–58; and Paul Knitter, "Is the Pluralist Model a Western Imposition?," chap. 3 in *The Myth of Religious Superiority: Multifaith Explorations of Religious Pluralism*, ed. Paul Knitter (Maryknoll, NY: Orbis, 2005).
7. See Jeannine Hill Fletcher's chapter in this volume, "The Promising Practice of Antiracist Approaches to Interfaith Studies," and Deanna Ferree Womack's chapter

in this volume, "From the History of Religions to Interfaith Studies: A Theological Educator's Exercise in Adaptation."

8. See Knitter, *Myth of Religious Superiority.*
9. Peggy McIntosh, "White Privilege: Unpacking the Invisible Knapsack," *Peace and Freedom Magazine* (1989): 10–12.
10. See Kate McCarthy's chapter in this volume, "(Inter)Religious Studies: Making a Home in the Secular Academy."
11. See Michel Foucault, *Power/Knowledge*, ed. and trans. Colin Gordon (New York: Pantheon Books, 1980), 81; and Gayatri Chakravorty Spivak, "Can the Subaltern Speak?," in *Colonial Discourse and Post-Colonial Theory: A Reader*, ed. Patrick Williams and Laura Chrisman (New York: Columbia University Press, 1994), 66–111.
12. See Rosemary Ruether, *Faith and Fratricide: The Theological Roots of Anti-Semitism* (Eugene, OR: Wipf and Stock, 1996); Katharina von Kellenbach, *Anti-Judaism in Feminist Religious Writings* (Atlanta: Scholars Press, 1994); Jasmin Zine, "Between Orientalism and Fundamentalism," in *(En)Gendering the War on Terror: War Stories and Camouflaged Politics*, ed. Kim Rygiel et al. (Abingdon, UK: Routledge, 2016), 27–50; Deepa Kumar, *Islamophobia and the Politics of Empire* (Chicago: Haymarket Books, 2012).
13. Lewis Z. Schlosser, "Christian Privilege: Breaking a Sacred Taboo," *Journal of Multicultural Counseling and Development* 31 (2003): 44–51.
14. Jennifer Peace, "Coformation Through Interreligious Learning," *Colloquy* 20 (2011): 24–26.
15. Leonard Swidler, "The Dialogue Decalogue," *Journal of Ecumenical Studies* 20 (1983): 2. Although its name privileges Bible as scripture, the format is still popular.
16. See Jennifer Howe Peace and Or N. Rose's chapter in this volume, "The Value of Interreligious Education for Religious Leaders."
17. From a 1985 press conference in Stockholm decrying opposition to the construction of a Mormon temple.
18. Diana Eck, "Prospects for Pluralism," *JAAR* 75 (2007): 771.
19. Robert Orsi, "Everyday Miracles: The Study of Lived Religion," in *Lived Religion in America: Toward a History of Practice*, ed. David Hall (Princeton, NJ: Princeton University Press, 1997), 5.
20. In Edward Said, *Orientalism* (New York: Pantheon Books, 1978), Said contends that geopolitical power in the Christian West distorts perceptions of difference, making scholarship a tool of Western imperialism.
21. See Ninian Smart, *The Religious Experience of Mankind* (Upper Saddle River, NJ: Prentice Hall, 1969); and Smart, *Religion and the Western Mind*, 50. For more recent work, see Meredith McGuire, *Lived Religion: Faith and Practice in Everyday Life* (Oxford, UK: Oxford University Press, 2008); and Nancy Ammerman, ed., *Everyday Religion: Observing Modern Religious Lives* (Oxford, UK: Oxford University Press, 2007).
22. Tamar Saguy and Eran Halperin, "Exposure to Outgroup Members Criticizing Their Own Group Facilitates Intergroup Openness," *Personality and Social Psychology Bulletin*, February 28, 2014, 1–12.
23. See Mary Boys and Sara Lee, *Learning in the Presence of the Other* (Nashville: Skylight Paths, 2006).
24. William Faulkner, *Requiem for a Nun*, act 1, scene 3 (1951).
25. Ellie Pierce, "A Sign of Division," in "Selected Case Studies," Pluralism Project, http://pluralism.org/casestudy/selected-case-studies. *Iftar*: the meal eaten by Muslims after sunset during Ramadan.
26. Judith Plaskow, "The Academy as Real Life," *JAAR* 67, no. 3 (1999): 521.

27. Paul Hedges, "Interreligious Studies," in *Encyclopedia of Sciences and Religions*, ed. Anne Runehov and Luis Oviedo (Dordrecht: Springer Netherlands, 2013), 1077.

28. See Kimberlé Crenshaw, "Mapping the Margins: Intersectionality, Identity Politics and Violence Against Women of Color," *Stanford Law Review* 43 (1991): 1241–99.

THE PROMISING PRACTICE OF ANTIRACIST APPROACHES TO INTERFAITH STUDIES

1. Eck, *A New Religious America*.

2. Paulo Freire, *Pedagogy of the Oppressed*, 30th anniversary ed., trans. Myra Bergman Ramos (New York: Continuum, 2007), 126.

3. Michael Omi and Howard Winant, *Racial Formation in the United States: From the 1960s to the 1990s*, 2nd ed. (New York: Routledge, 1994).

4. For an overview of changes in race categories of the US census, see D'Vera Cohn, "Race and the Census: The 'Negro' Controversy," Pew Research Center, January 21, 2010, http://www.pewsocialtrends.org/2010/01/21/race-and-the-census-the-%E2%80%9Cnegro%E2%80%9D-controversy.

5. James W. Perkinson, "Reversing the Gaze: Constructing European Race Discourse as Modern Witchcraft Practice," *Journal of the American Academy of Religion* 72 (2004): 619.

6. Will Sarvis, "Americans and Their Land: The Deep Roots of Property and Liberty," *Contemporary Review* (2008): 41.

7. Eric Kades, "History and Interpretation of the Great Case of Johnson v. M'Intosh," *Law and History Review* 19 (2001): 72, http://scholarship.law.wm.edu/facpubs/50. John Winthrop, the Puritan governor of the Massachusetts Colony, used the biblical text of Genesis 1:28 to argue that God had given the land to "sonnes of men, with a general condition: increase & multiply, replenish the earth & subdue it," and since Native inhabitants had failed in this, God's plan could be rightly carried out only by Christian colonialists.

8. Daniel Murphree, "Race and Religion on the Periphery: Disappointment and Missionization in the Spanish Floridas, 1566–1763," in *Race, Nation and Religion in the Americas*, ed. Henry Goldschmidt and Elizabeth McAlister (New York: Oxford University Press, 2004), 35–60.

9. Craig S. Wilder, *Ebony and Ivy: Race, Slavery and the Troubled History of America's Universities* (New York: Bloomsbury, 2013), 177. The curse of Ham centered on a biblical figure who was cursed by his father, Noah. Biblical interpretation in the sixteenth through eighteenth centuries argued an etymological connection between 'Ham' and 'black,' rendering Ham as the accursed father of all of black Africa. Contemporary biblical scholarship finds no justification for this etymological connection. David M. Goldenberg, *The Curse of Ham: Race and Slavery in Early Judaism, Christianity, and Islam* (Princeton, NJ: Princeton University Press, 2005), 149.

10. Steven Newcomb, *Pagans in the Promised Land: The Roots of Domination in US Federal Indian Law* (Golden, CO: Fulcrum, 2008).

11. Kades, "History and Interpretation of the Great Case of Johnson v. M'Intosh," 70.

12. See, for example, Steven Newcomb's discussion of Native sovereignty and the Dakota Access Pipeline: Newcomb, "The Dakota Access Pipeline and the Law of Christendom," Indian Country Media Network, August 29, 2016, https://indiancountrymedianetwork.com/news/opinions/the-dakota-access-pipeline-and-the-law-of-christendom.

13. David Whitford, "A Calvinist Heritage to the 'Curse of Ham': Assessing the Accuracy of a Claim about Racial Subordination," *Church History and Religious Culture* 90, no. 1 (2010): 27.

14. William Waller Hening, ed., *The Statutes at Large: Being a Collection of All the Laws of Virginia, from the First Session of the Legislature, in the Year 1619*, vol. 2 (New York: R. & W. & G. Bartow, 1823), 491.

15. Larry R. Morrison, "The Religious Defense of American Slavery before 1830," *Journal of Religious Thought* 37 (1980–1981): 16–29.

16. As late as 1861, Auguste Martin, bishop in Louisiana, defended slavery theologically with the argument that "slavery [is] an eminently Christian work . . . [entailing] the redemption of millions of human beings who would pass in such a way from the darkest intellectual night to the sweet . . . light of the Gospel." Cited in Cyprian Davis, "God of Our Weary Years: Black Catholics in American Catholic History," in *Taking Down Our Harps: Black Catholics in the United States*, ed. Diana Hayes and Cyprian Davis (Maryknoll, NY: Orbis, 1998), 25.

17. Aaron Augustus Sargent, *Chinese Immigration: Speech of Hon. A. A. Sargent of California, in the Senate of the United States, March 7, 1878* (Washington, 1878), 23.

18. O. Gibson, *Chinaman or White Man, Which? Reply to Father Buchard [sic], Delivered in Platt's Hall, San Francisco, Friday Evening, Mar. 14, 1873* (San Francisco: Alta Printing House, 1873), 9, 13, 29, http://content.cdlib.org/ark:/13030/hb7c6005dw/?&brand=calisphere.

19. Alexander McKenzie, pastor of the Shepard Memorial Church, Cambridge, Massachusetts, in John Henry Barrows, *The World's Parliament of Religions*, vol. 1 (Chicago, 1893), 85. For further discussion of the religio-racial project at the Parliament, see Jeannine Hill Fletcher, "Warrants for Reconstruction: Christian Hegemony, White Supremacy," *Journal of Ecumenical Studies* 51 (2016): 54–79.

20. Daniel B. Lee, "A Great Racial Commission: Religion and the Construction of White America," in *Race, Nation, and Religion in the Americas*, ed. Henry Goldschmidt and Elizabeth McAlister (New York: Oxford University Press, 2004), 85.

21. During this time, arguments were regularly made that a group or individual's Christian identity brought them closer to the American ideal. In 1914, when a group of Syrians sought citizenship through the American courts, they were granted citizenship in part because their "membership in the Christian fold" served as marker that they were part of the "Caucasian or white race." See Sarah Gualtieri, "Becoming 'White': Race, Religion, and the Foundations of Syrian/Lebanese Ethnicity in the United States," *Journal of American Ethnic History* 20 (2001), 42. Just five years later, Bhagat Singh Thind was recognized as "Aryan" and therefore "Caucasian" on the basis of linguistic and genealogical criteria, but his case for citizenship was overturned on the basis that his "Hindu-ness" would render him inassimilable to white culture. See Jennifer Snow, "The Civilization of White Men: The Race of the Hindu in *United States v. Bhagat Singh Thind*," in Goldschmidt and McAlister, *Race, Nation, and Religion in the Americas*, 259–80. The Supreme Court case is accessible online at http://www.bhagatsinghthind.com/court01.html. We might note that Christians painted others with broad (and inaccurate) brushes—Thind was not Hindu but Sikh.

22. Douglas S. Massey and Karen A. Pren, "Unintended Consequences of US Immigration Policy: Explaining the Post-1965 Surge from Latin America," *Population and Development Review* 38 (2012): 1. Massey and Pren explain: "Countries of the Western Hemisphere had never been included in the national origins quotas, nor was the entry of their residents prohibited as that of Africans and Asians had been. . . . The 1965 amendments were intended to purge immigration law of its racist legacy by replacing the old quotas with a new system that allocated residence visas according to a neutral preference system based on family reunification and labor force needs."

23. Simran Jeet Singh chronicles this contemporary religio-racial project in his essay "Muslimophobia, Racialization, and Mistaken Identity: Understanding Anti-Sikh Hate Violence in a Post-9/11 America," in *Muhammad in the Digital Age*, ed. Ruqayya Yasmine Khan (Austin: University of Texas Press, 2015), 158–73. See also Jaideep Singh, "A New American Apartheid: Racialized, Religious Minorities in the post-9/11 Era," *Sikh Formations* 9 (2013): 114–44.

24. For a further discussion of the structural outcomes of America's religio-racial project of White Christian supremacy, see Jeannine Hill Fletcher, "When Words Create Worlds," chap. 3 in her *The Sin of White Supremacy: Christianity, Racism and Religious Diversity in America* (Maryknoll, NY: Orbis, 2017).

25. Wilder, *Ebony and Ivy*.

26. The "Undoing Racism" training of the People's Institute for Survival and Beyond explains: "Persons who work in institutions often function as gatekeepers to ensure that the institution perpetuates itself. By operating with anti-racist values and networking with those who share those values and maintaining accountability in the community, the gatekeeper becomes an agent of institutional transformation." "Our Principles," People's Institute for Survival and Beyond, http://www.pisab.org/our-principles#gatekeeping.

27. Ibid.

THE POSSIBILITY OF SOLIDARITY

1. See Kate McCarthy's chapter in this volume, "(Inter)Religious Studies: Making a Home in the Secular Academy."

2. See, for example, Gregory A. Smith and Jessica Martínez, "How the Faithful Voted: A Preliminary 2016 Analysis," *Fact Tank*, Pew Research Center, November 9, 2016, http://www.pewresearch.org/fact-tank/2016/11/09/how-the-faithful-voted-a-preliminary-2016-analysis.

3. The campaign was started in the fall of 2015, by students taking a course on the modern Middle East at Bethel University.

4. John Azumah, "Evangelical Christian Views and Attitudes Towards Christian-Muslim Dialogue," *Transformation* 29 (2012): 128.

5. Charles Taylor, "The Politics of Recognition," in *Multiculturalism and the Politics of Recognition*, ed. Amy Gutmann (Princeton, NJ: Princeton University Press, 1994), 25.

6. Patel, *Interfaith Leadership*, 93.

7. Taylor, "The Politics of Recognition," 26.

8. Patel, *Interfaith Leadership*, 93–94.

9. There is notable disagreement among evangelicals on issues like sexuality, climate change, and the 2016 election. See, for example, Thomas S. Kidd, "Polls Show Evangelicals Support Trump. But the Term 'Evangelical' Has Become Meaningless," *Washington Post*, July 22, 2016.

10. Wesley Wildman, "When Narrative Identities Clash: Liberals Versus Evangelicals," *Congregations* (2005): 30.

11. R. Khari Brown and Ronald E. Brown, "The Challenge of Religious Pluralism: The Association Between Interfaith Contact and Religious Pluralism," *Review of Religious Research* 53 (2011): 328.

12. Christopher Lamb, "Ninevah Revisited: Theory and Practice in Interfaith Relations," *International Bulletin of Missionary Research* 8 (1984): 156.

13. Brown and Brown, "The Challenge of Religious Pluralism," 337.

14. Brian McLaren, *Why Did Jesus, Moses, the Buddha, and Mohammed Cross the Road?* (New York: Jericho Books, 2012), 15.

15. Azumah, "Evangelical Christian Views and Attitudes Towards Christian-Muslim Dialogue," 131.

16. Ibid.
17. Charles Soukup and James Keaten, "Humanizing and Dehumanizing Responses Across Four Orientations to Religious Otherness," in *A Communication Perspective on Interfaith Dialogue*, ed. Daniel S. Brown Jr. (Lanham, MD: Lexington Books, 2013), 51.
18. Iris Marion Young, *Inclusion and Democracy* (Oxford, UK: Oxford University Press, 2000), 52.
19. Ibid., 55.
20. Christian Smith, *Christian America? What Evangelicals Really Want* (Berkeley: University of California Press, 2000), 4.
21. Robert Wuthnow, "Living the Question—Evangelical Christianity and Critical Thought," *CrossCurrents* 40, no. 2 (1990), http://www.crosscurrents.org/wuthnow .htm.
22. Nicholas Kristof, "A Confession of Liberal Intolerance," *New York Times*, May 7, 2016.
23. Scholarship in interfaith studies could explore whether all instances of apparent religious discrimination are treated consistently. For example, should we treat the case of Muslim taxi drivers in Minneapolis refusing to transport alcohol in the same way we address the case of Christian bakeries refusing to make cakes for LGBTQ weddings? While we do not propose that the answer to this question is automatically clear, simply asking the question can draw attention to issues where inclusion and solidarity may be lacking.
24. Smith, *Christian America?*, 21.
25. Wendy Martineau, "Misrecognition and Cross-Cultural Understanding: Shaping the Space for a 'Fusion of Horizons,'" *Ethnicities* 12 (2012): 164–65.
26. Young, *Inclusion and Democracy*, 59.
27. Eboo Patel and Cassie Meyer, "The Civic Relevance of Interfaith Cooperation for Colleges and Universities," *Journal of College and Character* 12 (2011): 5.
28. Young, *Inclusion and Democracy*, 70.
29. See McCarthy's chapter in this volume, "(Inter)Religious Studies."
30. Young, *Inclusion and Democracy*, 74.
31. Ibid., 222, 197.
32. Ibid., 225, 226.
33. Ibid., 117.
34. Martin Luther King Jr., "Palm Sunday Sermon on Mohandas K. Gandhi," March 22, 1959, in *Martin Luther King, Jr., and the Global Freedom Struggle*, Stanford University, Martin Luther King Research and Education Institute, https://king institute.stanford.edu/king-papers/documents/palm-sunday-sermon-mohandas-k -gandhi-delivered-dexter-avenue-baptist-church.

WATER, CLIMATE, STARS, AND PLACE

1. On Christian hegemony, see the essay by Rachel Mikva in this volume, "Six Issues That Complicate Interreligious Studies and Engagement." On white Christian privilege in particular, see the essay by Jeannine Hill Fletcher in this volume, "The Promising Practice of Antiracist Approaches to Interfaith Studies." My own location places me as a scholar of Christian spirituality especially as it moves outdoors, a professor at a Lutheran-affiliated but strongly interfaith university, and a resident of the Calleguas Creek watershed, living in a place sacred to the Chumash people of Southern California.
2. Many recent works explore how various religious traditions engage the religious significance of the natural world. See, for example, the four-volume series edited by Roger Gottlieb, *Religion and the Environment: Critical Concepts in Religious*

Studies (New York: Routledge, 2010); and the ten-volume Harvard University Press series edited by Mary Evelyn Tucker and John Grim, *Religions of the World and Ecology* (Cambridge, MA: Harvard University Press, 1997–2004). Climate change and other looming catastrophes, such as the ongoing mass extinction crisis, are forcing us collectively to ask bigger questions of what it means to be human—and religious traditions are, after all, meant to respond to such questions. Other related questions not addressed in this essay but important for ongoing thinking include how climate change and ecological threats already affect particular religions, religious practices, and places on Earth; how these crises challenge or critique ecologically inadequate forms of religious belief, practice, or worldview; and how new forms of nonbelief or non-affiliation with religious community (the rise of religious "nones" and increasing numbers of professed atheists) shape these questions.

3. In January 2017, President Donald Trump issued an executive order to resume construction on the pipeline. At the time this essay was written, that order was facing challenges in court.

4. LaDonna Brave Bull Allard, "Why the Founder of Standing Rock Sioux Camp Can't Forget the Whitestone Massacre," *Yes! Magazine*, September 3, 2016, http://www.yesmagazine.org/people-power/why-the-founder-of-standing-rock-sioux-camp-cant-forget-the-whitestone-massacre-20160903.

5. I prefer the term "interreligious" to name the emerging field of study this volume explores. I find compelling the rationale for this terminology found in the chapter by Kate McCarthy in this volume, "(Inter)Religious Studies: Making a Home in the Secular Academy." Because of its currency in public life, I tend to use "interfaith" when describing the phenomenon or lived practice of encounter, dialogue, conflict, or collaboration between persons or communities of different religious orientations.

6. Linda Hogan, "We Call It *Tradition*," in *The Handbook of Contemporary Animism*, ed. Graham Harvey (New York: Routledge, 2014), 22.

7. To test your own bioregional knowledge, see "Bioregional Awareness Quiz," https://indigenize.wordpress.com/2013/03/21/bioregional-quiz.

8. Jennifer Price, *Flight Maps: Adventures with Nature in Modern America* (New York: Basic Books, 1999), 164. A convincing literature has documented the alienation from the natural world coded in Price's phrase, perhaps most hauntingly in books on childhood like Richard Louv, *Last Child in the Woods: Saving Our Children from Nature-Deficit Disorder* (Chapel Hill, NC: Algonquin, 2005) and Jay Griffiths, *A Country Called Childhood: Children and the Exuberant World* (Berkeley, CA: Counterpoint, 2014).

9. Kirkpatrick Sale, *Dwellers in the Land* (San Francisco: Sierra Club Books, 1985), 43. A classic work on love of place is Yi-Fu Tuan, *Topophilia: A Study of Environmental Perception, Attitudes, and Values* (New York: Columbia University Press, 1974). See also Michael S. Northcott, *Place, Ecology, and the Sacred: The Moral Geography of Sustainable Communities* (London: Bloomsbury, 2015). Theories of religion emphasizing place include Thomas A. Tweed, *Crossing and Dwelling: A Theory of Religion* (Cambridge, MA: Harvard University Press, 2006)—though this analysis remains mostly anthropocentric—and Graham Harvey, *Food, Sex, and Strangers: Understanding Religion as Everyday Life* (Durham, NC: Acumen Publishing, 2013).

10. In referring to animism, I am following the definition of Graham Harvey: "Animists are people who recognize that the world is full of persons, only some of whom are human, and that life is always lived in relationship with others." *Animism: Respecting the Living World* (New York: Columbia University Press, 2006), xi.

11. Such language also fails to represent religious diversity adequately, since it ignores so-called "Eastern" religious traditions and communities. I am limiting this section's

analysis to worldviews shaped broadly by or within the Abrahamic monotheistic traditions and more specifically the Christian tradition (the dominant architect, for better or worse, of the "Western" world). But the problems noted extend beyond Christians; they are visible throughout the overdeveloped West and its globalizing effects elsewhere.

12. The work of Potawatomi botanist Robin Wall Kimmerer brings together both dimensions of such attention. See, for instance, Kimmerer, *Braiding Sweetgrass: Indigenous Wisdom, Scientific Knowledge, and the Teachings of Plants* (Minneapolis: Milkweed Editions, 2015).

13. Many collections include perspectives from a range of indigenous communities. See John A. Grim, ed., *Indigenous Traditions and Ecology: The Interbeing of Cosmology and Community*, Religions of the World and Ecology Series (Cambridge, MA: Harvard University Press, 2001); and Harvey, ed., *Handbook of Contemporary Animism*. Better, however, is to get to know the history of one's own place, its pre-European inhabitants and their forms of life in that place, and—best of all—contemporary members of that community.

THE VALUE OF INTERRELIGIOUS EDUCATION FOR RELIGIOUS LEADERS

1. CIRCLE was founded in 2008 as a joint initiative of Andover Newton Theological School (ANTS) and Hebrew College, with generous and ongoing support from the Henry Luce Foundation. Although the center closed in 2017, when ANTS relocated to New Haven, Connecticut, both schools remain committed to interreligious education.

2. We wish to thank the following scholars and educators for responding to an open-ended query about the nature of religious leadership and interreligious education as we prepared this chapter: Justus Baird, Judith Berling, Rahuldeep Singh Gill, Heidi Hadsel, Celene Ibrahim, Sheryl Kujawa-Holbrook, Reuven Firestone, Gregory Mobley, Mary Elizabeth Moore, Nancy Fuchs Kreimer, Najeeba Syeed, John Thatamanil, and Homayra Ziad. While we could not include all of their insights, we are deeply grateful for their collegiality, mentorship, and leadership.

3. While we use the term "religious leadership" throughout this essay to refer primarily to those preparing for ordination and careers as religious professionals, we recognize that such leadership takes different forms. As Rahuldeep Singh Gill of California Lutheran University writes: "A religious leader could be a member of a congregation who wants to organize a food or clothing drive to benefit the local community. A religious leader could be someone who wants to make her workplace more amenable to prayer requirements and dietary restrictions of various peoples." Email to authors, October 30, 2016.

4. A version of this story was first published by Jennifer Peace in "Conversation Partners: We Need Each Other," *Reflections: A Magazine of Theological and Ethical Inquiry from Yale Divinity School* (2016): 40–42.

5. As Diana Eck has written, while religious "diversity" is a fact of life in the United States, religious "pluralism" is a self-conscious act of "energetic" engagement across lines of difference. See "What is Pluralism?," Pluralism Project, http://pluralism.org /what-is-pluralism.

6. On the use of this classical Jewish pedagogic practice in an interreligious educational context, see Melissa Heller, "Jewish-Christian Encounter Through Text: An Interfaith Course for Seminarians," *Journal of Inter-Religious Dialogue* 8 (2012): 29–42.

7. As sociologists have reported, when a person forges a positive relationship with even *one* member of a different religious group, it is much more likely that she will be open to others from that same group. See, for example, Putnam and Campbell, *American Grace: How Religion Divides and Unites Us*, 443–92.

8. Judith Berling of the Graduate Theological Union comments on such internal differences, using her own local parish as an example: "Even within my single parish, seemingly religiously monolithic, different convictions about what is vital to the . . . [community] are creating deep and dangerous ruptures. Religious leaders need skills to help parishioners learn how to understand persons who hold different religious views and practices, how to sustain relationships of mutual understanding and respect across lines of difference." Email to authors, October 30, 2016.

9. Encouraging our students to be honest about their questions is particularly important because of the pressure they often feel as emerging clergy and leaders to present themselves as experts and role models.

10. Jennifer Howe Peace coined the term "coformation" in the context of interreligious seminary education in the article. See Peace, "Coformation Through Interreligious Learning," *Colloquy* 20 (2011): 24.

11. It is important to add in this context that the CIRCLE staff has worked extensively with administrators, faculty, students, and board members at both of our schools to articulate *why* interreligious leadership education is vital to the missions of our institutions and reflective of the Jewish and Christian values we seek to inculcate in our graduates. Without such theological and pedagogic reflection, it is very difficult to weave this learning into the fabric of a school. This is especially true of a seminary (liberal or conservative), where there is a strong emphasis on the preservation of existing traditions and whose primary purpose is to supply their particular communities with new leaders. Hand in hand with this visioning work, there is, of course, the equally important task of thoughtfully integrating this educational element into the life of a school.

12. Several of the colleagues we contacted in the course of preparing this chapter reflected on the complex connections across religious traditions, past and present. As Justus Baird of Auburn Theological Seminary notes, "Our faith traditions did not develop in a vacuum; they were shaped by each other in negative and positive ways. . . . As the saying goes, to know one tradition is to know none." Email to authors, November 9, 2016. Gregory Mobley of Andover Newton expresses the benefits of uncovering this complexity through interreligious engagement in the following poetic reflection: "We find through interfaith learning that our neighbors have preserved certain stories we neglected but never discarded, stories and practices whose addition will allow our cathedrals to remain sanctuaries and portals into the future. Interfaith learning allows us to bring our beautiful cathedrals up to code." Email to authors, November 10, 2016.

13. A version of this story was first published by Jonah Pesner with Hurmon Hamilton, "A Community, Not Simply a Coalition," in Peace, Rose, and Mobley, *My Neighbor's Faith*, 249–51.

14. Ibid., 251.

15. Wilfred Cantwell Smith, *The Meaning and End of Religion* (New York: Macmillan, 1962), 9.

FROM PRISON RELIGION TO INTERFAITH LEADERSHIP FOR INSTITUTIONAL CHANGE

1. For a history of the case, see Rouser v. White 630 F.Supp. 1165 (E.D. Cal. 2009). To disrupt Rouser's efforts, officials moved him to various institutions and sent his "converts" elsewhere, thus spreading Wicca throughout the California correctional system. Wicca became the second or third largest religious group in several prisons.

2. Cruz v. Beto 405 U.S. 319 (1972), 322n2.

3. For a brief history, see Laura Magani and Harmon L. Wray, *Beyond Prisons: A New Interfaith Paradigm for Our Failed Prison System* (Minneapolis: Augsburg Fortress Press, 2006).

4. From 2005 until 2013, I provided legal expertise for McCollum v. CDCR, 647 F.3d 870 (9th Cir. 2011) and Hartmann v. CDCR, 707 F.3d 1114 (9th Cir. 2013).

5. The Religious Land Use and Institutionalized Persons Act (RLUIPA), 42 USC §2000cc, defined "religious exercise" as "any exercise of religion, whether or not compelled by, or central to, a system of religious belief" (§2000cc-5(7)(A)), and it also applied that definition to an earlier federal law, the Religious Freedom Restoration Act of 1993 (RFRA), 42 USC §2000bb. RLUIPA applies the "strict scrutiny" test for religious accommodations in prisons and in other limited areas. Government cannot "substantially burden" a "sincere" "religious exercise" unless the government has a very important reason ("compelling governmental interest") to do so. Even when there is an important reason, the government has to serve it with the lightest impact on religious exercise possible ("least restrictive means"). The RFRA also applies strict scrutiny to federal government institutions.

6. Inmates are able to obtain such items through gifts or purchase from approved vendors when allowed.

7. Patrick McCollum and Steve Herrick started the annual American Academy of Religion program in 2003. Rev. McCollum continues as session cofacilitator. Since 2015, Armed Services and Veterans Administration senior chaplains and endorsers have been included in the training.

8. Howard J. Ross, "If You Are Human, You Are Biased," in *Everyday Bias: Identifying and Navigating Unconscious Judgments in Our Daily Lives* (London: Rowman & Littlefield, 2014), 1–16.

9. I discovered this when I invited new religion scholars to our chaplaincy directors program in 2015.

10. For similar methods, see Carol A. Marchel, "Learning to Talk/Talking to Learn: Teaching Critical Dialogue," *Teaching Educational Psychology* 2, no. 1 (2007): 1–15; and Ellen E. Fairchild and Warren J. Blumenfeld, "Traversing Boundaries: Dialogues on Christian Privilege, Religious Oppression, and Religious Pluralism among Believers and Non-Believers," *College Student Affairs Journal* 26, no. 2 (2007): 177–85.

11. John C. Maxwell, *The Five Levels of Leadership: Proven Steps to Maximize Your Potential* (New York: Center Street, 2011), 2, 133.

12. See Barbara A. McGraw, "Toward a Framework for Interfaith Leadership," *Engaging Pedagogies in Catholic Higher Education* 3, no. 1 (2017), http://digitalcommons .stmarys-ca.edu/epiche/vol3/iss1/2. See also Susan R. Komives, Nance Lucas, and Timothy R. McMahon, "The Relational Leadership Model," in *Exploring Leadership: For College Students Who Want to Make a Difference*, 3rd ed. (San Francisco: Jossey-Bass, 2013), 93–149.

13. James MacGregor Burns, *Transforming Leadership: A New Pursuit of Happiness* (New York: Grove Press, 2003).

14. Of course there are inmates who use the law to see what they can get away with; however, in my experience, most often inmates' requests are sincere.

15. See cases in notes 2 and 4 above.

16. Devdutt Pattanaik, *East vs. West: The Myths that Mystify*, TED, video, November 19, 2009, https://www.ted.com/talks/devdutt_pattanaik.

17. See Wendy Cadge, *Paging God: Religion in the Halls of Medicine* (Chicago: University of Chicago Press, 2012).

INTERFAITH STUDIES AND THE PROFESSIONS

1. Patel, *Interfaith Leadership*, 39.

2. Matthew J. Mayhew, Alyssa N. Rockenback, Benjamin P. Correia, Rebecca E. Crandall, and Mark A. Lo, *Emerging Interfaith Trends: What College Students Are*

Saying about Religion in 2016 (Interfaith Youth Core, 2016), https://www.ifyc.org/ sites/default/files/u4/208423049283045.pdf.

3. Ibid., 7.
4. *Advancing Diversity and Inclusion in Higher Education: Key Data Highlights on Race and Ethnicity and Promising Practices* (Office of Planning, Evaluation and Policy Development, U.S. Department of Education, 2016), 36–39, https://www2.ed .gov/rschstat/research/pubs/advancing-diversity-inclusion.pdf.
5. *College Learning for the New Global Century* (Washington, DC: Association of American Colleges and Universities, 2007), 11–12, https://www.aacu.org/sites /default/files/files/LEAP/GlobalCentury_final.pdf.
6. *Interfaith Cooperation and American Higher Education: Recommendations, Best Practices and Case Studies* (Interfaith Youth Core, 2010), 13, https://www.ifyc.org /sites/default/files/best-practice-report.pdf.
7. Hart Research Associates, *Falling Short? College Learning and Career Success* (Association of American Colleges and Universities, 2015), 3, https://www.aacu.org /sites/default/files/files/LEAP/2015employerstudentsurvey.pdf.
8. "Remarks by President Obama in Address to the United Nations General Assembly," United Nations Assembly Hall, New York City, September 24, 2014, https:// www.whitehouse.gov/the-press-office/2014/09/24/remarks-president-obama-address -united-nations-general-assembly.
9. Ibid.
10. Benjamin P. Correia, Alyssa N. Rockenbach, and Matthew J. Mayhew, "Bridging Worldview Diversity through Interfaith Cooperation," *Diversity and Democracy* 19, no. 2 (Spring 2016), https://www.aacu.org/diversitydemocracy/2016/spring /correia.

TOWARD AN INTERRELIGIOUS CITY

1. An overview of the ICJS Imagining Justice in Baltimore (IJB) initiative, as well as links to digital content, is accessible online at http://www.icjs.org/programs/imagining -justice-baltimore.
2. Many people are fearful to directly engage in discussions of religious difference, or difference of any kind. Oftentimes this fear rests on a lack of personal connection and genuine encounter between people, and impressions of religious difference are filtered through larger narratives shaped by biases and prejudices that animate the media, as well as our religious communities. At the founding of the ICJS, careful pedagogical choices were made to confront anti-Judaism and anti-Semitism within Christian traditions (and Western thought) *prior* to raising religious literacy about Judaism with Christian audiences. This sequencing was based on the conviction that most Christians could not understand Judaism as Jews practiced it without first understanding the prejudicial lens through which they had perceived Judaism and Jews. Successful interreligious encounters must recognize existing power dynamics and educate majority cultures about the lens through which they see and understand minority cultures. The ICJS has committed to replicating this pedagogical practice, by educating our audiences in Islamophobia prior to, or alongside, literacy in Islam.
3. "Clergy Marches Against Violence" WBAL-TV 11, April 27, 2015, http://www .wbaltv.com/article/clergy-marches-against-violence/6923905.
4. Ibid.
5. Lawrence Brown, "Two Baltimores: The White L vs. the Black Butterfly," *City Paper*, June 28, 2016.
6. Antero Pietila, *Not in My Neighborhood: How Bigotry Shaped a Great American City* (Chicago: Ivan R. Dee, 2010).

7. Raj Chetty and Nathaniel Hendren, *The Impacts of Neighborhoods on Intergenerational Mobility: Childhood Exposure Effects and County-Level Estimates*, National Bureau of Economic Research (2015), http://www.nber.org/papers/w23001.

8. Emma Green, "Black Activism, Unchurched," *Atlantic*, March 22, 2016.

9. In Martin Luther King Jr., "The Power of Nonviolence," 1958, in *The Essential Marin Luther King Jr.: "I Have a Dream" and Other Great Writings* (Boston: Beacon Press, 2013).

10. In Kelly Brown Douglas's *Stand Your Ground: Black Bodies and the Justice of God* (New York: Orbis, 2015), she both explores the political, historical, legal, and theological contexts surrounding the shooting deaths of black boys and girls in America today, and offers a prophetic Christian theology in response, interrogating both the justice and freedom of God as experienced in black American life. Brown Douglas's theology grounds itself in her experience as a theologian, a church leader, and a mother, and is an important reflection of the possibilities of Christian leadership today.

11. Michael Lipka, "A Closer Look at America's Rapidly Growing Religious 'Nones,'" Pew Research Center, 2015, http://www.pewresearch.org/fact-tank/2015/05/13/a-closer-look-at-americas-rapidly-growing-religious-nones/.

12. Our participants included college students from HBCUs, public universities, and Catholic universities; college professors; retirees; young professionals with young families; educators; trustees of the ICJS; clergy; clergy-in-formation; local parishioners; people already on our mailing list; and people from the general public.

13. Ron Cassie, "A Tale of Two Cities: West Baltimore Before and After Freddie Gray," *Baltimore Magazine*, April 11, 2016.

14. Tom Hall, "Inter-Faith Dialogues Seek a Vision of Justice in Baltimore," WYPR, Baltimore, December 19, 2016.

15. Tom Hall, "Imagining Justice in Baltimore: A Jewish Perspective," WYPR, Baltimore, March 28, 2016; Tom Hall, "Imagining Justice in Baltimore: A Christian Perspective," WYPR, Baltimore, January 25, 2016; Tom Hall, "Imagining Justice in Baltimore: An Islamic Perspective," WYPR, Baltimore, April 25, 2016.

16. ICJS's Huffington Post blog is accessible online at http://www.huffingtonpost.com/author/icjs.

INDEX

To reflect the different authors' varying usages, the term "interreligious" in this index should be understood to mean interreligious/interfaith.

Figures are indicated by "f" following the page number.